P9-CBG-458

GREAT GARDEN COMPANIONS

GREAT GARDEN COMPANIONS

A Companion-Planting System for a Beautiful, Chemical-Free Vegetable Garden

Sally Jean Cunningham

Rodale Press, Inc.
Emmaus, Pennsylvania

OUR PURPOSE

"We inspire and enable people to improve their lives and the world around them."

© 1998 by Sally Jean Cunningham

All rights reserved. No part of this publication may be reproduced or transmitted in any form or by any means, electronic or mechanical, including photocopy, recording, or any other information storage and retrieval system, without the written permission of the publisher.

The information in this book has been carefully researched, and all efforts have been made to ensure accuracy. Rodale Press, Inc., assumes no responsibility for any injuries suffered or for damages or losses incurred during the use of or as a result of following this information. It is important to study all directions carefully before taking any action based on the information and advice presented in this book. When using any commercial product, *always* read and follow label directions. Where trade names are used, no discrimination is intended and no endorsement by Rodale Press, Inc., is implied.

Printed in the United States of America on acid-free ∞, recycled ♲ paper

We're happy to hear from you. For questions or comments concerning the editorial content of this book, please write to:

Rodale Press, Inc.
Book Readers' Service
33 East Minor Street
Emmaus, PA 18098

For more information about Rodale Press and the books and magazines we publish, visit our World Wide Web site at:
http://www.rodalepress.com

Editor: **Fern Marshall Bradley**
Senior Research Associate: **Heidi A. Stonehill**
Cover and Interior Book Designer:
Nancy Smola Biltcliff
Interior Illustrators: **Kathy Bray,
Louise M. Smith, Amy Bartlett Wright**
Stylist for Author Photo: **Evelyne Barthelemy**
Digital Cover Imaging: **Judy Reinford**
Photography Editor: **James A. Gallucci**
Copy Editor: **Jennifer Hornsby**
Manufacturing Coordinator: **Patrick T. Smith**
Indexer: **Lina Burton**
Editorial Assistance: **Jodi Guiducci, Liz Leone**

RODALE HOME AND GARDEN BOOKS

Vice President and Editorial Director:
Margaret J. Lydic
Managing Editor, Garden Books:
Ellen Phillips
Director of Design and Production:
Michael Ward
Associate Art Director: Patricia Field
Studio Manager: Leslie M. Keefe
Copy Director: Dolores Plikaitis
Book Manufacturing Director: Helen Clogston
Office Manager: Karen Earl-Braymer

**Library of Congress
Cataloging-in-Publication Data**

Cunningham, Sally Jean.
    Great garden companions : a companion planting system for a beautiful, chemical-free vegetable garden / Sally Jean Cunningham.
        p.   cm.
    Includes bibliographical references (p.   ) and index.
    ISBN 0–87596–781–7   (hardcover : acid-free paper)
    1. Vegetable gardening.   2. Companion planting.   3. Organic gardening.
4. Companion crops.   I. Title.
SB321.C9   1998
635—dc21   97–33933

Distributed in the book trade by St. Martin's Press

2 4 6 8 10 9 7 5 3 1   hardcover

With love and gratitude to my mom, Jean Seibert, who opened all the doors, and to my daughter, Alice, my window to the future.

RODALE PRESS
Organic Gardening Starts Here!

Here at Rodale Press, we've been gardening organically for over 50 years—ever since my grandfather, J. I. Rodale, learned about composting and decided that healthy living starts with healthy soil. In 1940, J. I. started the Rodale Organic Farm to test his theories, and today, the nonprofit Rodale Institute Experimental Farm is still at the forefront of organic gardening and farming research. In 1942, J. I. founded *Organic Gardening* magazine to share his discoveries with gardeners everywhere. His son, my father, Robert Rodale, headed *Organic Gardening* until 1990, and today, the fourth generation of Rodales is growing up with the magazine. Over the years, we've shown millions of readers how to grow bountiful crops and beautiful flowers using nature's own techniques.

In this book, you'll find the latest organic methods and the best gardening advice. We know—because our authors and editors are all passionate about gardening! We feel strongly that our gardens should be safe for our children, pets, and the birds and butterflies that add beauty and delight to our lives and landscapes. Our gardens should provide us with fresh, flavorful vegetables, delightful herbs, and gorgeous flowers. And they should be a pleasure to work in as well as to view.

Sharing the secrets of safe, successful gardening is why we publish books. So come visit us at the Rodale Institute Experimental Farm, where you can tour the gardens every day—we're open year-round. And use this book to create your best garden ever.

Happy gardening!

Maria Rodale

Maria Rodale
For Rodale Garden Books

Contents

Acknowledgments

I WANT TO EXTEND SPECIAL THANKS to the following people and organizations:

- my husband, Brendan, who works in the jungle (while I grow one) and who provided support in many ways— particularly those fine Sunday dinners, and a bit of manure shoveling, too.

- my editor, Fern Bradley, without whom this book might never have been born. She was tactful and supportive, direct and strong, finding the best in the work without ever taking "me" out of it.

- Deanne Cunningham, whose keen eye and wonderful photography made my garden look its best ever.

- the Erie County Master Gardeners and my other gardening friends, who continue to inspire me with their enthusiasm, and who so freely share their ideas, their gardens, and their passion for plants. Specifically, I appreciate the contributions of Mary Giambra, Skip Murray, John Holnbeck, Peg Giermek, Seymour Sunshine, and Roxanne McCoy, whose ideas show up in this book and in my garden.

- my garden helpers who showed up for "planting day," among them Barb Baker, Jen Pultz, Bernie Giermek, my sister Margie, and especially Craig Vogel, builder of raised beds and tiller of soil.

- Cornell Cooperative Extension, for the opportunity to learn, as well as teach, every single day. (May Cooperative Extensions be recognized and funded as the educational treasures they are!)

- Chris Metz, for her kind encouragement, daily support, and a million thoughtful details.

- the grandpas and grandmas who pass on their secrets, especially my Grandpa Harper, who put the gardener in my psyche, and to Grandpa Maynard, who sharpened the tools.

- all the gardeners who treasure living things besides plants. If we take care of the insects and the frogs, the birds and the snakes, we can all garden in joyful wonderlands.

Introduction

IN MY GARDEN, there are three kinds of harvests. The first harvest is the vegetables: lettuce and peas in the spring; summer's bonanza of broccoli, tomatoes, potatoes, beans, and corn; and the fall finale of carrots, brussels sprouts, and pumpkins. My garden's bounty includes plenty of flowers and herbs (they're some of my "great garden companions"), from zinnias and cosmos to dill and basil.

The second harvest from my garden is the satisfaction and peace of mind that I get from creating something that's beautiful and beneficial. My system of *companion gardening* keeps my little piece of the earth and its inhabitants healthy and thriving. I never use chemicals in my garden, because companion planting and other natural techniques keep pest problems at a minimum. I'm happy just knowing that my daughter can eat tomatoes right off the vine from my garden.

The third harvest is the techniques and secrets that I can teach other gardeners. In this book, I've gathered a rich harvest from my years of gardening experience. My aim is to help you get the very best from your garden by using companion planting and other organic gardening techniques to grow vegetables safely and easily. Once you learn my companion-gardening system, each year you'll see your harvest get bigger while the work gets smaller.

What You'll Find

In the first four chapters of *Great Garden Companions*, you'll discover how to use companion planting, intensive planting, organic soil building, and natural pest-control techniques to create your own companion garden. But that's just the start. Here's a sampling of some of the exciting features in the rest of the book:

- For detailed information on beneficial insects and the plants that attract them, see Chapter 5, "Bringing in the Good Guys."

- To learn how to combine perennial flowers and herbs in your vegetable garden, see Chapter 6, "Perennials in the Pumpkins, Shrubs on the Side."

- For some fun and fanciful companion-garden designs, turn to Chapter 7, "Having Fun with Companion Gardening."

- For great tips on using mulch and cover crops to improve the soil and cut down on watering and weeding chores, read Chapter 8, "The Four Fundamentals of Companion Gardening."

- For seasonal to-do lists of garden activities and projects, check Chapter 9, "Seasonal Care."

- For specific techniques and tricks for growing crops from asparagus to turnips, turn to Chapter 10, "Sally's Top Crops and Companion-Garden Secrets."

Asking the Right Questions

As a garden lecturer, TV "garden answer lady," and Extension educator, I'm constantly answering questions from gardeners. One of the most common questions I hear is, "I have a bug on my tomatoes (or beans, or roses, or lilacs…). What should I spray?" My answer: "The question is not what to spray. The question is what kind of insect is it?" It's a very important question, because in most cases, that insect isn't a threat to the plant. Believe it or not, most of the insects in your garden are great garden helpers!

In *Great Garden Companions*, you'll learn a lot about the "good bug" companions that "make their living" by eating insect pests. In fact, my fascination with beneficial insects was one of the driving forces behind my study of companion planting and the development of my gardening system.

One of the lessons I've learned through gardening is that working with nature can lead to a very successful garden. If we fight nature's rules, we're forced to rely on chemicals to keep our crops productive. But if we cooperate with nature, we can have it all: a beautiful garden, a great harvest, and lots of fun along the way.

So please enjoy *Great Garden Companions*. It's my chance to invite you to "visit" my garden, and it's a practical how-to guide to growing bumper crops of garden-fresh vegetables, improving the soil, attracting beneficial insects, and lots more. You can browse the chapters as you wish, or you can start right out in Chapter 1 with a walk through my "wonderful wonderland garden." I know I'll enjoy welcoming you as another one of my great garden companions!

Welcome to Wonderland

My garden is a wonderland. There are no Mad Hatters or March Hares, but to me, it's a magical place. I grow vegetables, herbs, and flowers in cooperation with nature and without ever using chemicals—either pesticides or chemical fertilizers. In my garden, you'll find a wonderful variety of plants and animals. Each one of them has food, a home, and a job to do in the special gardening system I call *companion gardening*. My system starts with traditional companion planting, but it goes a lot further.

In this chapter, I'll take you on a special tour of my garden, and I'll show you how all these gardening companions work together to keep my garden thriving. And in the next few chapters, you'll move on to selecting "great garden companions," so that you can garden in a wonderland, too.

WONDERLAND FARM

My Wonderful Wonderland Garden

I LOVE GARDENING. I love the little pea plants that poke up out of the last snow, the lime-green leaves of young buckwheat, and the incomparable taste of a sun-warmed tomato. I love to throw on yesterday's dirt-smudged gardening clothes at 6:30 in the morning, get out in my garden, and work until I'm starving.

Gardening is such an important part of my life that I want to be sure it's a safe and healthy activity for all the living beings around me. I share my home, Wonderland Farm, with some precious people and animals. There's my daughter, Alice, my mom, Jean, my husband, Brendan, two horses (Becky and Filo), two dogs (Moby and Ginger), and six cats (Buddy, Owl, Muffin, Teddy, Simba, and Toes). Birds, toads, and many helpful insects and other kinds of wildlife are welcome to visit my garden. I take care of the life in the soil, too—earthworms and other tiny critters that help my plants grow.

Always Organic

To me, gardening safely means gardening organically. I use no pesticides or herbicides. When I decided to garden organically, I still wanted to reap a good harvest, so I studied methods for avoiding pest problems without using chemicals. The result of my studying and experimenting is a gardening system that lets me grow plenty of vegetables and flowers in a chemical-free, environmentally friendly way. I call my system *companion gardening*.

As you might have guessed, my system starts with good old-fashioned companion planting. Companion planting is a mix of gardening fact and folklore that advocates growing certain plants together for their mutual benefit.

More than just vegetables. My vegetable garden includes lots of flowers and herbs that attract helpful insects and animals. I plant crops in wide rows, use plenty of mulch, and lay down old boards in the pathways to protect the soil.

The reasons for pairing up companion plants can be quite practical. For instance, planting pole beans with corn gives the beans a built-in trellis. Planting fragrant herbs like basil may confuse or repel pest insects that are looking for vegetable plants to munch on. Other companion pairings are harder to explain. They're vaguely based on the idea that one plant promotes the growth of another; for example, parsnips may grow better when planted beside peas.

But companion gardening goes well beyond random companion planting. I've discovered reliable groups of plants that grow well together, and I've developed techniques that attract a host of pest-eating insects to my garden. The end result is a beautiful and unusual sort of vegetable garden where I rarely even have to think about controlling insect pests. Let me take you on a tour of my garden, and you'll begin to see what I mean.

The Well-Mixed Look

Approaching my garden, you'll see right away how colorful and full it looks. Although it's a vegetable garden, there are lots of flowers among the crops. However, there are no tidy rows, and the layout seems haphazard. Some people may call it confusing, mixed up, or even messy! I say this because of a conversation I once overheard between my husband, Brendan, and one of his associates in the real estate business. They're both used to very neat suburban homes with tidy landscapes primed for showing. The conversation went like this:

Brendan: *This is Sally's vegetable garden. It's kind of messy, but...*

Realtor lady: *Look at all those flowers. Oh, but that's goldenrod, isn't it? She must not have too much time for weeding.*

Brendan: *Well, those wildflowers—and even some of the weeds—they are there on purpose. See, it's a system that mixes plants together. It's all for some reason.*

Realtor: *I see. Well, she sure has a lot of things growing in there, anyway.*

I admit I'm not the neatest gardener in the world, but Brendan had things right. All the plants in my garden are there with good reason—and once you understand the reason, my garden changes from messy to marvelous!

Watch Those Wide Rows

You won't see any long, straight, single rows of crops in my garden. In single-row plantings, people can tread anywhere and everywhere through the garden, and that's hard on the soil. Good soil is hard to come by (especially when you start with the kind of clay I have), so I'm careful to protect it. I plant crops in wide rows or beds (usually about 3 feet wide), and I make clear paths between the beds. I use old boards for the paths. Usually the beds are raised slightly above the paths. I work lots of organic material into the soil, so it stays loose and I don't have to till.

My wide rows may look crowded to people who are used to long single vegetable rows with 1-foot walkways in between. I space the plants just far enough apart to thrive, but not so far apart as to waste space or leave bare soil. In one bed, you may see a 3- by 6-foot solid patch of lettuce or mixed salad greens. Beside it, there's a jungle of bean and potato plants mixed together. In yet another bed, you'll spot

Sally Says

"Remember: Anytime you leave bare soil, weeds find it."

broccoli planted in a zigzag pattern. There's a mat of old grass clippings covering the soil between the plants, and the vegetables' leaves overlap slightly, shading the soil.

Flowers in the Vegetables

Are those zinnias poking up among the broccoli leaves? Yes—that's how we get to the "mixed-up" look.

I plant flowers everywhere in my vegetable garden. Why? One reason is that they're pretty—and for many of us, that is reason enough to plant flowers anywhere! However, there's a much more important reason to have flowers as well as herbs scattered among the vegetables.

The main reason I plant flowers and herbs in my garden is to create *biodiversity*. Now that's a fancy word, but it's easy to explain. Biodiversity simply means having many different plants and animals in an area. In nature, biodiversity is the normal state of things. In fields and forests, a huge range of plants grow all mixed together. One important benefit of this mixing of plants is that pests have a hard time finding the plants they like to eat. So, what's a logical way to camouflage the crops in your vegetable garden and confuse the pest insects? Mix them up!

Another benefit of the flowers and herbs I choose for my vegetable garden is that they attract and maintain a population of beneficial insects. These are the insects we *want* in our gardens because they hunt and eat other insects, including many common garden pests. There are beneficial beetles, flies, wasps, and more. Their pest-control power in my garden is amazing!

Flowering companions. Tansy, Queen-Anne's-lace, cosmos, and nasturtiums are four of my favorite companion plants. They're pretty and easy to grow, and they attract loads of beneficial insects.

Weeds and Wildflowers

Weeds are usually the last things gardeners want in the garden! But perhaps the definition of "weed" needs changing—or at least we should list some exceptions. In some cases, weeds and wildflowers are even more valuable than cultivated annuals and perennials for attracting beneficial insects and birds. So in my garden you'll see plenty of goldenrod, wild daisies, Queen-Anne's-lace, tickseed, and New England asters.

SALLY'S HELPFUL HINTS

Don't Waste the Dandelions!

You may curse dandelions, but they can also be a blessing. They have taproots, which reach down into the subsoil—the earth below the topsoil—where your crop roots usually don't penetrate. Dandelion roots can absorb important nutrients from the subsoil, which then become part of the dandelion plant. So when you pull or cut off the dandelion (before it flowers!), *use it*—either by adding it to your compost pile or working it back into the topsoil. You'll be adding some hard-to-find nutrients back into your garden beds.

Weeds also have roles as mulches and soil builders. To build a healthy, organic soil, you'll need to add organic matter (decomposed plant or animal material) on a regular basis. When I weed, I make sure that I uproot or cut off the weeds before they produce seeds. Then I let the weeds lie as mulch between rows and turn them under the soil when they dry.

Especially Insects

Any tour of my garden is a real stop-and-start process. When you least expect it, I'll exclaim "Oh, look!" but you won't have the faintest idea what I've spotted. The next thing you know, I'll have you squinting through a magnifying glass at a little insect doing something I find amazing.

These good-guy insects are important garden friends and a big part of why I spend next to no time controlling pest insects. If there are lady beetles and their larvae on the tansy and in the corn, I know that aphids won't trouble my crops. If there are spined soldier bugs galore in the goldenrod and tiny wasps hovering around the dill, I know I won't have problems with bean beetles. These beneficial insects show me that my garden is in harmony, a healthy little universe. These bugs and wasps are on pest duty, and I know I'll have plenty of vegetables again this year.

Inevitably, we will find some pests. There are a few slugs under the lettuce, perhaps because of the generous mulch of straw in the adjacent row. The broccoli that I didn't protect with row covers was visited by little white butterflies, so I may eventually see cabbageworms on the plants. On the other hand, a variety of predators may eat up the worms before I ever spot them.

Listen to the Buzz

My garden can be noisy. There's a steady hum or buzz of bees and flies. Don't worry! I'm not talking about nasty horseflies.

The flies are predatory flies, like hoverflies. Hoverflies actually look like bees, but they can't sting or bite you. Their larvae feast on aphids. So flies are welcome in my garden—with the exception of biting blackflies in spring and horseflies and deerflies in summer!

There are wasps in my garden, too, but they don't sting either. They're parasitic wasps, like the braconid wasps. These tiny, harmless (to us) wasps land on and lay eggs in pests like tomato hornworms. When the eggs hatch, the larvae feed on the tomato hornworms, and that's good news for me and my tomatoes.

I know that many of you may be scared of bees, but they play a valuable role. Bees (and flies) pollinate plants, and without insect pollination, we'd never harvest crops like cucumbers, melons, and squash.

Two of my favorite plants for attracting bees are borage and buckwheat. Borage is a lovely herb with edible, brilliant blue flowers that bees just love. If you buy it once, it will self-seed forever after, but you can easily pull out the new seedlings that you don't want. My garden has a bluish haze in summer because of all the borage I let roam.

As for buckwheat, I don't plant it so that I can make buckwheat flour. No, buckwheat is a cover crop in my garden, a crop grown especially to cover up the soil when it's not in use for a vegetable crop. The buckwheat keeps down weeds, and because I till the plants back into the beds, the soil gets an extra boost of organic matter. That buckwheat's flowers attract bees and beneficial insects is an added plus.

Perennials for Pest Fighters

After admiring the insects, I'll show you the small perennial garden next to my asparagus. There's a birdbath in the center surrounded by coreopsis, yarrow, more borage, volunteer Queen-Anne's-lace, asters, and even some annuals like dwarf sunflowers. As with any perennial garden, it's never finished. Every year, I add this and move that—but as a concept, the perennials stay!

Sally Says

"Insects are the pulse of the garden, the measure of how successful my garden will be."

I created a perennial grouping in the midst of my vegetable garden because a permanent planting is the best hideout for beneficial insects, as well as for my resident toad and the passing birds. I've discovered that I can't do much weeding or dead-heading in this garden to neaten it up for guests because I keep disturbing something important. First, I stopped just short of wrecking a work of art: the web of the common yellow and black garden spider. Then I stepped on the pine needle mulch and heard a squeak, which was a very annoyed large toad (she was unharmed). And when I started to pull out an excessively large borage plant that was keeling over after a hard wind, I almost grabbed a huge praying mantis. He looked at me with his big, quizzical eyes as if asking, "Why would you mess with that?" So I didn't!

Watch out when you weed. Borage and other herbs and wildflowers can self-sow and get weedy looking, but check before you pull! They may shelter helpful critters like praying mantids.

A PLACE FOR SNAKES

When I find rocks in my garden beds, I stack them in piles and leave them there. Rock piles help to welcome and shelter toads and lizards, as well as some other pest eaters that have a bad reputation—snakes! Snakes give many people the creeps. But most snakes are not poisonous. And they aren't slimy or sneaky or interested in you at all. (Where I live in western New York, virtually no snakes are dangerous—certainly *not* the ones we see around our gardens.)

I was lucky to learn as a child that snakes are great to have around. My Grandpa Harper taught me how to pick up snakes behind the head and showed me that they are dry and cool to the touch—and very interesting. I've taught my daughter, Alice, about snakes too.

Country homes need snakes to control rodents in outbuildings and basements. Snakes are very valuable around the garden, where they eat insects as well as rodents. Snakes like the shelter of rock piles, brush piles, woodpiles, and sometimes black plastic or boards, so I purposely set up a few such snake-friendly locations around the garden.

A Birdbath for the Bugs

The birdbath is for birds, right? Well, partly. Most gardeners love to watch birds. Birds also help with pest control, so they're always invited to my garden. They like the birdbaths and the large farm pond I'm lucky to have nearby.

However, the birdbaths here and there in my gardens have another purpose: to attract and support all those beneficial insects. Part of maintaining an army of helpful insects like lady beetles is giving them water. Flying insects need water at flying level—about waist height—so a birdbath is a perfect source. Crawling insects need water at soil level, which is why you'll see pie plates, a dog dish, a used horse-feed bucket, and a one-time ashtray sunk into the soil here and there around my garden. These shallow containers all have sand or rocks and pebbles in them to provide perches so the insects can drink without drowning. The "bug baths" also attract butterflies, and while butterflies don't eat insect pests, their color and beauty make them a pleasure to have in any garden.

Other creatures profit from these watering holes, too. Frogs, toads, and lizards visit the little pools and may set up residence nearby. Even my cats find the water dishes convenient for a cooling sip as they conduct "mole patrol." Somehow it all works together.

All in the Family

Cats, dogs, horses, and people are part of my life and part of my garden—sometimes invited, sometimes not! Most gardeners have to adjust their plans to accommodate their families. For instance, if you have little children, you may want to avoid planting certain poisonous plants, like castor bean or foxglove. If you have active older children in the neighborhood who may run through your garden, you may decide to build high raised beds to save your plants from destruction.

Cats for Mole-Patrol

I strongly believe that healthy neutered cats, who stay home because they are not out seeking mates, are the best single control for moles and rodents. Only two of my cats have outdoor privileges, but they really pull their weight as hunters. We often find mole and mouse "trophies" proudly laid out on the deck for us to admire. And we are pleased that our cats almost never hunt birds. The moles are hunted for display purposes only, as I am informed that they taste most unpleasant!

Horses, of Course

My horses also play a role in my Wonderland gardens. I really enjoy the friendly snorts that greet me when I walk out

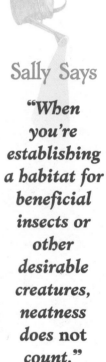

Sally Says

"When you're establishing a habitat for beneficial insects or other desirable creatures, neatness does not count."

Managing dogs in the garden. As long as my dogs have clear paths to follow, I find that they don't trample over plants, even when a tempting target is in sight.

to the garden, which is right next to their pasture. Those snorts are more than "Hello." They also mean "How about some dandelion greens and quackgrass?" Caution, horse lovers: Some weeds are poisonous, so don't feed horses weeds unless you know exactly what you're giving them.

So my horses are good company and good weed eaters. But even more important, their manure is downright wonderful fertilizer, whether composted or just aged and spread.

Dealing with Dogs

While we treasure our doggy pets, we know they can spell trouble in the garden. An exuberant year-old Lab can wreak havoc as he chases a ball through rows of tender young seedlings, and there is nothing quite like the excavations (always under favorite perennials) by puppies with the urge to bury toys. But I've found ways to keep my dogs from doing much harm. I've discovered that they're less likely to run over plants as they get older, and I'm surprised by their willingness to stay on the board or mulch pathways through the garden. Generally, if you show a dog who loves you what you want—as in "Moby, get out of that horse manure!"—he tends to cooperate. Dogs around the garden can be a plus: The scent of a dog is an effective deterrent to deer and other wildlife that can trample—or worse, eat—your plants.

Training the People

People in your garden are another story. They are definitely harder to train and impossible to fence out, plus they require tact and a nice tone of voice. Sometimes non-gardeners just don't understand why they shouldn't walk through your lettuce bed. Often, they can't tell a weed from a just-bought transplant. What's even worse, sometimes they "help" you!

It takes patience to encourage others (especially children) to learn gardening and find the joy in it, while not compacting your soil and weeding out the French tarragon. But with a little planning and ingenuity we can welcome our human guests and not be tempted to put tomato cages around them. Here are some tips that help keep the peace.

Friendly companions.
My daughter, Alice, has learned to respect the helpful insects and animals that help keep pesky insects from devouring her favorite strawberries!

- Put labels on your plants, especially those not in obvious rows or clumps.

- Make some little signs like "Don't tread on me," and display them on stakes in your garden beds.

- Provide obvious paths that are wide enough for people to use, in the direction they would tend to walk across the garden.

- Raise the soil of the planting beds higher than the paths, or build enclosed raised beds.

- Finally, at planting and harvest time—good times to have help—remember that the plants can be replaced, but people can't.

An Ever-Changing View

Sally Says

"Change is an important part of my companion-gardening system."

THAT'S THE END of the tour for now. (To see more of my garden, check out the photos beginning on page 55.) I wish you could sample some of the harvest!

Next year, my garden will look quite different. In the bed where pole beans are climbing the cornstalks, you may see tomatoes and basil with clover growing underneath. The potato patch will give way to lettuce, carrots, and dill. Each year, I plant my groups of plant companions in different beds. You may be familiar with this technique of *rotating* crops—it helps to reduce pest and disease problems and also lets me make the best use of my soil.

I also make some changes just for fun every year. I try new varieties, like the wonderful blue potatoes I discovered last year. And I experiment with new companions, like hollyhocks in my asparagus bed!

Next year's garden is also sure to be even better than this year's. That's because I learn new things about gardening all the time. I've resolved that I'll use more calendulas and cosmos—two powerful companion plants for pest control. And I'll have great new framed raised beds so I can raise my earliest-ever crop of peas, spinach, and lettuce.

Your next garden will be a great one, too, as you begin to try out the techniques of companion gardening. Read on to learn how my system works and how you can apply my ideas in your own garden.

Chapter 2

From Companion Planting to Crop Rotation

Companion planting captivates gardeners. We're charmed by the notion that plants have "friends" who help them grow better. And as organic gardeners, we're eager to try simple, nonchemical methods that may repel pests. There's also something satisfying about learning from old-time gardeners—and companion planting certainly has deep roots in history. I've discovered that companion planting makes my garden better, but it's not the whole story of my system. I also rely on insects, birds, earthworms, and even fungi and bacteria to create a healthy, bountiful organic vegetable garden. So companion planting is only part of the picture. It's inter-twined with techniques like attracting beneficial insects, building soil, and planting intensively—all vital to my companion-gardening system.

Starting with Companion Planting

I FIRST STUDIED companion planting on doctor's orders. I was confined to bed during a rough pregnancy—during gardening season, too! I decided that if I couldn't garden, at least I could read about it. There was plenty to read. I found books full of recommendations for pairing up vegetables with other vegetables, flowers, and herbs. There were even companion-planting suggestions for fruit trees. I tried to memorize every possible companion-planting combination, but the recommendations were sometimes confusing and very unscientific. There were even contradictions and impossibilities. For instance: One source said that bush beans grow well with cucumbers. Another recommended pairing bush beans with potatoes but said that potatoes should not be planted with cucumbers. So what's a gardener to do?

My answer was to dig hard into the research on companion planting. I sorted through hundreds of recommendations, trying to find the ones that were recommended by several sources and backed by research. Some companion-planting suggestions made lots of sense, such as planting cucumbers and broccoli together to make it harder for cucumber beetles to find the cucumber plants. Others were more like fairy tales. For example, petunias, especially pink petunias, are supposed to repel squash bugs and Mexican bean beetles. (Maybe they don't like the color pink!) And planting lettuce and squash together is supposed to put rabbits to sleep so they won't be able to eat the crops. I think I'd rather put my money on a garden fence or rely on my dogs' frequent tours around the garden to deter rabbits.

By the end of my pregnancy, I'd compiled some important reasons why companion planting works and had listed hundreds of companion-planting combinations to try. Testing those combinations and choosing the best took a few seasons of experimentation. And while I experimented and refined my choices, I developed my system of companion gardening.

Great garden companions. Basil and tomatoes are a traditional companion-planting duo that I like to use in my garden—they need similar soil and weather conditions, and they're a great pair in recipes, too.

Searching for Answers

When I decided to study companion planting, I was searching for help with my own garden. I was trying to garden organically and was failing miserably. There were horrendous holes in the broccoli leaves, the potatoes were puny, and the weeds made August a nightmare! I was even teaching organic gardening at the time, and what I did and taught were fine—as far as they went. But I made a mistake that beginning organic or "switching over" gardeners often make. I substituted organic products like bonemeal for synthetic products like chemical fertilizers—*but I gardened the same otherwise*. Somehow I thought that if I avoided pesticides, used manure, and planted my rows of vegetables, Mother Nature (knowing I'd been good to her) would keep the pests in line. So wasn't I dismayed when the Colorado potato beetles arrived in droves, every ear of corn had earworms, and there were embarassing little green worms floating in the pot when I cooked my broccoli!

The problem was that I had a very *unnatural* garden: a flat rectangle of straight single rows of plants with bare soil between. This gardening style works when you rely on chemical pesticides to kill pests and chemical herbicides to wipe out weeds. But for

COMPANION PLANTING: A GREAT TRADITION

Companion planting is one of the oldest gardening traditions. Even ancient Roman historians wrote about companion planting. And you've probably heard of the "Three Sisters" gardening style of the Native Americans, which involves planting corn, beans, and squash together. Surely such a time-honored tradition must work; yet some people dismiss it as "old wives' tales." But I say that those old wives were quite smart, and just because something is folklore doesn't mean it's fiction!

So how does companion planting help make your garden better? Here are some of the benefits of companion planting:

Companion crops "lend a hand." For example, corn planted beside lettuce shades it from hot summer sun.

Companion plants use nutrients efficiently. In late summer you can plant cabbage, which needs lots of nutrients, at the same time you plant garlic—and get good crops of each from a single bed. (You harvest the cabbage in the fall, and the garlic keeps growing until the following summer.)

Companion plants can help prevent pest problems. Some companion plants supposedly repel pests, especially odoriferous plants, like onions. I often use chives and onions as companions to discourage carrot rust flies or Japanese beetles. Other companion plants may lure pests away from a crop. For example, you can plant mustard to lure flea beetles away from cabbage, broccoli, and related crops.

Companion plants attract beneficial insects. For example, tansy always has a place in my garden because it's a magnet for lady beetles, which eat lots of aphids and other pests.

me, the few organic products or tricks I substituted (insecticidal soaps, black plastic to kill weeds, and home remedies for pests) just wouldn't cut it. I had to rethink the whole system. I needed a garden that could take care of itself without lots of artificial help from me.

Learning from Nature's "Garden"

So the season after my enforced bed rest, I started experimenting with companion planting in my garden. I was hooked on the idea of mixing and matching plants to create a beautiful garden with practically no pest problems. But I discovered that while companion planting was a great idea, it wasn't enough. I also needed to build up the diversity and richness of my garden soil and to create a diverse environment both in and around my vegetable garden. I began to study the examples of nature, paying close attention to what was happening around the pond and in the woods beside my garden.

I'd like you to imagine some of the things I saw in the woods. There were fallen leaves and hemlock needles covering the soil surface. When I bent to poke a finger under the leaves, I saw earthworms tunneling in the moist surface soil. Under a fallen tree limb, I saw centipedes and pillbugs doing some of the decomposing that turns

NO SPRAYS ALLOWED!

When I started gardening, I had no trouble making up my mind about whether to use chemical pesticides and herbicides. I just read the labels! There were so many warnings and cautions about potential harm to birds, fish, water quality, and human health, I knew that chemicals weren't worth the risks. I would cope with all pests, including weeds, another way.

What about organic sprays like pyrethrins, rotenone, and neem? Many of the official organic certification programs for organic farmers allow use of these sprays. However, these substances still pose some environmental or health risks. A quick reading of a rotenone label, for example, mentions danger to fish. So what happens if we spray or dust rotenone and it rains? The rotenone may wash off the plants and end up in storm drains, streams, or the pond...Even neem and pyrethrins, which are relatively safe for humans and animals, can kill or harm several beneficial insects.

I work hard to set up a truly diverse system in my garden, full of predatory insects and other creatures that will keep pests in line. The last thing I'm going to do is use a product that can upset the delicate natural balance. So the bottom line for me is: No sprays allowed!

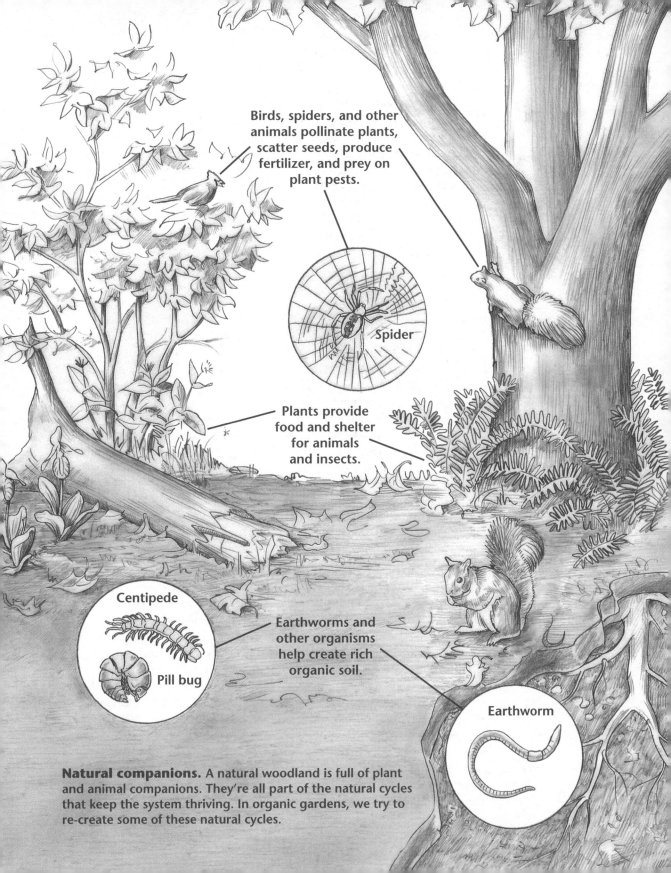

Birds, spiders, and other animals pollinate plants, scatter seeds, produce fertilizer, and prey on plant pests.

Spider

Plants provide food and shelter for animals and insects.

Centipede

Pill bug

Earthworms and other organisms help create rich organic soil.

Earthworm

Natural companions. A natural woodland is full of plant and animal companions. They're all part of the natural cycles that keep the system thriving. In organic gardens, we try to re-create some of these natural cycles.

dead plants into a rich type of organic matter called humus. There were ferns growing in the rich humus and wild blackberries clustered at the sunny edges of the woods. Both those plants thrive in the acid soil beneath the evergreens. I heard sounds, too: the hum of insects, the chattering of squirrels, and the warble of birds that were searching the woods for berries, seeds, and insects to eat.

Now, think what would happen in the woods if Joe Gardener came along with a pesticide to "get rid of those bugs?" What if he raked up the pine needles, added some lime, and planted roses or tomatoes? I'm sure you know the answer: Interfere with the links in the living chain, and the natural system starts to collapse.

So if modern human gardening styles ruin natural systems, should we move back into caves or walk around feeling terribly guilty all the time? Of course not! There aren't enough caves for all of us anyway, and feeling guilty won't make things any better. What we *can* do is set up gardens that take advantage of the natural processes that make the woods a successful, self-sustaining system. We can make a difference by planning gardens and landscapes that won't need chemicals to keep them looking good. And a very good way to start is by creating a more diverse environment in your own yard and garden.

Sally Says

"Once you start studying how plants grow together in woods and meadows, you'll see that Mother Nature was the first companion planter!"

Gardening with Nature

Can we re-create a natural forest or meadow in the vegetable garden? Not really—and we don't want to if we plan on producing a harvest. In our gardens, we want to choose which crops we're going to grow, after all. To mimic Mother Nature but still grow *your* choice of food and flowers, there are several techniques that will help.

Break up mono-crops. If you're growing a lot of one crop, plant several small plots in different parts of your garden, and mix the crop with at least one other vegetable crop.

Plant flowers and herbs. Interplanting flowers and herbs among your vegetables attracts natural predators such as birds and beneficial insects and makes it harder for pest insects to find the crop.

Shelter beneficials. Provide water, food, shelter, and breeding places for beneficial insects, toads, birds, lizards, and even snakes. Possible habitats can be hedgerows, perennial plantings, groundcovers, or rock piles. Putting out bird feeders, birdhouses, and birdbaths also helps.

Swear off pesticides. Even organic sprays like pyrethrum can kill beneficial insects. Butterflies have nearly *no* pesticide tolerance. And killing all the "pests" wipes out food that your beneficial insects might have eaten. Basically, if you spray, what you'll destroy is your effort to attract beneficials.

Leave some weeds. Learn which weeds or wildflowers provide habitat for natural predators, and leave a few of them in place when you weed. (Warning: Some weeds compete too well for nutrients, harbor pests or diseases, or take over too aggressively—so learn to identify weeds like Queen-Anne's-lace and goldenrod that are safe to leave in place.)

Companion Planting Creates Diversity

Creating diversity brings us right back to companion planting. My study of nature revealed the two best reasons for using companion planting in my vegetable garden, and I'll boldly state them here.

First, almost any combination of plants grown together is better than segregating crops into separate blocks. Combining plants increases biodiversity—the variety of living things in an area. And this variety is one of the big secrets of companion gardening! If you start mixing up your vegetables and adding in herbs and flowers, you'll also attract a variety of birds and beneficial insects to your garden. This alone will do a great deal to ensure a successful garden.

This leads to my second bold statement: When companion planting works to minimize pest problems, it is usually because the companion plants confuse the pest insects or attract beneficial insects. Certain plants do a good job of confusing pest insects in search of your crops. Other plants attract the beneficial insects that destroy those pests. In fact, I'll bet that many of the traditional companion plants that "repel" pests really work because the

Getting companion planting right. It's said that planting marigolds will discourage bean beetles, but a half-hearted approach, like the one in the right-hand bed, won't do the job. If you want to deter pests, strive for a truly diverse mix of plants, as shown in the left-hand bed.

mixed-up planting confused the pest or because the companion plant harbored predatory or parasitic beneficial insects. So either Mr. Pest never found his dinner or he was eaten before he got there!

Sorting Out the Companions

As I played with companion planting and increasing diversity in my garden, I still found myself searching for a way to simplify what I was doing. I didn't want to review all the companion-planting books each year and re-create my garden from scratch! I decided to create plant groupings that worked well together and to keep using those groups from year to year.

I started with the vegetable crops that I wanted to grow. I broke these up into groups I call *families*. Then I chose *friends* that would complement and assist the vegetables by attracting beneficial insects, confusing pests, and enriching the soil. Most of these are herbs and annual flowers, and many of them are traditional companion plants. However, I also drew from recent research on the best plants to attract beneficial insects, so my friends even include some perennial flowers, as well as cover crops, like buckwheat.

A plant family with its friends forms a *neighborhood*. I sometimes make small changes in the members of a neighborhood. For instance, one year I became very interested in fancy salad greens other than lettuce, so I added them into my lettuce neighborhood. I move my neighborhoods from bed to bed each year, a practice called crop rotation, which also plays a role in controlling insect and disease problems. I'll show you the details of how to choose your own plant families and friends in Chapter 4, "My Special System."

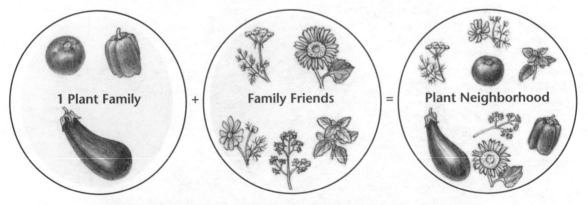

Adding up the system. My planting system starts with vegetables grouped as a *family* and adds in herbs and annuals that make good *friends*. Planted together in a raised bed, they make a garden *neighborhood*.

1 Plant Family + Family Friends = Plant Neighborhood

Taking Care of Your Soil

PLANT NEIGHBOR-HOODS are the heart of my system, but they're not the whole of it. My early attempts at organic gardening showed me that there's more to it than just not using chemicals, and there's more to it than mixing up your plants. Even if you plan wonderfully diverse planting beds, if your soil is in poor shape, your harvest will be poor, too. Soil is the source of food and water for my crops, so covering and protecting the soil are a big part of my companion-gardening system.

Keep Your Soil Covered

I always cover my soil. Sometimes I'm tempted not to, especially when the garden looks so fresh and orderly, with neat little seedlings pushing through the soft, raked earth. The trouble is, the garden won't look like that for long. Not only do weeds sprout, but rain and wind start to batter the soil surface. Soon that soft, raked planting bed has gullies in it where topsoil has eroded. Or if the weather's been dry, the soil surface is baked, crusty, and hard. It will be impossible for seedlings to poke through, for roots to grow, or for water to soak in. And if you cultivate to fix things, you end up stepping on the soil, and it becomes even more packed down. To prevent this destructive sequence of events, I always cover my soil.

Make the Most of Mulch

Most gardeners use mulch to cover their soil. There are many kinds of mulch. I mulch with grass clippings, straw, news-paper (shredded or in sheets), leaves, pine needles, cocoa shells, and sometimes black plastic. (I leave bark chips for the landscape plantings.) I know gardeners who use rugs, carpet runners, tarps, and shower curtains for mulch. If you don't like the looks of these "recycled" mulches, just cover them with a more attractive natural mulch. That way you can use what you have available.

Cover Up with Cover Crops

Cover crops or green manures are special crops that we plant especially to keep the soil covered. I love using cover crops in my garden because they also shelter those all-important beneficial insects, and they're prettier than many mulches.

You can choose from many grasses and grains for a cover crop, including annual ryegrass, hairy vetch, buckwheat, clover,

Sally Says

"Whether it's the end of a spring planting day or the end of the gardening season, I just don't feel I'm finished if the soil is still exposed."

and alfalfa. You can plant some of these in fall to cover the soil during the winter, and then turn them under in the spring to build the soil's organic content. Or you can plant them in beds that need to "rest" for all or part of the growing season. They cover and protect soil, block weeds, and add organic matter.

I think the best trick with cover crops is to plant them next to or among your vegetable crops. This is called intercropping, or interseeding. It works particularly well with legume crops like clover and alfalfa. These crops improve soil fertility by "fixing" nitrogen. This means that with the help of special bacteria in the soil, their roots can change nitrogen gas from the air into nitrogen compounds plant roots can use. (Nitrogen is a building block of protein, which plants need to live and grow, just like animals.) In Chapter 8, "The Four Fundamentals of Companion Gardening," you'll find descriptions of several cover crops and instructions on how to plant them.

Keep Crops Close Together

Still another way to cover the soil is by planting your vegetable crops close together—intensively—in wide rows. Wide rows can be anywhere from 1½ to 4 feet wide. You can space individual plants so closely that their leaves touch or overlap when they reach full size. This leaf canopy shades the soil so weeds can't get enough sunlight to grow well, and less moisture evaporates from the soil. You can plant a single crop intensively—for example, a 3-foot-wide row of beans planted 6 inches apart in all directions. Or you can plant two or more different kinds of plants intensively for the same effect. For instance, you can plant zinnias to fill in bare spots in the broccoli bed, or plant lettuce and spinach together across a whole bed.

Be a Soil Builder

In a forest or meadow, the natural system works to continually build up the soil. Plants grow and die, then insects, bacteria, and fungi cause the dead plants

Interplanting saves soil. Plant a cover crop like clover or alfalfa between rows of corn and other vegetables to prevent soil erosion. Interplanting also reduces water loss and enriches the soil.

to decompose, returning nutrients to the soil. Animals die, too, and their bodies also contribute nutrients as they decompose. Even rocks break down gradually and add minerals. But when we farm or garden, we use up the soil about 16 times faster than nature rebuilds it. In part, that's because we keep removing plants as we harvest, instead of letting them decompose and return to the soil. Poor agricultural practices that waste soil and cause erosion are also to blame. So we need to build the soil in our vegetable gardens all the time!

Building soil can be a lot of work, and common sense says it's easier to protect the good soil you already have. Covering the soil is a good start toward preventing soil loss. However, it's important not only to keep your soil but also to keep good soil structure. Soil with good structure has lots of pores, tiny openings that roots can grow through and that can hold water and air (yes, plants need air in the soil or they can't grow!).

Once soil structure is destroyed, it can take two years or more to re-create it. Good structure, or tilth, is something that you can feel, especially as you gain experience with gardening. Good soil crumbles in your hand because it's made up of lots of little clumps of particles that contain both moisture and air.

The best way to protect soil structure in your vegetable beds is to *stay off them*. When we step on the soil, our body weight compresses it, crushing all those tiny openings that hold water and air. That's why I raise my beds slightly and put clear paths between them. It shows me and visitors to my garden where it's safe to walk.

Your Soil Is Full of Life

Imagine that you're in your garden, where you can scoop up a handful of soil and look at it. Aside from a centipede, grub, or pill bug, you might not see anything that looks alive, but that's only because your eyes aren't powerful enough to see most of the tiny organisms at work there.

In that handful of soil, there are millions of bacteria and fungi that help break down organic matter, making nutrients available to plant roots. Special nitrogen-fixing bacteria work with the roots of leguminous plants to fix nitrogen. There are microscopic wormlike creatures called nematodes—some helpful and some destructive. Root-knot nematodes infest roots of many vegetable crops and can stunt their growth, while beneficial nematodes kill termites, grubs, and many other pest insects.

Feeding the Soil

When I was a little girl, my Grandpa Harper taught me to "feed the soil and not the plant." So when I saw him put kitchen scraps into trenches in the garden, I thought he was

Sally Says

"There are 900 billion microorganisms in a pound of soil. As a teacher, I've found that once gardeners realize that soil is alive, they treat it with a lot more respect."

actually "feeding" the soil! But what he was really doing was feeding the microorganisms, insects, and animals in the soil. They feed on organic matter—which can be anything from apple peels to those overgrown zucchini that you couldn't manage to give away.

For organic gardeners, getting organic matter into the soil probably takes more time than any other single gardening activity. That's because we know that our soil is our garden's gold—our most precious resource. We make and spread compost, sow cover crops, put down mulch, and dig spent crops back into the soil. One year, I used my gardening journal to jot down how I spent my time in the garden. My notes showed that I put about half my time into gathering and moving organic matter (manure, leaves, yard debris, mulch from the town), making compost, and getting the stuff into the garden!

Once we add the organic matter, the soil life takes over. The microorganisms, insects, and other soil-dwelling animals munch on it, eventually decomposing and converting the organic matter into simple forms that plants can use. Earthworms are the best-known soil-building organisms. They can process or digest their weight in organic matter daily, converting it into nitrogen, phosphorus, potassium, and other nutrients, which they leave behind in a material called castings. If you supply organic matter, you'll have a soil neighborhood of earthworms and other happy organisms that will create a rich, productive soil.

WORKING FOR THE WORMS

In the cast of characters in garden soil, earthworms are the stars. They are like miniature tillers that turn the soil and aerate it—and even better, they work for free! All we have to do is provide organic matter to feed them. As we haul in all those leaves and other kinds of organic matter, it may seem like we're working awfully hard for the worms, but helping them is a guarantee of wonderful soil. Here are some of my favorite amazing facts about earthworms.

- An earthworm produces nitrogen, phosphorus, and potassium (the same three nutrients found in standard bagged fertilizer) in the perfect form that plants can use.

- One earthworm can produce $1/3$ pound of fertilizer a year. In an earthworm-rich garden, that translates into 50 to 75 pounds of fertilizer each year in a 10- by 20-foot plot.

- Earthworm castings are 5 times richer in nutrients than standard soil.

- Worms secrete a natural lubricant as they tunnel through soil. The lubricant helps bind soil particles together, improving soil structure.

- Some worms bring minerals up from as far as 8 feet below the soil surface—places where no garden tiller ever reaches.

Making the Most of Your Garden

MY SYSTEM OF companion gardening relies on some tried-and-true techniques that increase productivity and add pest-protection insurance to your garden. These methods are succession planting, relay planting, and crop rotation. Using these techniques helps make the most of garden space and also makes the garden more diverse and naturally pest resistant. That fits right in with companion gardening!

Succession and Relay Planting

Successions and relays are two planting techniques that use space well and keep the soil covered. Succession planting is planting a new crop as soon as you pull up the plants from a crop that's finished. A typical routine would be to harvest a cool-weather crop like peas and then plant a warm-weather crop like beans or squash in their place.

Relay planting takes a bit more strategic planning. When you plant in relays, you start one crop next to, or under, an existing crop that will finish soon. For example, you may plant bush-bean seeds under broccoli plants two weeks before the broccoli harvest. That way, the beans will already be growing when you pull out the finished broccoli plants.

Another sequence I like involves overlapping plantings of early spring lettuces, onions, carrots, and more lettuce. As your harvest leaves spaces among one crop, just plant a few of the next.

Relays speed your harvest. About two weeks before harvesting broccoli or other cool-season crops, I poke seeds of warm-season crops, like beans, into the beds beneath the mature plants. It gives me a great head start on my next harvest.

Crop Rotation Pays Off

For me, crop rotation is a gardening basic: It just makes sense to locate your crops in a different part of the garden each season. Crop rotation minimizes disease and insect infestations. For example, if you plant tomatoes in the same bed every year, you'll probably end up fostering a tomato disease like Verticillium wilt. The fungi that cause the disease will remain in the soil over the winter and will just start up again if you plant more tomatoes in the same spot in the spring.

On the other hand, if the tomatoes are in a new bed as little as 15 feet away, the fungi may not find their target in time to survive. The same is

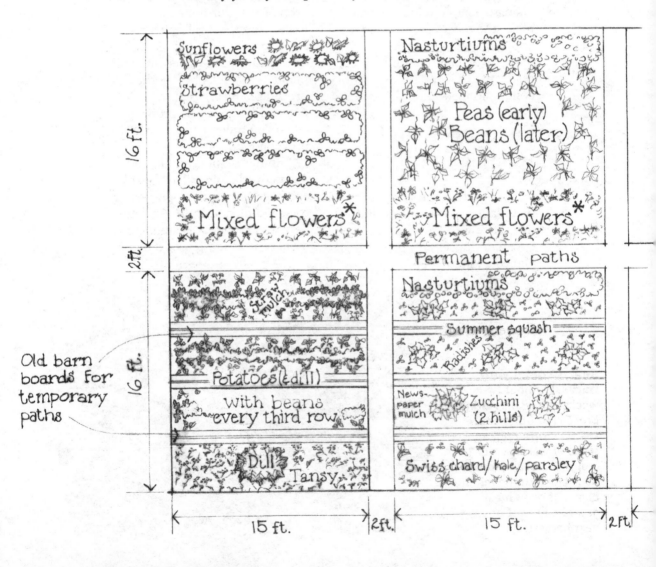

true for pests. How soon to re-peat the same crop in one location varies by the crop and the situation. I recommend waiting at least four years before re-planting a crop in the same spot, especially if a soilborne disease has been present.

Smart rotations also help make the best use of soil nutrients. That's because different crops have different nutrient needs. Some crops, such as cucumbers and tomatoes, use up lots of nutrients, while others, such as beans and potatoes, use very few or actually add nutrients. I group my vegetable crops as heavy feeders, light feeders, or soil builders when I plan rotations with soil in mind. I've built crop rotation right into my companion-gardening system, as you'll see when you create your own crop groups.

Basil

Tomatoes in tall cages

Heavy mulch or black plastic

Mixed flowers*

Try:
Clover interplanted
with tomatoes

My companion garden.
My garden has six blocks of beds. In each block I inter-plant herbs and flowers and mix my crops to create a diverse system that's full of natural pest-control power. Each year, I rotate crops from one block to another.

Broccoli
(lettuce tucked under)

Cauliflower
Interplant onions

Cabbage

Brussels sprouts

Allow:
·goldenrod
·Queen-Anne's-lace
·lamb's-quarters
to grow
around edges

All under
row covers

← Marigolds

15 ft.

* Mixed Flowers:
cosmos, asters,
coreopsis, zinnias,
bachelor's buttons,
chrysanthemums for
transplanting in fall

Summing Up My System

By now you know that my companion garden has a mixed-up look, and it's a real mix of gardening techniques. Companion planting is a key element, but feeding and protecting the soil are equally important. I've also worked to make special areas to attract and shelter beneficial insects and animals. And of course, I plant all my crops intensively, I plant crops in successions and relays, and I rotate crops from year to year.

The techniques themselves aren't new, but the way I've combined them is, and it adds a sense of adventure to my gardening. I'm always on the lookout for beneficial insects I might not have seen before, and I'm always thinking about new ways to make my vegetable garden even more self-sustaining. For example, one new technique I'm experimenting with is planting a hedgerow next to my vegetable garden specifically to attract and shelter those good insects and animals that prey on insect pests (I'll tell you more about that in Chapter 6, "Perennials in the Pumpkins, Shrubs on the Side").

It's easy to enjoy experimenting because my basic system works so well. As I plant cosmos with my eggplant and add compost to my intensively planted raised beds, it's nice to know that I'm part of a long tradition of gardening wisdom. The techniques and principles were always there. It's just our turn to apply them.

And in the next two chapters, we'll do just that. We'll start with garden layout and making raised beds, then move on to the nitty-gritty of setting up plant families, friends, and neighborhoods. The end result will be a successful, diverse garden, full of food and flowers and *lots* of life!

Chapter 3

Getting Ready to Garden

Spring fever is a real and serious condition at Wonderland Farm. I have exhilarating "fever"-induced moments when I buy and plant without reason or control. But despite my occasional spontaneous planting binges, I'm usually quite thoughtful and organized about setting up my garden in the spring. I'm lucky enough to have plenty of room to expand my garden each year, and I plan where to build my new beds.

I also look for nooks and crannies around the yard, even in my flowerbeds and borders, where I can tuck in some vegetables and herbs. After all, mixing up the vegetables and flowers is what companion gardening is all about!

I build up raised beds, mark and mulch my paths, and check the condition of my soil. And I make sure that the hoses are in place so I won't find myself stuck without water when the results of my planting binges have sprouted.

—29—

Setting the Scene for Gardening

THE FIRST STEP in creating your companion garden is choosing a location and laying out the growing beds. If you're an experienced gardener who already has an established vegetable garden, don't worry. It's easy to transform an existing garden into a companion garden. You don't have to choose a new site.

If you're starting a new garden, keep in mind that full sun is a must for most vegetables. It also helps to choose a site that's close to your kitchen door and to a source of water. I advise new gardeners to start small—a 10- by 15-foot plot is plenty to tackle the first season.

Try Mini-Gardens

Companion gardening works really well when you're gardening in small beds in several parts of your yard. So even if you don't have lots of space, you can still grow plenty of vegetables. Place mini-gardens here and there around your yard where the sun or other conditions suit them or where you can see and enjoy them from your patio or through a window. Try a few small beds along pathways, or put salad and herb beds near your kitchen door. And don't ignore the front yard—check the design for a Front-Yard Salad Garden on pages 130–131, and you'll see what I mean.

Unconventional vegetable beds. Add a few vegetables and herbs to your foundation plantings and flowerbeds. You'll love your yard's new look when you tuck lettuce, basil, and Swiss chard among the flowers and shrubs!

Why Be Square?

Rectangular garden plots filled with tomatoes, peppers, carrots, and lettuce are a rather monotonous but standard feature of backyards from California to New England. They're like farm fields in miniature, with long, straight rows of crops. But your garden doesn't *have* to have four corners. After all, it's easier to guide a tiller or lawnmower around curves and circles than around sharp corners. So use your imagination when you plan your garden layout!

My own garden does have squared-off corners, but it's not a simple rectangle, and it includes a mix of low raised beds and taller framed beds. I've often thought that if I were starting from scratch, I'd enjoy a circular garden. I'd create a central sitting area or flowerbed with four or six garden beds radiating out from the center. In fact, I've even designed this garden! (It's the Wheel Garden on page 132.)

Raised Beds Are Basic

DID YOU KNOW that you can grow just as many vegetables in three 6- by 3-foot intensively planted raised beds as in a conventional 10- by 20-foot row garden? Making raised beds and planting intensively— that is, in wide rows of closely spaced plants—can make a dramatic difference in your garden's productivity. It will increase yields per square foot and make your garden easier to tend at the same time.

Wide-row gardens require less weeding and watering than regular gardens, so they're less work. Plus, once you build soil quality in your raised beds by adding organic matter, you can say good-bye forever to tilling and heavy digging!

While you can apply my system of companion gardening to a standard narrow-row garden, I strongly urge you to switch to raised beds planted in wide rows. It's one of the best changes I ever made in my gardening style. If you have a rotary tiller, you can use the hilling attachment to make raised beds. I shape my low raised beds using hand tools.

Preparing Your Site

Before you make raised beds, you need to thoroughly work your garden soil—unless your garden already has rich, well-worked soil. Then it may need only a light fluffing with a garden fork.

Sally Says

"Making raised beds doesn't have to be a major construction project."

Don't turn on that tiller or get out your shovel without first checking the soil moisture level! The soil should be dry enough to crumble in your hand. If the soil is so wet that a handful clumps or cakes when you squeeze it, it's too wet for digging or tilling. Be patient—overdoing the digging in wet soil can ruin soil structure.

If your soil is dry enough, it's best to shape it into beds two weeks before planting day. I recommend working the soil no deeper than 7 inches.

Working the soil always brings up a new crop of weed seeds and exposes them to light, which makes the seeds sprout. By working the soil in advance, you allow that new weed crop to germinate. Then you can cultivate the soil lightly on planting day to kill the weed seedlings and create a nearly weed-free bed for your vegetable seeds and transplants.

Starting from Scratch

If you're new to gardening, or if you're expanding your garden, you'll probably face the tough task of turning a patch of lawn into a vegetable garden. That usually means stripping off sod and digging soil that may be heavy and compacted. But I've sworn off such heavy work and rely on an easier alternative, which I call "quick and dirty bed building." You'll find the instructions for this technique on page 34.

Making Raised Beds

After you've worked your beds with a tiller or digging fork to create loose, crumbly soil, it's easy to form raised beds with just a rake and hoe. Make the beds 2 to 3 feet wide, depending on how far you're comfortable stretching your arms to plant, water, spread mulch, and

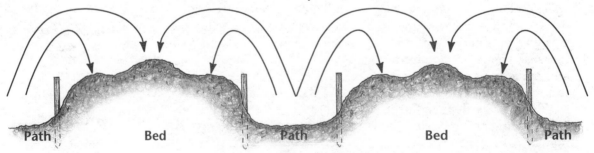

Shovel soil from center of path to center of beds.

Path   Bed   Path   Bed   Path

Use a hoe to pull soil up and form bed edges.

Shaping raised beds. To form low raised beds, first move soil from the areas that will be pathways to form the edges of the beds. Then scoop more soil from the paths into the centers of the beds.

harvest. I recommend making the widest bed you can manage, because then you'll have more room for planting a variety of crops and companion plants.

Here's how to shape your raised beds:

1 Mark the layout. Using stakes and string, mark the edges of your beds and paths. The paths should be at least 1 foot wide. You may want to make some paths wider so that you can maneuver your wheelbarrow or garden cart along them.

2 Form the beds. Your objective is to move the loose topsoil that's in the pathways onto the bed areas, creating beds that are 4 to 6 inches taller than the pathways. To do so, work along a pathway, using a wide hoe to pull soil from the path into the bed. After you work the length of one bed, turn around and pull soil into the adjacent bed. Do this for all the beds. You can also use a rake for this step, as shown in the illustration below.

3 Finish digging out the paths. Now make one more sweep down each path with a shovel, dumping the soil from the paths into the center of the beds.

4 Level the top of the bed. You can smooth the surface of the beds with the back side of a wide rake, or improvise with materials you have on hand. I know a gardener who drags the bed springs from a crib over the bed (this does require a helper!). This method is great for lifting rocks and evening the surface. Just remember, from this point on: NO stepping in the bed!

Perfecting Your Paths

As a finishing touch for your garden, cover all bare soil in the pathways. Bare soil compacts quickly, so water won't penetrate well. If you leave the paths bare, you'll end up with standing puddles or sticky muck that ruins your shoes and clothes (not to mention what happens to your floors

Bed making with a rake. Stand in a garden pathway, and rake the soil from the opposite pathway into the bed. This method works well with loose soil, but if you have heavy clay, try shaping beds with a hoe instead.

when the dogs track it inside!). Weeds also sprout quickly in bare paths.

Fill your paths with straw, wood chips, sawdust, gravel, or leaves. If your garden has had lots of weed problems in past seasons, you may need an extra layer to block the heavy crop of weed seedlings or persistent

perennial weeds. Spread cardboard, newspaper at least five sheets thick, or even old carpet on the paths before you put down the mulch.

One great alternative to mulching is planting dwarf white clover in your paths. The clover will add organic matter to the soil, fix nitrogen, and help many beneficial insects.

SALLY'S HELPFUL HINTS

Plank Paths

My top choice for path coverings is wooden planks—preferably aged barn boards. Here's why I use them:

- My garden cart is easy to maneuver on them.
- I often sit in a path when I plant or weed, and planks stay drier than clover or straw.
- Planks disperse the weight of carts, dogs, and people over a larger area, which helps preserve soil structure and protects the homes of those all-important earthworms.
- Planks make great slug traps. (Just flip them over and pick off the slugs—or let the birds picnic!)
- It's handy to secure the edges of row covers or black plastic by tucking them under the boards.
- I have boards on hand from a barn-repair project, and I love to recycle!

One final tip: If you have a serious weed problem in your garden, spread newspaper before you put down the boards. It will help block weeds that may sneak up through spaces between the boards.

Quick and Dirty Bed Building

One year when I was struggling with a serious back problem, I wanted to make a new perennial island around a beautiful crabapple tree in the lawn. There was no way I was going to strip sod, let alone double-dig! So, I simply *built* soil—by a sort of in-place composting—right on top of the lawn.

It's All in the Hugel

My technique is similar to an old German technique called the hugel method (*hugel* means hill in German). It's like making a special compost pile that you never turn and that can be planted directly. While there is a waiting period between building the bed and planting it, the building process is *much* quicker and less strenuous than digging and tilling unworked soil.

When you build a "quick and dirty bed," the all-important first step is to cover the site by spreading newspaper five or six sheets thick. I failed to do this with my first pile, and I learned about the power of perennial grasses. I still struggle with the occasional weed that finds its way to the light—even through a bed originally built 2 feet tall!

Cover the newspaper with a 6- to 12-inch layer of coarse material such as brush or twigs. Then pile on layers, from the coarsest to the finest organic materials, until you have a 2- to 4-foot-tall hill of the desired width and length. (As in regular composting, decomposition happens most effectively in piles at least 3 feet tall, long, and wide.)

My bed consisted of brush followed by 12 inches of slightly aged leaves, 4 inches of manure, some straw, grass clippings, a little topsoil, and compost. Your materials will vary depending on what you have, but the concept remains the same—and it works! I built my hugel in August of one year, planted into it the following spring, and had a lovely first-year perennial bed that summer. And I will *never* double-dig again!

Do You Need a Soil Test?

If you're starting a brand-new garden, you may want to do a complete soil test. Cooperative Extension offices throughout the country usually provide a soil test for a small fee. The results will tell you about soil fertility levels and recommend soil amendments to correct any nutrient deficiencies. (Be sure to ask for recommendations for organic amendments.) Contact your local Extension office and tell them you want a soil test. They'll tell you how to prepare a sample of your soil for testing.

Don't assume that you always need a full soil test for new garden beds. If you've been growing flowers and vegetables successfully in your yard and want to start a new bed, you can assume that the soil will be similar (unless your yard is several acres in size). Also, if you add organic matter to your soil regularly, you have been feeding the

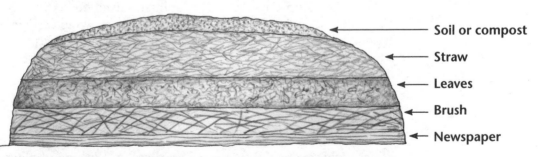

Soil or compost
Straw
Leaves
Brush
Newspaper

Quick and dirty bed building. In late summer, layer brush, shredded leaves, grass clippings, or other organic materials in a pile. Put coarse materials on the bottom and fine materials on top. By the next spring, you'll have a raised bed ready for planting.

earthworms and other soil life—and *they* ensure soil fertility.

The truth is, I've never had my soil fully tested. That's because everything grows! Also, I know the clues that might signal a deficiency, and I'm not seeing them. I add so much organic matter that I know my soil is fertile. I also add rock phosphate and greensand every four years on a "can't hurt" basis.

Checking Soil pH

One thing I do like to test is soil pH. A pH test measures how acidic or alkaline the soil is. For most crops, your soil pH should be between 6.0 and 7.0—slightly acidic to neutral. No matter how fertile your soil is, if the pH is much higher or lower than this range, the plants can't absorb nutrients from the soil efficiently.

Cooperative Extension offices, with the help of Master Gardeners, typically provide free or inexpensive pH testing. Or you can buy a pH test kit or pH paper at garden centers or from garden supply catalogs. Just follow the instructions in the kit.

If your soil pH is off, you can change it by adding lime (to raise the pH) or sulfur (to lower the pH). There's no simple formula for predicting how much to add because the effects of lime and sulfur vary with soil type. For example, you may need to add more lime to a heavy clay soil than to a sandy loam soil. Again, check with your local Extension office for advice on what you should add.

Sally Says

"Testing your soil may be optional, but adding organic matter is mandatory!"

Building Framed Raised Beds

LOW RAISED BEDS serve well for most companion gardens, and they're very easy to make. But there are some good reasons to build at least one tall raised bed that has solid sides.

Framed raised beds make it clear that people and dogs should *stay off*, which protects soil structure!

Tall raised beds are perfect for very early spring planting because they drain better, dry out faster, and warm up earlier than regular garden beds or low raised beds. If you have clay soil and cold, late springs (as I do in western New York), a framed raised bed is your best chance for growing early lettuce, spinach, and peas.

Framed beds make gardening easier and more enjoyable for children, senior citizens with physical limitations, or anyone who has difficulty stooping, squatting, or digging. With good planning and some help building, raised planting beds can even be made wheelchair-friendly.

Best Bed Sizes

Building a framed raised bed is a big project, so be sure you build a bed that's a convenient size. To decide on the right width, think about these questions: How long are your arms? How flexible is your back?

I like to set bed width with the "Three Bears" in mind. A bed that a big Papa Bear will tend can be up to 4 feet wide. For Mama Bear, keep beds about 3 feet wide, and for Baby Bear, build a bed no more than 2 feet across. That way nobody will be tempted to step up on the beds (and crush the soil) when planting, weeding, or stealing a strawberry!

When it comes to bed length, remember that the longer the bed, the less likely someone will be to walk all the way around it. So, a 12-foot-long raised bed will probably have footprints in it sooner or later. That's why I recommend 8-foot or 10-foot beds: because they're short enough to walk around. They're also convenient to build if you're working with wood because lumber is sold in 8-foot and 10-foot lengths. Why design anything that requires a lot of unnecessary sawing when you'd rather be gardening?

Preparing Your Site

Before you start building, prepare your site by removing large rocks, leveling the soil, and removing weeds. Then mark the boundaries of the bed. If you're building more than one bed, be sure to leave enough space between them for your garden cart or wheelbarrow to pass through.

Preparing the site. Before building a framed raised bed, you must level the site. Use a shovel to move soil from high areas to low areas, and then rake the bed areas smooth. If you've changed the grade by more than a few inches, let it settle for a few weeks before planting.

Straw, Blocks, or Wood?

For fast and easy raised beds, you can simply outline the inside with bales of straw and fill it with soil. But for a more durable bed, you'll probably want to make a long-lasting frame of wood, stone, or cement blocks, or even invest in a ready-made bed-building kit from a catalog.

If you can get cement blocks cheaply, they're useful for outlining beds. Just arrange them with the open sides facing up and fill in the center area with soil. You can plant flowers or herbs—especially invasive ones like mint—right in the holes in the blocks where they'll stay contained. My friend Peggy Giermek even used cement blocks to edge flowerbeds in front of her house. She planted snow-in-summer (*Cerastium tomentosum*), a lovely trailing perennial, in the holes in the blocks. It draped beautifully down the sides of the beds and hid the blocks.

My first choice for raised bed frames is wood. Generally, the most-available wood types are rough-sawn hemlock, spruce, pine, and selected hardwoods such as pallet-grade red oak, beech, or maple. You may also be fortunate enough to acquire some timbers of a really decay-resistant native wood, like cypress or cedar. But even if you select a less decay-resistant wood, like pine, maple, or ash, you can build a raised bed that will last for many years.

Sally Says

"My new raised beds are the best home improvement I ever made. Now I can plant in April!"

Craig's Raised Beds

I'm lucky to have an excellent builder in my family, my brother-in-law, Craig Vogel. Craig built me some wonderful raised beds using hemlock landscape timbers that will probably last 20 years. The beds are 11 feet long and 3 feet wide (inside dimensions). You can adapt Craig's beds to the size that suits your garden.

Step-by-Step Bed Building

To make a bed like the one shown in the illustrations, you'll need 6- by 6-inch hemlock landscape timbers cut to the following lengths (if you don't have the tools or experience to cut timbers, ask the lumberyard to cut the lengths you need): two 12-foot pieces, two 11-foot pieces, two 4-foot pieces, and two 3-foot pieces. You'll also need a roll of 4-mil builder's plastic and fourteen 10-inch landscape nails (also called landscape spikes).

Step 1. Lay out the first level of timbers. Use two 12-foot timbers for the sides and two 3-foot pieces for the ends of the bed. Nail these together by inserting a landscape nail horizontally near each corner.

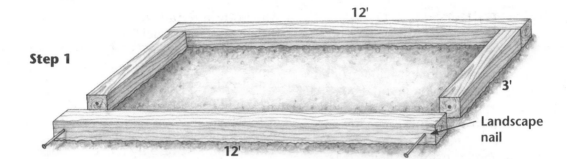

Step 1

12'

3'

12'

Landscape nail

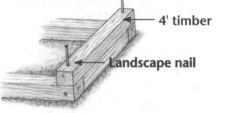

4' timber

Landscape nail

Step 2. Add the end pieces for the second level. Place the two 4-foot sections at the ends of the bed. Drive landscape nails through the timbers to secure them to the timbers below.

Step 2

Bow saw

Step 3

Step 3. Prepare the side pieces for the second level. Measure the distance between the end pieces, and if needed, trim the two 11-foot timbers so they'll fit tightly in that space.

Step 4. Secure the side pieces for the second level. Put the 11-foot timbers in place along the sides of the bed, and drive landscape nails through them to secure them to the timbers underneath.

Step 4

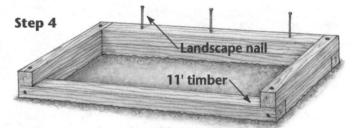

Landscape nail

11' timber

Step 5. Line the inside of the bed. Cover the inside of the timbers with 4-mil-thick black plastic to protect the wood from direct contact with the soil. Staple the plastic along all inside walls, letting some plastic overlap onto the soil level about 2 inches. Lay newspaper several sheets thick on the floor of the bed to discourage any weed seeds lying in wait.

Step 5

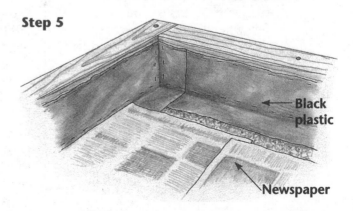

Black plastic

Newspaper

Filling the Beds

Perhaps you have lots of fine topsoil just lying around ready to fill a bed. (If so, lots of us would like to move in with you!) But for many gardeners, it's a struggle to find good topsoil in their yards. You can buy topsoil, but commercial topsoil varies in quality. It's smart to get the topsoil tested for nutrients and pH before you buy a large quantity.

I suggest that you fill the bed with organic material that will compost in place, creating the soil you need. Start by assessing what you can get: some aged manure? Some nearly finished compost? Aged leaves from your town's recyling area? A lot of brush and yard waste from spring cleanup? If new homes are under construction in your neighborhood, you can ask a friendly builder if you can take some topsoil from the building site. While some builders have arrangements to sell the soil, others don't and may be glad to give or sell it to you. The few wheelbarrows-full that you need aren't much compared to what they dig out in preparation for building a house.

Whatever your sources, fill the new bed with at least 12 inches of soil and organic matter. Put the least-decomposed material, such as twigs and sticks, kitchen scraps, and shredded paper, on the bottom. Gradually layer other materials, such as leaves, aged manure, and grass, until you reach the top. The top layer should be the best compost and topsoil you have.

If you have a lot of unfinished compost or only partially decomposed organic matter in your bed, let the bed settle and mature for several weeks before planting. This will allow any "hot spots"—the hot parts of the pile where material is decomposing rapidly—to cool down to avoid burning plant roots. The bed materials may sink a few inches, but that won't be a problem.

SALLY'S HELPFUL HINTS

Supercharge Your Soil

The bed you've built may have plenty of nutrients—but if you're like me, you'll want a "soil insurance policy." If so, whip up a special organic fertilizer that will fortify your soil and ensure a good supply of nutrients for your plants. Just mix 2 gallons of cottonseed meal with ⅛ cup of kelp meal. This is enough for 50 cubic feet of soil, or about two 12- by 3-foot beds. Spread the mix over the soil surface, and use a garden fork to work the mix into the top 12 inches of soil.

Planning for Water

ALL TOO OFTEN, watering the garden is an after-thought. We don't think about it until a sudden hot spell in spring leaves our seedlings drooping and in danger of sudden death. I know, because I've been guilty of it myself. So now I plan my garden-watering system before I plant.

I envy gardeners who have sophisticated high-tech irriga-tion systems. The pipes are buried, the connections fit neatly together, and drip hoses deliver water to each and every plant. But these systems can be expensive and take lots of early planning. I know that in my real-world garden, it will be a while before I have one.

What I do have are hoses! My hoses are in 50- or 100-foot lengths. I connect several together and attach them to my water source. And I must say, out of all gar-dening activities, I've had more moments of teeth-gritting frustration from hose problems than I've ever had from pest problems. My mistakes have included buying cheap hoses, buying some ½-inch and some ⅝-inch hoses, buying dif-ferent types of hoses that don't connect easily, and failing to check and set up my hose system well before planting day.

Sally's Hose Rules

Based on my many mis-takes, I've come up with some hose rules that I now abide by religiously. Although I don't enjoy taking care of my wa-tering equipment, I know that my beloved plants will suffer and the yield from my veg-etables will be poor if I don't. So if you're more interested in taking care of "plant ware" than hose hardware, you may want to push yourself to follow my rules, too!

Homemade hose guides. I use old pieces of pipe stuck in the ground at the corners of my garden to keep hoses out of the beds.

Here are my seven essential rules for successfully managing garden hoses:

🐦 Buy only good quality, weather-resistant, ⅝-inch hoses.

🐦 Select one brand of hose and watering products and stick with it. That way you'll know that all the parts will fit together. Metal or plastic ends and accessories are both fine; just stick with one kind.

🐦 Test your hoses and watering accessories before you move them out to the garden, and test them well before planting day in case you discover problems!

🐦 Set up hose guides at the ends of your paths or at the corners of your beds so you can water without dragging a hose over precious plants.

🐦 Consider installing permanent drip-irrigation hoses around some plantings. (I haven't made this investment yet, but I believe that drip irrigation is water-wise and effective, and it's on my to-do list!)

🐦 Learn how to repair a hose (you can check my method on page 162).

🐦 Stick to 50- or 100-foot lengths of hose, because 200-foot hoses are too heavy and cumbersome to drag around.

Doing the Prep Work

I REALLY LIKE the "getting ready to garden" tasks, like making beds, arranging paths, and fixing hoses, that I've covered in this chapter. These garden-preparation tasks challenge me to be innovative and solve problems, and—unlike other parts of life—there's no right or wrong, just *my way* to do it! I've also learned to love the preparation because doing it well sets up the garden for success. It's like going into a test when you have really studied. And once I've done the work, I can smugly say, "I'm ready...bring on the plants!"

All Ready to Plant

With beds built, soil in shape, and hoses in hand, we're ready to plant! Now it's time for us to get on to the heart of companion gardening: figuring out just which plants you want to pair up in your beds to create a beautiful, high-yield garden.

Chapter 4

My Special System

My family and friends are quite tolerant of my passion for plants, insects, and gardening. Sometimes my human companions even help me in my garden. But most of the time, my gardening companions are beneficial insects, frogs, birds, and a few other creatures. When I talk about companion gardening, the "family and friends" I'm referring to are the plant kind. I group vegetable crops that work well together and call them a *family*. Each crop family has a special set of *friends*—flowers and herbs that I plant among the vegetables. Some plant friends come and go, but most stick around for a long time. Now and then, I try out a few newcomers in my garden, and some of them become permanent plant friends, too. These plant families and friends make up my garden *neighborhoods*, and they're the secret to successful companion gardening. Once you learn how to create your own garden neighborhoods, garden planning is a breeze!

Setting Up Plant Families

CHOOSING PLANTS and grouping them into "families" and "friends" to make garden "neighborhoods" is one of my favorite parts of companion gardening. My garden comes alive with color and life because I plant so many flowers and herbs along with my vegetables. When I'm paging through seed catalogs and making plant lists, I can picture how beautiful my garden will look.

The first time you set up plant groups for your companion garden, plan on spending a couple of hours studying plant lists, charts, and catalogs. You'll learn a lot! Just be patient, and follow my guidelines. They'll help spare you the hair-pulling struggles I suffered while first creating my system. After you get your plant families and friends set, you'll use them year after year. That makes garden planning a cinch! You just take out your garden plan, add or change a few crops and companion plants, rotate your neighborhoods, and you're done.

A companion garden is a vegetable garden at heart, so start your garden plan by creating crop families from the list of vegetables you plan to grow. From there, you can pick plant friends and set up a rotation scheme that will help you prevent nearly all pest problems and get the most from your crops.

Sally Says

"When you're planning your garden, take a second look at your crop list. Do you really want cabbage? And does anyone need more than two zucchini plants?"

Deciding What to Grow

When it comes to growing vegetables, we tend to plant what we've always planted or what our grandma planted. But if you have limited time for gardening (and who doesn't?), it pays to decide what vegetables you truly appreciate picked fresh from the garden. For instance, I usually grow sweet corn, because there's nothing like the sweetness of just-picked corn at a summer picnic. But there have been years when I've decided that growing corn was too much work, especially when I can buy high-quality, inexpensive sweet corn at the farm down the road.

Only you know the appetites and favorite crops of the people you grow for. Perhaps you need a constant season-long supply of carrots for your children's lunches and snacks. And are there ever enough fresh-picked snap peas?

As you make your crop list, choose a few crops just for fun, too. Try some new varieties of your favorite vegetables, and sample some of the heirloom varieties of crops like tomatoes and beans—the choices of colors, shapes, and flavors are amazing!

Four Kinds of Families

Once you've finalized your crop list, you're ready to set up crop families. In my companion-gardening system, there are four ways to group vegetable crops into families.

Botanical families. Crops that are genetically related belong in the same botanical family. They often have similar cultural needs and pest problems.

Feeding families. Nutrient needs are the common ground for crops in a feeding family. Some crops need highly fertile soil; others do fine in average or fairly poor soil.

Performance families. Grouping plants in performance families is very practical—they're crop combinations that literally help each other grow better. You may recognize some of these combinations as familiar companion-planting recommendations.

Pest-fighting families. In a pest-fighting family, one family member may help repel pests that attack another family member. Or one crop may lure pests away from another crop.

My Crop Families

It's not hard to sort your crops into families, even if it seems confusing at first. I use all four kinds of families in my garden. I group tomatoes, eggplant, and peppers together as a botanical family. Cabbage and its relatives are another, and vine crops, like squash, are a third. I make a family of potatoes and beans because they're a great pest-fighting duo. Onions, carrots, and greens are a good feeding family. Perennial crops like asparagus and strawberries are a performance family that needs a permanent bed. You'll find a detailed rundown of my crop families in "Sally's Garden Neighborhoods" on pages 46–47.

A traditional trio. Corn, beans, and squash or pumpkins are a crop combination created by Native Americans that makes a great companion-garden family.

SALLY'S GARDEN NEIGHBORHOODS

Setting up your first companion garden can take some trial and error. I remember my first attempt. I had 3- by 5-inch cards spread all over my kitchen table. Each card represented a crop, herb, or flower. I shuffled those cards many times before I finished! But I finally settled on crop families and plant friends that I really liked together. Each year, I try some new plants in the garden because I'm always curious and because I like variety. It may help you to know how I set up my basic garden neighborhoods, so here's a summary of what I do. You can incorporate some of the combinations I use into your garden.

The Tomato Neighborhood

Family: Tomatoes, peppers, eggplant, greens

Friends: Basil, cleome, cosmos, parsley, Queen-Anne's-lace, any tall Aster Family flower

Mulch/Groundcover: Black plastic or clover

Rotation: To avoid spreading viral disease, a four-year rotation is wise

Notes: Early in the season, plant lettuce, spinach, or other greens around the edges of the bed. By the time the tomato plants grow large, the greens will have been harvested. When using black plastic as mulch, stuff compost or shredded newspaper and kitchen scraps underneath to enrich the soil.

The Potato Neighborhood

Family: Potatoes, beans, peas

Friends: Calendulas, cosmos, daisies, dill, rosemary, sweet Annie

Mulch/Groundcover: Straw

Rotation: Minimum of three years

Notes: Plant potatoes in single rows with room for hilling. Plant beans or peas in wide rows. Use potatoes to break in new garden areas. All the trenching and digging really works the soil and helps reduce weeds.

The Cabbage Neighborhood

Family: Cabbage Family crops, lettuce, root crops

Friends: Asters, calendulas, chamomile, chrysanthemums, cosmos, marigolds, rosemary, sage, thyme

Mulch/Groundcover: Sweet alyssum or dwarf white clover

Rotation: Minimum of two to three years; remove spent plants from beds at the end of the season, because they can harbor pests and diseases over winter

Notes: Plant the crops in 2-1-2 or 3-2-3 patterns with groundcover in between, or tuck onions, carrots, or beets around the crops. Lettuce grows well in the shade of broccoli leaves. Cover all crops with row covers from planting until harvest.

The Squash Neighborhood

Family: Squash Family crops, corn, pole beans

Friends: Borage, dill, nasturtiums, sunflowers

Mulch/Groundcover: Straw around vine crops; clover between corn rows; plant buckwheat or alfalfa nearby

Rotation: Use a three-year rotation

Notes: Beans will climb corn, especially on an outside row. Plant vine crops and nasturtiums in hills or 3-foot-wide sections among corn. If you don't grow corn, use stakes, teepees, or trellises to support the beans.

The Roots and Greens Neighborhood

Family: Carrots, greens, onions

Friends: Caraway, chamomile, cleome, cosmos (dwarf), dill, fennel, Queen-Anne's-lace, Iceland poppies, short Aster Family flowers

Mulch/Groundcover: Grass clippings

Rotation: These crops aren't disease prone, but root maggots can affect carrots, so a two-year rotation is smart; you can plant greens in the same bed repeatedly without a problem

Notes: Interplant greens, carrots, and onions, or plant them in blocks side by side. Use thinnings in salads. After harvesting lettuce, plant kale or fall greens.

The Perennial Crop Neighborhood

Family: Asparagus, horseradish, strawberries, rhubarb (and possibly raspberries)

Friends: Borage, sweet alyssum, chives, Swan River daisies (for strawberries); asters, bee balm, black-eyed Susans, chamomile, creeping thyme, lovage, tansy, yarrow (for horseradish); cosmos, dill, hollyhocks, sweet Annie (for asparagus)

Mulch/Groundcover: Pine needles or straw for strawberries; buckwheat or black plastic for horseradish; grass clippings, finely chopped leaves, or pine needles for asparagus

Notes: This permanent bed is a good place for perennial herbs and flowers. Match an aggressive spreader like horseradish with equally competitive tansy or bee balm. Use tall but noncompeting hollyhocks and cosmos sparingly in the asparagus patch.

If you're daring, another perennial crop you can try is Jerusalem artichokes. These sunflower relatives produce crunchy, nutty, nutritious tubers (for eating raw or cooked). But watch out—this family member can be a real troublemaker, hogging all the space it can, and it's impossible to eradicate. Unless you have a very large garden, consider planting Jerusalem artichokes in a tub or an isolated corner.

How to Get Started

You'll probably find it helpful to refer to my crop family setup as you decide on your own crop families. In fact, you may want to group your crops the same way I do.

However, if your crop list doesn't jive well with mine, or if you're feeling adventurous, work out your own family groups. If you grow a wide range of vegetables, start by grouping your crops in botanical families; if you have a small crop list, try grouping your crops in feeding families first. From there, you may decide to rearrange them into performance or pest-fighting families.

Just remember that there are really no *wrong* choices, and with experience, you'll discover which combinations of plants work best in your garden.

Botanical Families

Most vegetable gardeners have heard of the Cabbage Family and the Legume Family. They're two examples of botanical families—related plants that have been grouped together by botanists. Botanists give fancy scientific (Latin) names to these groups of genetically related plants, like Solanaceae for the Tomato Family and Brassicaceae for the Cabbage Family.

I use common names for botanical familes, but I try to know the scientific names, too, because the common names can vary. For example, some gardeners call the Cabbage Family the "Crucifer Family," while others call them "cole crops" or "brassicas." You'll find a rundown of botanical families in "Botanical Families" on the opposite page.

Botanical Benefits

There are good reasons to cluster plants in botanical families: By doing so, you'll help prevent pest woes. Grouping plants botanically makes it easy to

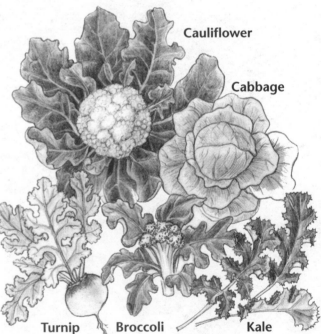

Botanical families. It's not always easy to guess which crops are botanically related. Did you know that cabbage, broccoli, cauliflower, kale, and turnips all belong to the Cabbage Family?

Botanical Families

Here's a rundown of the classic botanical groupings of vegetable crops. I've included the scientific names because you'll sometimes see them used in books when crop rotation is discussed. The names can be tongue twisters, so you'll also find phonetic pronunciations in parentheses. You'll see that plants in the same botanical family often have the same soil and temperature needs, with a few notable exceptions. They're also prone to the same pest problems.

Botanical Family Names	Family Members	Family Characteristics
Aster Family Asteraceae (as-tir-AY-see-ee)	Chicory, endive, lettuce, sunflowers	Leafy crops, usually do best in cool weather or in light shade in hot weather; family also includes many common flowers, including asters and zinnias
Cabbage Family Brassicaceae (brass-ih-KAY-see-ee)	Broccoli, brussels sprouts, cabbage, cauliflower, Chinese cabbage, collards, kale, radishes, turnips	Heavy feeders; need protection from common insect problems
Carrot Family Apiaceae (ay-pee-AY-see-ee)	Caraway, carrots, celery, dill, fennel, parsley	Carrots and celery like cool weather and loose soil, but other family members do well in heat and tolerate most soils
Grain Family Poaceae (poh-AY-see-ee)	Corn	Demanding crop, labor-intensive, a heavy feeder, a glutton for water; needs a lot of space for effective pollination
Legume Family Fabaceae (fa-BAY-see-ee)	Beans, peas	Nitrogen-fixing crops that enrich the soil; this family also includes a few trees and cover crops (such as alfalfa)
Onion Family Liliaceae (li-lee-AY-see-ee)	Asparagus, chives, garlic, leeks, onions	As a perennial, asparagus has different needs; other family members are susceptible to onion maggots, don't tolerate weed competition, and are light feeders
Spinach Family Chenopodiaceae (kee-noe-poe-dee-AY-see-ee)	Beets, spinach, Swiss chard	Leafy crops that prefer cool conditions; beets are a root crop as well
Squash Family Cucurbitaceae (kew-kur-bih-TAY-see-ee)	Cucumbers, melons, pumpkins, squash	All need warm weather and lots of space; need protection from common insect and disease problems, including cucumber beetles and squash borers
Tomato Family Solanaceae (sow-luh-NAY-see-ee)	Eggplant, peppers, potatoes, tomatoes	Heat-loving crops; similar soil requirements; subject to many serious fungal diseases; potatoes tolerate cool weather and need acid soil

choose plant friends and makes sense in terms of plant care.

Reducing pest problems. Plants that belong to the same botanical family often have the same pest and disease problems. For example, tomatoes, potatoes, and eggplant (Tomato Family crops) can all suffer from a nasty fungal disease, early blight. If you plant these crops all over your garden, you may end up with early-blight fungi in the soil of every bed. Each year, the fungi will build up until your whole garden is infected. But when you plant the Tomato Family crops in a single bed and move them to a new bed each year, the fungi will die out in the beds without these crops, giving you a better chance of growing a healthy crop in the future.

I keep my Squash Family crops together because I like to cover them all with row covers (to keep out pests) until they flower. I also group my Cabbage Family crops and cover them with row covers as a preventive measure, sometimes for the whole growing season.

Choosing plant friends. Grouping plants in botanical families also helps when it's time to choose plant friends. Continuing our Tomato Family example, you can choose friendly herbs and flowers that do the best job attracting beneficial insects that prey on or repel Tomato Family pests.

Providing care. Plants in the same botanical family often have similar needs for light, moisture, and fertility. But there *are* odd ducks—or should I say, plants—that don't act at all like the rest of the family! In the Tomato Family, potatoes are the oddball—they prefer quite different growing conditions than tomatoes, peppers, and eggplant.

Feeding Families

When we go out to eat, some of us choose the all-you-can-eat buffet, while others turn straight to the "light and healthy" portion of the menu. It's the same with plants. Some are big eaters, while others have small appetites. There are even a few crops

Feeding families. Crops in a feeding family have similar nutrient needs. Garlic, turnip, and carrots are light feeders. Basil, cilantro, and most other herbs are also light feeders.

that hardly eat anything and leave food behind...for the next group!

In a practical sense, grouping plants in feeding families helps you make the most of your soil fertility. There are heavy feeders, moderate feeders, light feeders, and even soil improvers. To find out which crops belong in each group, check "Veggie Appetites," below.

Grouping crops in feeding families is simple, so it works well for small gardens. It's a good way to group your crops if you have poor soil that you're gradually improving—you can put the heavy feeders in the richest bed. You can also plan a crop rotation according to feeding needs. You can plant soil improvers in a bed the year after the heavy feeders, and the following year, put moderate and light feeders into that bed.

Pest-Fighting Families

In my garden, certain crops always share a bed for one reason only: safety. The crops provide mutual defense against pest problems, or one protects the other. While none of these combinations is foolproof, I can attest to good results in my garden.

VEGGIE APPETITES

Some vegetable crops need highly fertile soil to produce good yields, while others can get by with less feeding and fertility. If you grow a limited number of crops, you may find it easiest to group them by feeding families. Here's a rundown of crops by their "appetites." To learn when and how much to feed each of these crops, refer to Chapter 10, "Sally's Top Crops and Companion-Garden Secrets."

Heavy Feeders

Celery	Peppers
Corn	Pumpkins
Cucumbers	Squash
Eggplant	Tomatoes
Melons	

Moderate Feeders

Broccoli	Lettuce and other greens
Brussels sprouts	
Cabbage	Parsley
Cauliflower	Spinach
Chinese cabbage	Swiss chard
Kale	

Light Feeders

Beets	Onions
Carrots	Potatoes
Garlic	Radishes
Leeks	Turnips

Soil Builders

Beans	Peas

Beans and Potatoes

Research studies show that planting bush beans and potatoes in alternating rows significantly reduces the numbers of Colorado potato beetles and Mexican bean beetles compared to single-crop plots. Is this because the companion crops repel the pests or because the interplanting just mixes up the pests so that they don't find the target crop? I don't know the answer, but I am very pleased that it works! I have a special interplanting technique for beans and potatoes. For instructions, see page 225.

Sacrificial Eggplant

Colorado potato beetles love eggplant. So if you don't love eggplant, try planting some among your other Tomato Family crops. Watch and wait for the beetles to accumulate on the eggplant, and then destroy the plants. Or watch for the cavalry of predatory insects to arrive. That little cavalry may not get there in time to save your eggplant trap crop— but they will be ready to handle the potato beetles when they try to feast on your tomatoes and potatoes.

Radishes to the Rescue

Radishes are a classic player in companion-planting folklore. Radishes are easy to tuck under or around most vegetable crops. Radishes planted among hills of squash or pumpkins are supposed to deter cucumber beetles.

I use radishes for bed markers by planting them at the ends of sections of lettuce or other direct-seeded vegetables (the radishes germinate and grow quickly, so I can tell where one crop ends and another begins). And since flea beetles love radishes, I use radishes as a "trap crop" to catch the beetles early and keep them off other tender seedlings. (I just pull up the infested radishes and destroy them to get rid of the flea beetles). This can also work with cabbage maggots. The maggots go straight to the radishes, which may save your broccoli and other Cabbage Family crops.

A protection family.
A circle of radishes planted around cucumbers may act as a protective shield that keeps cucumber beetles out.

Odoriferous Onions

All the Onion Family crops, including chives, onions, and garlic, make great protectors. They're reported to repel carrot rust flies, Colorado potato beetles, Japanese beetles, and aphids. This odoriferous family may also discourage wildlife from eating your plantings, and onion/garlic sprays can actually kill some pests and repel others.

Performance Families

Sometimes one crop can help another grow better just by being close by. For example, if a crop like lettuce needs shade in hot weather, it can grow well next to a tall, sun-loving crop. Some of my best performance-family arrangements involve teepees made with 8-foot poles. I simply tie three to five poles together and plant climbing peas or beans at the base of the poles. Then I plant lettuce, spinach, or other greens in the middle, where they'll be shaded by the teepee sides as the climbing crops grow. Many of these performance families are based on companion-planting tradition. For more possibilities like this, see "Growing in the Shadows" on page 54.

Performance families often have a bonus—they help you make the best use of limited garden space. You can create a performance family by matching a crop that needs to climb with a crop that stands straight or that grows inside a cage. Three examples of plants that can support climbers are corn, sunflowers, and tomatoes (the climbers can climb the tomato cages). The climbing crops I've used on living trellises like these are snow peas, cucumbers, pole beans, and scarlet runner beans.

Performance families, which often match totally unrelated crops like beans and lettuce, may offer yet another benefit. Insects that attack one crop but not the other may be confused by the close placement of the two different crops, so the pests may not find their target crop.

The Three Sisters

One classic example of a companion-garden family is the "Three Sisters." Native Americans developed this interplanted group of corn, beans, and squash, which benefits all three crops. They planted pole beans and corn together in large planting hills and added squash or pumpkin vines to cover the ground between the hills.

The dense, prickly squash vines protect the corn from animal invaders and have the benefit of open ground to grow on between the hills of corn and beans. The corn plants act as living stakes for the beans to climb, and the beans help the corn by "fixing" nitrogen. It worked traditionally and still works in my garden.

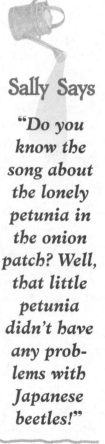

Sally Says

"Do you know the song about the lonely petunia in the onion patch? Well, that little petunia didn't have any problems with Japanese beetles!"

GROWING IN THE SHADOWS

We think of vegetable crops as sun lovers, but some crops can tolerate shade or even grow better in partial shade during hot weather. You can create performance families by pairing tall crops with shade-tolerant crops.

To make a performance sun/shade family, just pair a tall crop from the list below with a midsize or short crop. Or match up a midsize crop with a short crop. Plant the shorter crop between rows of the taller crop or on the eastern side of the tall crop (protected from hot afternoon sun). You can also plant short crops under teepees or trellises that support tall crops.

Most of the midsize and short plants grow just fine in full sun but will tolerate the shade of a nearby tall plant. Lettuce and spinach are two crops that really benefit from partial shade in hot weather.

Tall Crops

Corn

Cucumbers (on a trellis)

Melons (on a trellis)

Peas (vine-type)

Pole beans

Scarlet runner beans

Sunflowers

Tomatoes (caged or staked)

Midsize Crops

Broccoli

Brussels sprouts

Cauliflower

Celery

Chinese cabbage

Eggplant

Peppers

Short Crops

Beets	Lettuce
Cabbage	Radishes
Carrots	Spinach
Cucumbers	Swiss chard
Gourmet greens	

A cooperative family in a teepee. Pole beans climb a teepee, shading lettuce and New Zealand spinach from the hot summer sun. I plant flowers that attract beneficials in the center area under the teepee where I can't reach to harvest.

Great Plant Companions

Choosing flower and herb companions to grow with your vegetables is lots of fun because there are so many beautiful—and often edible—flowers to choose from. There are no wrong choices when you select plant companions, but certain herbs and flowers are better choices than others because they offer more than just beauty. The best choices of all are the companions that attract and shelter beneficial insects like lady beetles and lacewings. In this section, we'll take a look at some of my favorite plant companions.

Traditional companion-planting recommendations list marigolds as pest repellents. I'm convinced, however, that marigolds and other strongly scented plants, like basil, really work because they *confuse* the pests that are looking for your vegetables.

Companion planting can produce wild color combinations, like this mix of purple kale, rich green parsley, red-stemmed Swiss chard, and orange marigolds.

▼

Follow my simple rule for choosing plant companions: Just pick one Parsley Family member (like parsley, dill, or coriander) and one Aster Family member (like marigolds, daisies, and sunflowers) to match up with each of your vegetable groups. Voilà—it's a garden neighborhood!

The Aster Family (Asteraceae) offers a wonderful variety of flowers that attract beneficial insects, including lady beetles, spined soldier bugs, assassin bugs, and predatory wasps. Two of my favorites: Sunflowers (*left*) can do "double duty" as bean poles, and blanket flowers (*below*) create a long-blooming, low-maintenance bright spot in any garden.

Purple coneflowers, black-eyed Susans, and other perennials from the Aster Family attract beneficials, too. Try planting a permanent cluster of perennials near, or right beside, your vegetable garden. It's a "good-bug hideaway" where beneficials can retreat after the hunt.

◀ For a beautiful contrast, try the fine, feathery leaves and delicate blossoms of cosmos among some stocky eggplants with their glossy, purple fruits. Tuck in some crinkly leaved basil to add extra interest—and pest protection.

Cosmos are one of my top ten picks for all-around good companions. They provide nectar for insects, don't take up much space, and their sweet flowers keep coming all summer long.
▼

Onions don't really need much help from plant companions because their pungent odor repels many garden pests. But petunias look pretty weaving among onion stems, and they help cover the soil and harbor some insect helpers.

'Purple Wave' petunias shelter spiders and ground beetles (great warriors against slugs). The petunias also mix beautifully with nectar-rich chamomile. 'Purple Wave' is cost-effective, too: One plant easily spreads 3 feet in all directions.

Nasturtiums are a must in my garden. Their vining stems make them a great companion rambling among the cucumbers and squash. They're reputed to repel cucumber beetles, but I depend more on their value as a habitat for predatory insects. In a traditional Three Sisters planting of corn, beans, and squash, I consider nasturtiums a "kissing cousin!"

One way to make room for plant companions in gardens with limited space is to go—and grow—upward. Cucumbers climb a string trellis easily, leaving plenty of room for fennel and an edging of nasturtiums. For even more color, you can add tall annuals like cleome or cosmos among the fennel.

Calendulas (*bottom*) are ▶
another workhorse
companion plant. Their
cheerful yellow and orange
blossoms attract many
beneficials, and the plants
are easy to start from seed.
Plus, they often reseed
themselves from year to
year. They bloomed among
my squash all summer.
What's not to like?

Dwarf zinnias nestle beautifully alongside cauliflower. Their nectar lures lady beetles and other predators. And to protect against slugs (who love to feast on cauliflower leaves), I use a straw mulch, which shelters slug-eating ground beetles.

▼

▲

Straw mulch also helps keep low-hanging fruit clean and prevents fruit rot. I especially like it under peppers and tomatoes. Delicate cleome completes the pretty picture and attracts the tiniest of the beneficial wasps and flies.

Sweet alyssum has tiny flowers that are just the right size for delicate beneficials like chalcid wasps. Plant it alongside bushy crops like potatoes, or let it spread to form a living groundcover under arching plants like broccoli. ▶

Gazanias (sometimes called treasure flowers) bloom prolifically from June to October. They attract beneficials and fit neatly among medium-size plants like these 'Sweet Banana' peppers. ▼

Dill is a great companion for Cabbage
Family crops, like brussels sprouts.
The pairing is mutually satisfying: The
brussels sprouts support the floppy dill,
while the dill pulls in the predatory
wasps like a magnet.

▲
Botanically speaking, angelica is a perennial member of the Carrot Family, along with dill, fennel, and caraway. All of these herbs are proven "good-bug magnets." Angelica requires special placement because it can reach 6 feet tall. Try it as a centerpiece in your perennial cluster.

◄ I keep a permanent border of perennial herbs along the front of my vegetable patch. Chives, thyme, artemisia, and garlic chives are welcome plant friends.

German chamomile is a dependable, easy-to-grow herb, and I love its cheery white-and-yellow blossoms. It's a popular traditional herb with many uses, but in my garden its job is to attract hoverflies and tiny beneficial wasps.

Borage is one of my favorite plant companions. Its periwinkle blue blossoms are delightful—and edible (they're great in salads). It self-seeds freely every year but it isn't aggressive. Bees (important for crop pollination) love borage. It's as pretty as a picture with coreopsis 'Early Sunrise'.

I wouldn't dream of a companion garden without tansy, probably the single best attractor for beneficial insects. I've found lady beetles, spined soldier bugs, spiders, hover-flies, a praying mantis, predatory wasps, and other beneficials on the tansy in my garden.

Every companion-garden bed is unique, and the more diverse the planting, the more successful you'll be. This bountiful garden includes leeks, pumpkins, and deep green Italian kale along with nasturtiums, pansies, marigolds, Italian basil, parsley, and borage as plant friends. Wherever you plant a diverse mix of food crops, flowers, and herbs, you can enjoy a beautiful and productive garden while you observe the fascinating world of beneficial insects at work.

You can apply companion-gardening ideas anywhere in your yard. Try mixing some colorful leaf lettuces or other vegetables among your flower beds. Or tuck them in a shrub border or foundation planting.

Finding the Right Friends

ONCE YOU'VE SORTED your crops into families, you'll move on to choosing plant friends for them. The most important group of friends is the insect-attractors, the plants that draw beneficial insects to your garden. You can also choose protector plants that help keep pests away from your crops and helpers that feed the soil and block weeds.

Your choices range from popular annuals like marigolds and cosmos to culinary herbs like dill and basil. I even find ways to include perennial flowers and herbs in the garden, sometimes in permanent beds adjacent to my crop beds.

You'll find the plant listings on pages 247–265 helpful in choosing plant friends. You can also refer to the entries on individual crops in Chapter 10, "Sally's Top Crops and Companion-Garden Secrets." For each crop, you'll find some specific friends recommended. If you've had problems in the past with particular pests, you may want to consult "Plants for Beneficial Insects" on page 247 to find out which plants attract the beneficials that prey on your problem pest.

As with your crops, there really are no wrong choices—so be sure to include generous helpings of your personal favorite flowers and herbs!

Friends That Attract Good Bugs

"Good bugs"—beneficial insects—are the reason I have so few pest woes in my garden. We want beneficial insects standing by in our gardens at all times—sort of a National Guard ready when pest protection is needed—so we have to feed them. And when beneficials aren't eating pests, they eat pollen, and that's why plant friends are so important.

Friends from the Aster Family. Cheerful flowers from the Aster Family add bright colors to a vegetable garden, and they draw a wide variety of beneficials, too.

Most of the beneficials are very tiny or have short mouth-parts, so the best attractant flowers have nectar and pollen that's easy to reach. These plants have wide, open, daisy-shaped flowers, like asters, or broad clusters of delicate flowers, like Queen-Anne's-lace and dill.

Two Rules for Choosing Ally-Attracting Friends

I use two basic principles in choosing plant friends that draw beneficials. First, I keep something flowering from spring through fall, so the beneficials always have something to eat. Second, for every neighborhood, I choose at least one friend from the Aster Family and one from the Carrot Family, because their flowers are especially attractive to tiny beneficials.

Rule #1: Strive for season-long bloom. The earliest flowers around my garden are dandelions. I allow some of these weeds to flower around the perimeter of my garden. There are plenty of spring-blooming perennials you can fit into permanent beds near your garden. Summer is full of flowers, including cosmos, marigolds, calendulas, and yarrow. For late bloom, I use fall-blooming asters, goldenrod, purple coneflowers, and boltonia. Be sure to include tansy. I think it's the single best plant for luring beneficials to the garden and keeping them there once they arrive.

Rule #2: Include Aster and Carrot Family plants. The Aster Family is one of the largest plant families, and you'll find plenty of Aster Family choices in "Plants for Beneficial Insects" on pages 247–257. The Carrot Family includes many familiar herbs, such as angelica, caraway, coriander, dill, fennel, lovage, and parsley. Queen-Anne's-lace is a valuable member of this list, so learn to recognize its seedlings, and don't weed them all out!

Plants from other botanical families are also helpful. Choose

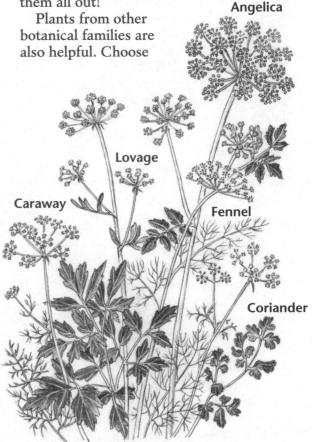

Angelica

Lovage

Caraway

Fennel

Coriander

Friends from the Carrot Family. Carrot Family herbs and flowers have lovely, lacy flower heads that are powerful lures for beneficial insects like lady beetles and parasitic wasps.

some Cabbage Family flowers, such as sweet alyssum or mustard—or let some broccoli plants go to flower. (Parasitic wasps will love it!) Include some Mint Family plants near your garden—in pots or inside root barriers—such as bee balm, catnip, and spearmint, which attract many beneficials. Bee balm will also attract hummingbirds. A pot or hanging basket of lantana will not only attract butterflies but will also harbor lady-beetle larvae until it's time for them to go hunting for your pests.

Friends That Protect Your Plants

Just as there are certain vegetable crops that repel pests, companion-planting tradition includes many reports of flowering plants that ward off pests. By planting these companions near the target crop, the folklore claims, you create a protected zone that pests won't enter.

Scientific evidence on repellent plants is mixed. Do I count on repellent plants to protect my crops from pests? No! To my mind, using repellent plants is a backup technique—but it never hurts to have a backup. And many of these plants really do help—if only by mixing up a pest that may be looking for your crops. For a rundown on plant friends that repel pests, see "Plants That (May) Keep Pests Away" on pages 258–259.

Four-o'Clocks Trap Japanese Beetles

Flowers and herbs can also protect crops by serving as trap crops. For example, nasturtiums are a trap crop for aphids and flea beetles, and mustard plants attract cabbageworms and harlequin bugs.

One of the best tips on a trap crop came to me from an internationally known Japanese-iris judge, Clarence Mahan, who knows a lot about Japanese beetles—in this country as well as in their country of origin. He taught me that the best traps for Japanese beetles are the old-fashioned annual four-o'clocks.

A protective combo. Planting squash with plant friends, like dill and nasturtiums, gives the squash a competitive edge against pests. The nasturtiums help repel squash bugs, and the dill attracts aphid predators.

The beetles just love them! I keep a coffee can filled with soapy water on hand, and when the plants are beetle-loaded, I just flick the beetles into the can. While it may be sad to see lovely flowers covered with Japanese beetles, it's even sadder to lose a wonderful rose bush or a crop of corn, potatoes, or raspberries.

Get More Eggplant with Marigolds

Marigolds have many claims to fame in a companion garden, but they're stars in my garden because they're tops at repelling flea beetles from eggplant. Having had several years of flea-beetle battles and eggplant whose leaves looked like they were used for target practice, I tried an experiment. I planted some eggplant in one area of the garden by itself. In another area, I interplanted eggplant with lots of tall, strongly scented marigolds and basil. There was a big difference. The interplanted eggplant looked great; the others had buckshot-riddled leaves from flea beetles. So, while we watch for what scientists report on the flea-beetle challenge, why not mix in those marigolds?

Friends That Help You Garden

While pest prevention is the major role of plant friends, there are some that also help by keeping down weeds and improving the soil. Other plant friends help out by attracting pollinating insects. Many of these crops also help attract beneficial insects, making them very good friends indeed!

Living mulch. When you plant ground-covering crops, you're growing a living mulch. In addition to fighting weeds, living mulches prevent soil erosion, improve soil texture, and even enrich the soil. My favorite living mulches are clover, buckwheat, and alfalfa. I plant buckwheat or alfalfa between rows of corn. Sometimes I use clover instead of black plastic as a living mulch around my tomatoes. Also, these crops' flowers attract beneficials.

I also love planting sweet alyssum to use as a living mulch. There's nothing prettier than a sea of white, pink, or purple alyssum flowers under broccoli, cauliflower, or brussels sprouts. Sweet alyssum shelters beneficial insects like ground beetles and is a pollen source for beneficials.

Bee plants. If you grow cucumbers, melons, squash, pumpkins, sunflowers, or strawberries, you need bees to pollinate your crops, or you won't harvest any fruit. And if you save your own seeds from year to year, you also need pollinating insects for your Cabbage Family plants.

Any nectar-producing flower will attract bees. Borage, sunflowers, and clover are three of my favorites. It's especially good to have some of these flowering around vine crops like squash or melons at pollination time.

Sally Says

"When you use catnip as a plant companion, be sure to leave room for an ecstatic cat to roll around without flattening the veggies!"

Planting Your Neighborhoods

S O NOW WE'VE COVERED all the ins and outs of creating companion-garden neighborhoods. If you've reached this point in the chapter but still aren't sure about some of your choices, go back and compare them to "Sally's Garden Neighborhoods" on pages 46–47. Make sure that each of your neighborhoods includes vegetables, flowers, and herbs.

When you're satisfied with your choices, you can celebrate the fact that you've created a garden plan that will continue to work as long as you care to garden. I fiddle with choices of family groups and plant friends each year, but the changes aren't major. I may substitute one flower for another or add a new crop to my list. But it's easy to make these substitutions. The tough job of setting up the neighborhoods only happens once.

This is especially nice for gardeners who want to rotate their crops. All you do is move each plant neighborhood to a different bed each year. It's easiest to do that in a continuing pattern, like the one shown in the illustration on page 76, which shows a basic layout for a companion garden that's very like my own.

Putting Your Plan into Action

Planting companion-garden neighborhoods can be quite different from planting a conventional garden. You'll be planting your vegetables in close spacings and planting flowers side-by-side with vegetables. In the end, you're still sowing seeds and planting transplants. It's just the spacing distances and planting patterns that change.

Intensive planting. Traditional gardeners plant carrots in single rows with lots of bare soil between (left). I plant carrots with onions, scattering carrot seeds around the onion sets (right). I thin the carrots over time, but no soil shows once the crops become established.

YEAR I

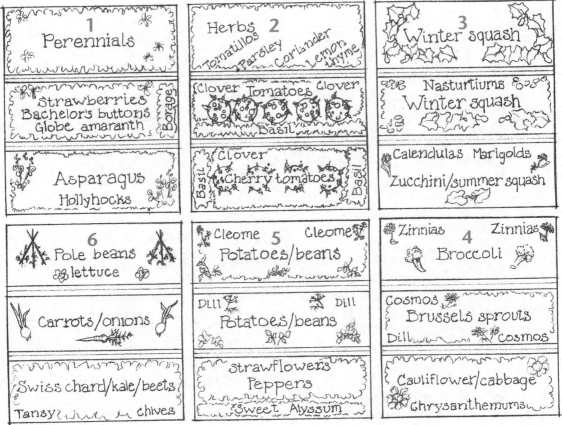

1 Perennials

Strawberries
Bachelor's buttons
Globe amaranth
Borage

Asparagus
Hollyhocks

Herbs 2
Tomatillos   Coriander
Parsley   Lemon thyme

Clover Tomatoes Clover
Basil

Basil Clover
Cherry tomatoes Basil

3 Winter squash

Nasturtiums
Winter squash

Calendulas Marigolds
Zucchini/summer squash

6 Pole beans
lettuce

Carrots/onions

Swiss chard/kale/beets
Tansy   chives

Cleome **5** Cleome
Potatoes/beans

Dill   Dill
Potatoes/beans

Strawflowers
Peppers
Sweet Alyssum

Zinnias **4** Zinnias
Broccoli

Cosmos
Brussels sprouts
Dill   cosmos

Cauliflower/cabbage
Chrysanthemums

YEAR II

1	6	2
Permanent plantings	Lettuce & friends	Tomatoes & herbs
5	4	3
Potatoes/ beans/ peppers	Cabbage family	Squash family

YEAR III

1	5	6
Permanent plantings	Potatoes/ beans/ peppers	Lettuce & friends
4	3	2
Cabbage family	Squash family	Tomatoes & herbs

Moving the neighborhoods. This companion garden has six neighborhoods, each made up of three raised beds. One neighborhood has perennial crops that stay in the same spot permanently. The other neighborhoods rotate to a new part of the garden each year.

Some gardeners may find it strange at first to plant as intensively as I do, especially when a seed packet says: "space every 18 inches in rows 24 inches apart." But as long as you've added lots of organic matter to your soil, there's more than enough "food" there to keep your plants healthy. And the closely planted crops and their friends will form a leafy canopy that maintains soil moisture longer and keeps weeds from becoming a problem. (Close plantings = blocked-out weeds!) That's a winning combination, especially in early summer, when weeds can easily get ahead of you and dry weather is coming.

In a nutshell, I have three basic techniques for planting. I scatter seeds in blocks, and I plant transplants in repeating patterns. For crops that sprawl, like squash and melons, I plant seeds in hills in double-wide beds. I'll describe these techniques here. You can also turn to the crop entries in Chapter 10, "Sally's Top Crops and Companion-Garden Secrets," to find specific directions on how to plant various crops.

Scattering Seed

I plant cover crops, lettuce, carrots, and sometimes peas and beans just by scattering the seeds. I sprinkle the seeds over the entire width of the bed as evenly as I can and then thin the seedlings to the proper spacing once they have a couple of true leaves. I may mix seeds of flowering friends right in with the crop seeds, or if I'm planting the flowers as transplants, I just add them in at intervals along the bed.

Patterns for Transplants

To plant transplants like brussels sprouts or broccoli, a little more calculation is needed. I use staggered planting patterns, which I call 2-1-2 or 3-2-3 patterns.

The 2-1-2 Scheme

I plant broccoli, brussels sprouts, and eggplant in a 2-1-2 pattern: To start, I plant two broccoli plants across the row, about 15 inches

2-1-2 spacing. Plant crops like broccoli in a pattern of two plants–one plant–two plants. Fill the gaps along the sides of the bed with flowering companions, like zinnias.

3'

apart. That leaves about 10 inches to the outside edges of the row—plenty of room for an under-planting of sweet alyssum or clover and for draping row covers and tucking them under the boards that I use in my pathways. Then I plant one broccoli plant in the center of the bed, about 15 inches from each of the two plants already in place. (The three plants will form a tri-angle, and each side of the triangle is about 15 inches long.)

I continue down the bed, planting two plants across, one centered, two across, and so on. I fill the empty spaces on either side of the single broccoli plants with a small companion plant like marigold or calendula. Or I may substitute a large companion plant like dill, borage, or cosmos for a few of the single broccoli plants.

The 3-2-3 Scheme

In a 3-foot-wide row, cabbage, cauliflower, and peppers grow well in a tighter spacing than 2-1-2. I use a 3-2-3 pattern. (I don't usually grow head lettuce, but it would be a good candidate for this spacing, too.) Here's how it works: Plant three transplants across the row about 10 inches apart and 8 inches from the out-side of the row. That still leaves enough room to drape row covers and tuck them under the walk-ways. Then measure about 10 inches *down the row* from the center plant, and plant two more plants about 10 inches apart, each one 13 inches from the outside of the row. Continue down the row, planting three across, two across, three across, until the row is full.

In every other pattern, I like to substitute plant friends for the center plant of the "three" group. There's lots of room for creativity with this scheme, and you can create some exciting patterns of crops and flowers.

Double-Wide Beds

I can combine 3-foot-wide beds to form a bed that's about 7 feet wide (two beds plus a 12-inch-wide path). I use double-wide beds for

3-2-3 spacing. Use a pattern of three plants–two plants–three plants for cauliflower. You can substitute an annual like Swan River daisies for the center plant in each row of three plants.

3'

large plantings of beans for can-
ning. I also use extra-wide beds
for sprawling vine crops.

Big Blocks of Beans

When I'm using beans as a
cover crop to improve the soil,
I plant them thickly in blocks
that are at least two wide beds
thick. I want bean-plant growth
and roots to really cover the
territory. So I practically eliminate the walkways and just
leave stepping stones or a thin
board in place to step on during
harvest. The beans make a solid
stand from which I harvest a
little and turn under a lot.

Wide Swaths for Pumpkins

Whether you're planting
pumpkins as part of a Three
Sisters plot or planting a whole
pumpkin field, there is no such
thing as a 3-foot-wide bed of
pumpkins! Pumpkins crawl,
sprawl, and stretch in all directions, regardless of paths and
neighboring plants. So I plan on
that and give them double-wide
beds, once again with a narrow
board or stepping stones down
the center for getting into the
bed when harvesting. I plant my
hills in alternating beds, leaving
plenty of open space for them to
fill as they grow.

But I don't let that space go
to waste! I either plant corn
and beans for a Three Sisters
combination, or I put wide
sheets of black plastic in and
around the pumpkin hills.

There are two ways to plant
the Three Sisters, as shown
below and on page 80. Both
methods start with a circle
of corn plants about 2 feet
in diameter. Once the corn
sprouts and reaches 6 inches
tall, you can plant beans
around the corn. Then, with
one method, you plant the
pumpkin seeds in a row between the hills.

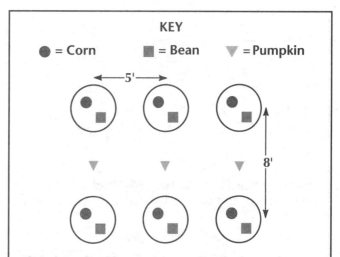

KEY

● = Corn   ■ = Bean   ▼ = Pumpkin

Planting the Three Sisters: Method 1. Plant
circles of corn and beans 5 feet apart in rows 8 feet
apart. Sow pumpkin seeds between the rows.

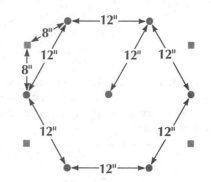

Method 1 planting detail. Each corn/bean circle
consists of seven corn seeds and four bean seeds.

With the second method, you plant the pumpkin seeds at the edge of every seventh hill, as shown below. When I use black plastic mulch around my pumpkins, I spread lots of aged or partially aged manure before I lay the plastic. Sometimes I put down leaves and shredded newspaper, too. (I'm careful not to let any "hot" manure touch my growing plants.) That way, I build the soil at the same time I have dedicated space to the pumpkins. Also, the plastic is wonderful for totally blocking weeds. I use it wherever weeds have been a problem and whenever I suspect the manure is not fully composted.

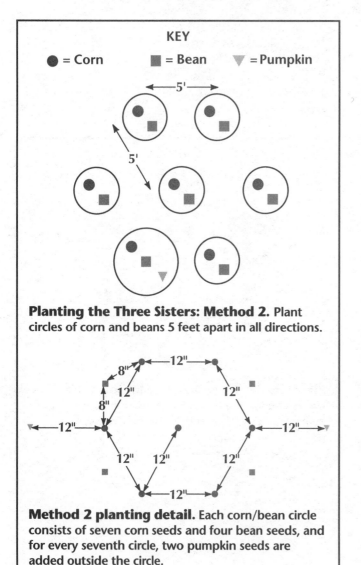

KEY

● = Corn   ■ = Bean   ▼ = Pumpkin

Planting the Three Sisters: Method 2. Plant circles of corn and beans 5 feet apart in all directions.

Method 2 planting detail. Each corn/bean circle consists of seven corn seeds and four bean seeds, and for every seventh circle, two pumpkin seeds are added outside the circle.

Watching Your Garden Grow

Planting a vegetable garden often seems to happen in a great flurry of activity. But once it's up and growing, you'll find that your companion garden is a great place to work, explore, and enjoy. There are always interesting surprises waiting to be discovered. Just the other day, I saw seven different kinds of lady beetles on one of my tansy plants! So get planting, and in the next chapter, we'll move on to some other exciting techniques you can use to make your garden a paradise for beneficial insects and a perilous place for pests.

Chapter 5

Bringing in the Good Guys

When you use my companion-gardening system, you group your crop families and their plant friends together in garden neighborhoods. That means they'll live and grow together in peace and harmony, right? Not always! Now the outsiders start to arrive—insects and animals, invited or not. They come flying, crawling, digging, and marching right into your happy plant community. But most of them will be welcome guests, those wonderful beneficial insects that you've attracted by planting flowers and herbs. They're your main line of defense against the pest insects that will also inevitably drop in. In this chapter, you'll learn all about the "good guy" insects: how they control pests, what they look like, where you'll find them in your garden, and more special techniques you can use to help them thrive. We'll tackle the bad guys in Chapter 9.

Taking a Bug's-Eye View

Sally Says

"The more we learn about beneficial insects, the less inclined we are to kill bugs, because that little wriggling critter might just be, and probably is, one of the good guys!"

INSECTS FASCINATE ME. When I first studied organic gardening, I was delighted to discover that most of the insects in my garden are my allies in fighting pests. But many people find it hard to believe that most insects are beneficial, because long ago somebody taught them to be afraid of insects and say "Eeeuuuw" when they saw a spider or an ant. Most of those in the insect-fearing crowd will concede that a few insects do good things—but don't let those "bugs" get too close!

Those folks would be surprised to learn about the major roles insects play in the survival of our planet. For example, without insect pollination, there would be food shortages, because about one-third of the food we eat comes from plants pollinated by insects. Insects are critical to the decay cycle that returns nutrients to the soil. They're also an important part of the food chain for birds, fish, frogs, and other animals.

Introducing the Good Guys

So who are all the "good guys?" Lady beetles probably top most people's lists, followed by praying mantids and honeybees. Of course, spiders are helpful, and so are pest-eating lightning bugs, and then there are earthworms—certainly worth their weight in gold, even if they're not insects. But they're just the beginning. Believe it or not, 95 to 99 percent of all insects are beneficial or harmless to human life and endeavors.

There are four main job descriptions for beneficial insects: predator, parasitoid, pollinator, and soil builder/garbage collector. Whether you see them at work or not, you can bet your companion garden employs thousands of beneficial insects carrying out these four important jobs.

Like all insects, beneficials have distinct stages in their life cycles. Some types of insects undergo a process called complete metamorphosis. These insects emerge from eggs as larvae, such as caterpillars, which look completely unlike the adults. A larva feeds and grows, then forms a pupa (a resting stage in which the insect covers itself with a hard shell). After resting awhile in the pupa, the adult emerges.

Other types of insects have a type of lifestyle known as incomplete metamorphosis. These insects emerge from eggs as nymphs, resembling tiny adults. The nymphs feed and molt several times before reaching adult size and form. All stages in the life cycle of a beneficial insect can be helpful to gardeners.

Lady beetles lay eggs on leaf undersides in the spring.

Lady-beetle larvae eat aphids and other pests.

Adult beetles eat both pests and nectar.

The larvae pupate in spring and early summer.

Insect life cycles. Insects have complicated life cycles, sometimes going through dramatic changes in size and shape. You'll see all stages of beneficial insects, such as lady beetles (above) and spined soldier bugs (below), in your companion garden.

In spring and summer, spined soldier bugs lay eggs on plants.

Nymphs feed on pests like Mexican bean beetle larvae.

Adults overwinter under mulch.

Adult bugs eat both nectar and pests.

Insect Predators

The most familiar beneficial insects—lady beetles and praying mantids—are predators. They hunt down and eat their prey just as the lion hunts the antelope. Predatory insects are usually larger than their prey, and often they hunt in the larval (caterpillar or grub) stage as well as in the adult stage.

Predatory insects usually prey on several kinds of insects. The praying mantis, for example, captures and eats just about anything it can wrestle to the ground—including another praying mantis! Many predators have names that are clues to their behavior: assassin bugs, ambush bugs, soldier beetles, and tiger beetles. Other colorful names describe the insect's appearance, like big-eyed bugs, dragonflies, and lacewings. Delicate lacewings can actually be fierce hunters. Certainly the larvae are voracious eaters—that's why they're nicknamed aphid wolves!

Paper wasps are also fine insect hunters. People are often afraid of these wasps, but they are rarely aggressive toward humans unless their lives are threatened. What paper wasps seek are full-size caterpillars, such as gypsy moth larvae and imported cabbageworms, which the wasps feed to their young.

Insect Parasitoids

Parasites are organisms that live their entire lives directly on the bodies of their *hosts*. Mistletoe is a well-known plant parasite that develops special rootlike structures that puncture tree bark and absorb water and nutrients from the trees. Fleas and lice are insect parasites.

Parasitoids, a special kind of parasite, live on the body of their hosts for only a part of their lives. Parasitoid insects lay eggs on or inside the body of a host insect, larva, or egg.

When the parasitoid larvae hatch, they feed on the host. The most common parasitoids are wasps and tachinid flies. Braconid wasps lay eggs in the bodies of tomato hornworms, and the larvae feed on the caterpillar. If you grow tomatoes in your companion garden, you will probably see tomato hornworms with little white bumps or growths attached, which are the wasp's pupae. The pupae develop when the hornworm is near death. More adult wasps will emerge from the pupae, ready to hunt down still more tomato hornworms.

Insect Pollinators

Bees pollinate about 75 percent of the world's food-crop plants. Most gardeners have no idea of the wonderful variety of bees—over 4,000 species of bees in North America alone. Bumblebees and a large group called "solitary bees," which includes mason bees, leafcutter bees, and squash bees, actually do much more pollinating than honeybees.

Flies are the second most important pollinators. Other pollinators include butterflies, beetles, moths, wasps, and even thrips. For the sake of pollination alone, never kill a bee, fly, or wasp in the garden—unless you're allergic to the stings, or unless it's a deerfly or horsefly that's about to bite you!

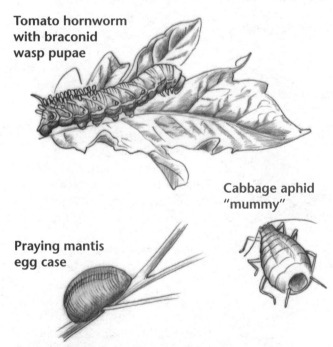

Tomato hornworm with braconid wasp pupae

Cabbage aphid "mummy"

Praying mantis egg case

Beneficials at work. Some of the distinctive signs of beneficial insects at work are white pupae of braconid wasps sticking out of tomato hornworms, the dead shells of aphids left after aphidiid wasp larvae feed on them, and the papery egg cases of praying mantids.

Soil Builders and Garbage Collectors

There is so much to praise about the insects and other creatures that build soil and break down decaying matter in nature and in our gardens. Anyone who has a compost pile has met some of these creatures, including millipedes, centipedes, beetles, sow bugs, and earwigs. They turn yard waste into "black gold." You can learn more about these insects and other organisms in Chapter 8, "The Four Fundamentals of Companion Gardening."

Keeping Your Good Guys Happy

ONCE YOU'VE PLANTED your beds with a mix of those flowers, herbs, and groundcovers, you can pretty much sit back, relax, and watch the garden happen. (If you needs ideas of what to plant, refer to Chapter 4, "My Special System.") The beneficials will control the pests, and your role will be to orchestrate, watch for situations that need extra help, and fine-tune the whole arrangement.

There are some extra things you can do to take care of the beneficial insects in your garden. Beneficials need the same things that all living creatures must have: water, food, shelter, and protection (particularly for breeding). Your garden will provide the food, and it's easy to make sure your beneficials can find water and shelter.

Water for Beneficials

Your companion garden should have water available at all times and at two levels. For flying insects, a waist-height water dish like a birdbath works well. However, while water a few inches deep is perfect for birds, tiny insects may drown in such "deep" water! Give beneficials plenty of places to land by adding rocks and pebbles. (Think of it as providing a beach and towels for your guests.)

For insects that live at ground level, put out a few shallow pans, and add water to them whenever you water your garden. Any

Set up a bug bath. To supply water for insects at ground level, just set out a large clay saucer or aluminum pie tin with pebbles and small rocks in it. Add just enough water to cover most of the rocks and pebbles, leaving some exposed as landing sites for tiny beneficials.

container will do, from old pie tins and plastic dishes to nice ceramic bowls. Choose a container with sloping sides and pebbly surfaces so that tiny beneficials have places to alight. If you're concerned about standing water allowing mosquitoes to breed, just stir up the water or refill it often with a vigorous stream of water from the hose.

Other beneficial animals will visit your bug baths too, including frogs, toads, birds, and maybe even a lizard or salamander. All of these will also dine on insects.

Food for Beneficials

Most beneficial insects need two types of food sources. One is pest insects, so we need to be sure there are some aphids, leafhoppers, plant bugs, slugs, and all kinds of caterpillars around our gardens. This can be tough for gardeners to accept, because who wants bugs in their produce? But if there are *no* pests in your garden, there won't be any beneficials either, and that can leave your crops vulnerable to attack. You'll need to be patient and trust in your unseen army.

To survive when the pest pickings are poor, beneficials will dine on nectar and pollen. The flower and herb "friends" in your companion garden will provide that in plenty.

Sheltering Beneficials

Be sure that beneficials have places to hide themselves and their eggs around your yard and garden all year. During the garden season, include some permanent plantings in your garden, like a cluster of perennials around a birdbath. Having permanent mulched pathways also shelters many insects like ground beetles.

The tough times to provide shelter for insects are fall and winter, when you want to pull out the spent crops and cut down the dead foliage. Leave some of the perennial foliage standing over winter—it may harbor beneficial insect eggs. You can also create a special mulch boundary around the edge of your garden that won't be dug or tilled. Many beneficial insects will overwinter under mulch or in the soil, and this boundary will give them a place to hide.

Winter mulch for beneficials. Beneficial insects need sheltered spots to overwinter, so each fall I lay a mound of straw and dried leaves along the edge of my garden to serve as a winter home for insects.

Buying Beneficial Insects

Raising beneficial insects for sale to farmers and gardeners is a booming business. You'll see insects for sale in many garden-supply catalogs and at some nurseries. Should you buy beneficial insects to release in your garden? I say no! I believe on a home-garden scale, we can attract all the helpers we need by planting the right attractant plants and supplying water and shelter.

One case where buying beneficials may help is in home greenhouses or large sunrooms. Gardeners who have indoor gardening areas like these can buy many effective pest controllers. One type is a lady beetle called a mealybug destroyer (*Cryptolaemus montrouzieri*). The larvae of these beetles look like giant mealybugs themselves, with a white, waxy cottonlike coating.

Both the shaggy-looking larvae and the adult beetles dine on mealybugs. They are active only in temperatures above 56°F, and they prefer humid conditions.

Checking Out Your Beneficial Buddies

How can you tell whether beneficial insects are at work in your garden? One way to tell is by what you don't see. If no holes appear in your plant leaves, it's probably because beneficials are keeping caterpillars, beetles, and other pests at bay.

Another way is to go on a beneficial-insect exploration tour in your garden.

"Backyard Garden Beneficials," beginning on page 88, is a run-down of 31 kinds of the most common beneficials found in backyard gardens. In this section, you'll find pictures of the insects, tips on identifying them, including their most distinctive features, and the likely spots where they hide in or near your garden. Pick a day when there's not much wind, grab this book or an insect field guide, a magnifying glass or lens (at least 10 power), and perhaps your reading glasses for close-up work.

You may want to keep a notebook to record what insects you see, and on which plants. You can also jot down any questions you have about the insects. One warning here: You may get less "gardening" done if you're like me. The more I look, the less I weed. But then so many of the beneficials are on those "weeds" anyway!

Bug-hunting tools. When you scout for beneficial insects, take along reading glasses or a good magnifying lens to help you make out the identifying features on the tiny beneficials and a ruler to judge size.

Backyard Garden Beneficials

Once you've planted a companion garden, there will be beneficial insects in it—whether or not you know who they are. In this section, you'll find information and illustrations to help you identify these small, hardworking gardening helpers. You'll also discover how they're helping out in your garden. Check the "Did You Know?" feature for my somewhat nonscientific interpretations of insect behavior and other tidbits of information I've discovered, plus a few of my own experiences with treasured insect guests. I've grouped the insects by family (like "Beetles" and "Wasps") to make it easy to look up the type of insect you're interested in.

BEETLES

Beetles are the largest group of insects—about one-third of all the insects on earth are beetles. Lots of them are beneficial predators and pollinators. Beetles lay eggs that hatch into larvae (an immature stage). After feeding, the larvae pupate, and adults emerge from the pupae. You can often identify a beetle by the straight dividing line that appears to run down its back from head to tail. The line is formed by the folding of the wings. Beetles have two pairs of wings, and both adults and larvae have chewing mouthparts. Beetles may be vegetarians, scavengers, predators, or parasites.

FIREFLIES (Lampyridae)

ADULT
Actual size =

LARVA

Distinctive features: While they are also called "lightning bugs," fireflies are really beetles. The adults are brown or black, long and flat, with a luminous, blinking organ on the tip of the abdomen. Larvae also glow, and they resemble flat beetles with impressive jaws. Adults are about ½ inch long.

Life cycle: Fireflies lay eggs in the soil, and the larvae hatch and overwinter there. The flashing of fireflies is part of their mating behavior, and there are different blinking patterns for different species.

Where to find them: Firefly larvae favor moist places under bark or debris. The adults are easy to spot flashing on summer evenings, usually at the edge of woods or a field, in your hedgerows, or even in lawn areas under trees.

How they help you: Adult fireflies don't feed, but the larvae are active predators of other insects, slugs, and snails. They hunt at night—just when slugs are also out attacking your garden.

Special notes: Of course, firefly larvae don't really have little lightbulbs inside their bodies. The light they produce is the result of a reaction of special chemical substances in the organ located at the tip of the abdomen. Perhaps it's the inspiration for those glowing plastic cartridges that children love to play with!

DID YOU KNOW? Two beetles are the subjects of old songs, rhymes, and stories— some fanciful, and others based on fact. "Glowworms" (firefly larvae) have a sweet image in the old song, but they are actually fierce hunters. They climb onto the backs of snails. When a snail pops its head out, the glowworm attacks, secreting an enzyme that paralyzes the snail so the glowworm can digest it.

On the other hand, the old poem about the ladybug (really a lady beetle) who's supposed to "fly away home" because her house is on fire and her children are burning is not so far from the truth. It refers to the practice of burning fields to prepare them for replanting. Undoubtedly, lady beetles and lots of other creatures have been destroyed in those fires.

No one's written a song yet about the multicolored Asian lady beetle, but she does have a nickname—the "Halloween Ladybug." That may be because she wears lots of disguises. These beetles can be yellow, orange, or red, with or without spots!

GROUND BEETLES (Carabidae)

**ADULT
Shown actual
size**

Distinctive features: Ground beetles are shiny and black or brightly colored. Some have prominent eyes, long antennae, and distinct "waists." Ground beetles hide under stones and run quickly when disturbed. Their larvae have distinct segments, strong legs, and visible "jaws" for grasping prey. Some give off strong odors. Adults are ¾ to 1 inch long.

Life cycle: Some ground beetles lay eggs in small cells made of mud, twigs, and leaves. The larvae may be active predators for about a year, and adults often live from two to three years.

Where to find them: During the day, look for ground beetles under rocks, logs, or boards. If you find them, don't disturb them. They are also attracted to goldenrod, pigweed, groundcovers, and brush. This large beetle family includes over 3,000 species in North America.

How they help you: Adults and larvae are valuable predators of Colorado potato beetles, root maggots, imported cabbageworms, diamondback moth larvae cutworms, cabbage loopers, asparagus beetles, aphids, flea beetles, gypsy moth larvae, spider mites, tent caterpillars, and many other garden pests.

Special notes: The best way to encourage ground beetles is to maintain perennials, hedgerows, or a small woodpile near the garden. It's best not to handle ground beetles for reasons beyond their fierce-looking jaws (yes, they do nip!). For example, the bombardier beetle (*Brachinus* spp.) emits a little cloud of toxic liquid that can stain your skin. And when disturbed, the green pubescent ground beetle (*Chlaenius sericeus*) gives off an odor that smells like leather.

LADY BEETLES (Coccinellidae)

ADULT
Actual size = ●

LARVA

Distinctive features: Also called ladybugs and ladybird beetles, these beetles are dome-shaped and round or oval. They may be red, orange, beige, or yellow, and many have black spots. Many species, such as the 11-spotted lady beetle, have a specific number of spots on their backs. The larvae are dark with orange or yellow marks and have six legs. They're sometimes called "alligators" because they look like alligators in miniature. The pupae are usually dark with orange marks. Adults are ⅟₁₆ to ⅜ inch long.

Life cycle: Lady beetles overwinter as adults, usually under leaf or woodpiles or in garden debris. Adults lay clusters of pointed, yellow eggs. The larval stage lasts 20 to 30 days, and the pupal stage, 3 to 12 days.

Where to find them: Every spring, I find handfuls of lady beetles in debris under my tansy and in the groundcover around my lilacs. In early spring they thrive on pollen from dandelions and other flowers. You'll also find them on yarrow, alfalfa, goldenrod, scented geraniums, and all types of daisies. There are over 450 species of lady beetles in North America.

How they help you: Lady beetles are general predators of aphids and many other insects, including thrips, mites, mealybugs, and scale. They also eat the larvae or eggs of many pests. Depending upon the species, adults may eat from 50 to hundreds of aphids per day, and larvae often eat even more. (The larva of the common convergent lady beetle, *Hippodamia convergens*, eats its weight in aphids daily.)

Special notes: Lady beetles will often disappear if all the aphids in the area are destroyed, so don't be too quick to spray aphids—even with mild organic controls such as insecticidal soap. To tide them over when insect prey is sparse, maintain permanent plantings of tansy, angelica, and spring-flowering shrubs.

ROVE BEETLES (Staphylinidae)

ADULT
Size varies with species

Distinctive features: Rove beetles have short antennae and prominent, pinching jaws used to seize other insects. You might have mistaken them for earwigs. They move rapidly, carrying the tip of their abdomens high above the ground. The gold-and-brown rove beetle is noted for its shiny golden hairs over the abdominal tip. Adults are ⅟₁₀ to 1 inch long.

Life cycle: Rove beetles overwinter as larvae, pupae, or adults. They lay eggs in soil or decomposing organic matter such as leaf litter. There can be several generations a year.

Where to find them: Rove beetles seek shelter in dark, damp places, such as compost piles or under leaves, stones, or boards. My garden's wooden pathways offer them a covered bridge for happy hunting. Planting dense groundcovers and providing mulched areas will also help to shelter them. Up to 2,900 species occur in North America.

How they help you: Both adults and larvae are active scavengers, dining on whatever insect larvae and soft-bodied insects they find. They are especially appreciated for consuming root maggots and other fly maggots. (One species studied gobbled up 80 percent of the cabbage maggots in the test plot.) Some species are also parasitoids.

Special notes: These beetles have very sharp jaws that look rather threatening and may be used to pinch you if you handle them. A few also have an extra defense: They can spray a strong, smelly liquid in the direction their tails are pointing. So appreciate these hungry maggot-hunters when you spot them, but don't get too close!

SOLDIER BEETLES (Cantharidae)

**ADULT
Actual size =**

Distinctive features: These beetles resemble fireflies (without the glow). They are elongated, usually brownish yellow or tan, and display long antennae. The Pennsylvania leatherwing (*Chauliognathus pennsylvanicus*) has a long dark spot at the base of each wing, and the head and area behind the head also have black spots. The downy leatherwing (*Podabrus tomentosus*) is a bluish gray beetle named for its fuzzy, hairy appearance. Adults are ⅓ to ½ inch long.

Life cycle: Adults lay eggs in clusters in the soil, and the larvae live in the soil. There are one or two generations per year.

Where to find them: Milkweed, goldenrod, hydrangeas, catnip, and many other flowers will attract soldier beetles to your garden. You'll spot the beetles frequently on flowers in late summer. The pupae need permanent plantings (perennials, cover crops) where they will not be disturbed. The Pennsylvania leatherwing is only found east of the Mississippi, but many other species are common throughout North America.

How they help you: Adults and larvae are usually predators, feeding on many kinds of insects, including cucumber beetles, grasshopper eggs, caterpillars, root maggots, rootworm larvae, and most soft-bodied insects.

Special notes: If you've had bad cucumber beetle problems in your garden, make a special effort to attract soldier beetles to your cucumbers. Try planting catnip, or let milkweed or goldenrod spring up among your cukes.

DID YOU KNOW? To buy and release lady beetles in your garden, thoroughly wet the area where you plan to release the beetles, and release them in the evening. Try putting out a sponge spread with commercial beneficial insect food (available from suppliers of beneficial insects), and release some of the insects under a damp straw mulch. This will maximize the chances that the lady beetles will stay in your garden instead of flying away.

TIGER BEETLES (Cicindelidae)

ADULT
Actual size =

Distinctive features: These big-eyed beetles have long antennae and vary in color from bronze, green, and blue to black. Some have yellow markings. They have long legs and can run fast and fly well. The larvae are noticeably S-shaped, with strong hooklike projections on their abdomens that they use to anchor themselves in the soil while they grab their prey. Adults are ½ to ¾ inch long.

Life cycle: Adults and larvae overwinter in the soil. Females lay eggs singly in burrows in the soil. The larvae dig burrows in open areas from which they hunt. Each generation takes two to three years to complete its cycle.

Where to find them: Tiger beetles move fast, but you may spot them flying or running after predators in sunny, open areas or napping in the sunshine on bare, sandy or dusty spots on pathways or beaches. They also swarm around lights at night. There are about 100 species of tiger beetles throughout North America.

How they help you: Adult tiger beetles eat ants, flies, caterpillars, grasshoppers, aphids, and any other insect that they can catch. The ferocious larvae seize grubs or insects, sometimes even chasing after the prey and then dragging it back to the den for dinner.

Special notes: These beetles and their larvae could star in fast-action movies and exciting chase sequences—if only we could catch up with them! They are rather violent, however. The adult grabs its victim with sharp, sickle-shaped jaws and then whacks it against the ground until it stops moving. As predators go, this one is a real ally for gardeners—but quite a brute! To give tiger beetles a safe spot to overwinter, maintain some perennials, groundcovers, and undisturbed areas around the garden.

BUGS

This group of insects is often referred to as "true bugs" because many people call all insects "bugs." True bugs have shield-shaped bodies with a triangular area on top, above the point where the wings cross. Bugs have mouthparts designed for sucking—some are spearlike, carried under the insects' bodies, but pointed straight out for feeding. Predatory bugs impale their prey and suck out the body fluids. The life cycle includes egg, nymph, and adult stages. The nymphs are often different colors from the adults but change gradually as they molt several times, shedding their outer skins until they emerge as winged adults.

AMBUSH BUGS (Phymatidae)

ADULT
Actual size =

Distinctive features: These aggressive predators have pale yellow or greenish yellow bodies and a wide, dark band across the abdomen. Their well-developed front legs are especially strong for seizing prey. Adults are less than ½ inch long.

Life cycle: Not much is known about ambush bug life cycles. Adult bugs attach their black oval eggs to leaves; nymphs emerge through the tips of the eggs.

Where to find them: These bugs are masters of camouflage, but I've spotted many on New England asters in the field near my garden. Also look in goldenrod. Ambush bugs are found throughout the United States.

How they help you: Ambush bugs eat flies, butterflies, day-flying moths, and other bugs. Beekeepers consider ambush bugs pests because the bugs eat bees.

Special notes: Ambush bugs get their name from their behavior of lying in wait in flowers and snatching victims that fly near. An ambush bug injects its prey with saliva, which paralyzes the victim so the bug can feed without struggle.

ASSASSIN BUGS (Reduviidae)

ADULT
Actual size =

Distinctive features: These long, oval bugs have thin heads that look stretched out. They have large eyes and spiny front legs that are veru powerful—they use the legs to grasp prey. The adult bugs have curved mouthparts that are carried under their heads. There are several kinds in several colors, from dull brown through yellow, green, or black. The nymphs are often brightly colored, in shades of red. The adults are usually ½ to ¾ inch long.

Life cycle: Assassin bugs overwinter as adults, nymphs, or eggs in garden litter, fields, or beneath perennial plantings. Depending upon the species, the complete life cycle takes one year or more.

Where to find them: Assassin bugs frequent meadows, fields, and gardens. Watch for them in your hedgerows, perennials, or groundcover plantings. You may spot their eggs—rusty-colored bundles topped with white caps—on leaves or in the soil. Assassin bugs are common throughout North America.

How they help you: Assassin bugs eat aphids, leafhoppers, flying insects (including bees), asparagus-beetle eggs and larvae, and other beetle larvae.

Special notes: Assassin bugs are fun to spot but not to handle. They can inflict a nasty bite that really hurts!

DID YOU KNOW? Assassin bugs come in a variety of colors and shapes. Some are long and stretched out like walking sticks; others are oval or rectangular. The wheel bug (*Arilus cristatus*) is huge (1⅛ to 1⅜ inches long) and can capture and devour large caterpillars such as tomato hornworms. Wheel bugs also eat Japanese beetles and European chafer beetle larvae. They are found east of the Rocky Mountains. A smaller assassin bug, called the bee assassin, is more common in the western United States. It is generally red with black or brown markings, or brown with yellow marks. It's not popular with beekeepers, because it attacks honeybees along with a variety of other insects.

BIG-EYED BUGS (Lygaeidae)

ADULT
Actual size =

Distinctive features: These tiny oval bugs are named for their huge eyes that point sideways. They are off-white through tan, gray, and brown, with small black spots on head and thorax. The bugs drop to the ground when disturbed. The eggs have distinctive red spots and are laid singly. Adults are ⅛ to ¼ inch long.

Life cycle: Adults overwinter in garden litter. They eat nectar and seeds when prey isn't available. There are several generations per year.

Where to find them: Look for big-eyed bugs under potato plants, clover, and other low-growing groundcovers or cover crops. The best-known species (*Geocoris* spp.) of big-eyed bugs is common in southern states north to Maryland, and in California.

How they help you: Big-eyed bugs prey on insect eggs, aphids, blister beetles, leafhoppers, and spider mites. Nymphs and adults can eat several dozen spider mites per day. Effective control for corn earworm eggs.

Special notes: The big-eyed bug isn't found where I live in western New York, but many of its relatives are found here. The big-eyed bug belongs to the insect family called "seed bugs." Its members eat seeds—hence the name—but many are also predators. If you have a butterfly garden with milkweed in it, you are sure to find the small eastern milkweed bug (*Lygaeus kalmii*), which has a bright red X on its black body.

DAMSEL BUGS (Nabidae)

ADULT
Actual size =

Distinctive features: Damsel bugs are fast-moving, thin, gray or brown insects with curving, needle-like beaks, powerful forelegs, and threadlike antennae. The wingless nymphs look similar but are smaller than adults. Adults are ⅜ to ½ inch long.

Life cycle: Adults overwinter in weeds, alfalfa, or grain fields and lay eggs in spring. Nymphs emerge after one week and dine on other insects. There are one or two generations per year.

Where to find them: Look carefully under groundcovers or cover crops, especially alfalfa and clover, for these small, nondescript insects. The only place I've found them is in my neighboring farmer's alfalfa field. Damsel bugs are found throughout North America.

How they help you: These little hunters are not frail "damsels in distress." In fact, they cause distress to aphids, caterpillars, thrips, leafhoppers, treehoppers, mites, redheaded pine sawflies, and plant bugs.

Special notes: If you find damsel bugs in nearby fields, try moving them into your garden—perhaps to beds of tomato plants underplanted with clover. Handle them carefully! These not-so-ladylike damsels can inflict a painful bite.

ADULT
Actual size =

NYMPH

MINUTE PIRATE BUGS (*Orius* spp.)

Distinctive features: To the unaided eye, these tiny bugs just look like black dots. With a magnifier, you'll see their oval black bodies with a black-and-white pattern of triangles, and very small heads. Nymphs are pinkish, yellow, or tan and have red eyes. Adult bugs are ¼ inch long.

Life cycle: Adults overwinter under perennials or groundcovers. Females lay eggs on stems and leaves. Nymphs feed on insects for two to three weeks. There are three or four generations per year.

Where to find them: Minute pirate bugs like the shelter of corn, alfalfa, clover, and vetch. Try looking for them on white flowers because it's easy to spot the black bugs against the white flowers. I found them gobbling thrips on daisies in my garden. Minute pirate bugs are found throughout North America.

How they help you: One research study counted over 50 varieties of prey for these active predators! Both adults and nymphs kill large numbers of aphids, thrips, leafhoppers, corn earworm eggs, and spider mites.

Special notes: Minute pirate bugs are sold commercially for greenhouse use in Europe and the United States, especially for thrips control.

ADULT
Actual size =

SPINED SOLDIER BUG (*Podisus maculiventris*)

Distinctive features: These shield-shaped bugs may be yellow, beige, or brown, with black speckles. They have long snouts that point straight forward. Their pointed shoulders—like a soldier's uniform with epaulets—distinguish them from a pesty relative, the stink bug. Adults are ½ inch long.

Life cycle: Adult spined soldier bugs overwinter under permanent plantings and lay eggs on leaves in spring. Nymphs start out eating plant juices or water but soon become predators. After six to eight weeks, they reach adult stage and continue feeding for another month or two. There are up to two generations per year.

Where to find them: In my garden, spined soldier bugs are easy to spot on, around, and under tansy! Also look for them on other flowering perennials. Spined soldier bugs are found throughout North America.

How they help you: These busy predators eat lots of pests, especially larvae of Mexican bean beetles and Colorado potato beetles. (Commercial growers even use them.) Other prey include European corn borer larvae, corn earworms, armyworms, imported cabbageworms, sawfly larvae, and—unfortunately—even a few beneficials, such as lady-beetle larvae.

Special notes: You can buy a special attractant substance called a pheromone to lure spined soldier bugs to your garden—but I'll bet you won't have to in your companion garden. Tansy does the job just fine.

TWO-SPOTTED STINK BUG (*Perillus bioculatus*)

ADULT
Actual size =

Distinctive features: This bug is also called the conspicuous stink bug, and it's easy to see why. This fellow really stands out with his shield-shaped, black body with a wide, curved, orangey band across the back. Nymphs are red and black. Adults are ⅜ to ½ inch long.

Life cycle: Females lay gray eggs in clusters on the undersides of leaves. There are two or three generations per year.

Where to find them: Look for two-spotted stink bugs in weedy areas, where they feed on plant juices to supplement their diet of insects. You may also spot them in your asparagus bed. These bugs occur throughout the United States.

How they help you: Nymphs and adults consume eggs or larvae of Colorado potato beetles, Mexican bean beetles, asparagus beetles, and cabbage loopers.

Special notes: One study on two-spotted stink bugs showed that they reduced Colorado potato beetle populations by up to 60 percent. It would be especially helpful to lure two-spotted stink bugs to your potato patch, asparagus bed, or cabbage neighborhood.

DRAGONFLIES
Dragonflies are long, slender insects with large, compound eyes that nearly cover the head or bulge out to the side. They have sharp, biting mouthparts and can eat their prey while in flight. All have four strong wings that move independently and can propel the insects forward or backward. Immature dragonflies, called *naiads,* are powerful predators that capture aquatic insects—and even small fish—by using a bristly lower "lip" that emerges at lighting speed to grasp the prey. This group of insects also includes damselflies. There are about 5,000 species worldwide and about 450 in North America.

DARNERS (Aeschnidae)

ADULT
Shown ⅓ actual size

Distinctive features: Darners are the fastest, largest dragonflies. They are usually green, brown, or blue, and have large, clear, finely netted wings that can span up to 5 inches in some species. Their large compound eyes meet on top of their heads. Their wings remain outstretched at rest. Adults are 2¾ to 3⅛ inches long.

Life cycle: Females hover above water and thrust their eggs below the surface, usually into slits in the stems of submerged plants. The nymphs, or naiads, live in water and crawl out in early spring or late summer to transform into adults.

Where to find them: Darners may lay their eggs in small ponds or even backyard water gardens. You may find the nymphs under stones or debris near water gardens or small streams. Brown darners (*Boyeria vinosa*) occur throughout most of the eastern United States. Green darners (*Anax junius*), also called darning needles, are common throughout most of North America.

How they help you: Darners prey on mosquitoes, bees, and many flying insects. Larvae eat mosquito larvae and other aquatic life.

Special notes: You may have a chance to witness the transformation of a darner naiad into an adult. The naiads emerge from the water—sometimes traveling only 1 foot from the edge—and split their skins down the center of the body so the adult can emerge. If you're interested in attracting darners, be sure your water garden has an appropriate open "shore" where the nymphs can emerge.

NARROW-WINGED DAMSELFLIES (Coenagrionidae)

**ADULT
Size varies
with species**

Distinctive features: Narrow-winged damselflies are brightly colored, often shiny blue or blue-green. They have two pairs of wings that taper to a narrow stalk at the base. They hold their wings vertically over their bodies when at rest. The nymphs, or naiads, live in water, using their fishlike gills to propel themselves. Adults are 1 to 2 inches long.

Life cycle: Females deposit eggs on plants above or below the water surface. The nymphs capture aquatic insects and tadpoles until fully grown. Adults of many species emerge from the water in July or August.

Where to find them: A backyard pond, water garden, or bog garden will attract damselflies. Since they are not strong fliers, adult damselflies usually stay close to a water source. You'll find nymphs of many species in quiet or slow-moving water.

How they help you: Naiads dine on many aquatic insects, including mosquito larvae. Adults are general predators who eat many other insects. They are especially effective at controlling aphids. Most North American damselflies belong to this family.

Special notes: Some familiar damselflies are nicknamed for their colors. Doubleday's bluet (*Enallagma doubledayii*) has a bright blue body. The red bluet (*Enallagma pictum*) has a bright red, reddish yellow, or brown and yellow body. If you live in the Northeast, you might have met it personally, as it often alights on a person's shoulder to nibble gently and harmlessly on clothing.

DID YOU KNOW? Damselflies and dragonflies mate in flight, and you may spot mating pairs flying together near ponds and water gardens. The males may also assist the females when it's time to lay eggs. The male holds the female while she dips her abdomen into the water to deposit the eggs. Then, like a helicopter, the male lifts the female straight up and away from the water's surface. In another species, the male and female submerge themselves in the water for up to 30 minutes in order to lay eggs.

LACEWINGS

The scientific name for this group of insects, *Neuroptera*, comes from the network of veins in the transparent wings of its members. There are over 300 species in North America. The ones we meet most often are lacewings, mantidflies, and antlions. Brown and green lacewings are generally considered the most valuable predators of garden pests. Insects in this order have two pairs of long, oval wings, which they hold like a tent over their bodies when at rest. They have chewing mouthparts, and the larvae are mostly predators.

BROWN LACEWINGS (Hemerobiidae)

ADULT
Actual size =

Distinctive features: These delicate insects have brown, transparent, netted wings covered by fine hairs. Their eggs are cream-colored ovals laid directly on the undersides of leaves. The larvae often camouflage themselves with debris, earning them the nickname of "trash collectors." Adults are ¼ to ⅜ inch long.

Life cycle: In the spring, females lay hundreds of eggs on the undersides of leaves. The larvae scavenge under organic matter for one to three weeks. Some species have several generations in a year.

LARVA

Where to find them: Adult brown lacewings fly in the evening and night, mostly in woods, orchards, or fields. Try poking under some leaves in these areas, and you may find the spindle-shaped larvae, fuzzy with organic "trash," just trundling along. Brown lacewings occur throughout North America.

How they help you: Both adults and larvae are generalists, eating aphids, mealybugs, nymphs of scale insects, and other soft-bodied insects. A single lacewing larva consumes 100 to 600 aphids in the course of its development.

Special notes: Brown lacewings are often described as shy or secretive, and not much is known about how effectively they control pests in gardens. However, they are effective aphid predators and are beneficial wherever they occur.

DID YOU KNOW? Bug zappers are marketed as control devices for mosquitos, gypsy moths, blackflies, and other pest insects. However, what they *really* kill are lots of innocent night-flying insects. Scientists at the University of New Hampshire who conducted "zapper counts" found dead lacewings as well as parasitic wasps that control gypsy moth and other caterpillars. They also found predatory beetles that prey on pest caterpillars. Other victims were caddis flies (an essential link in the ecology of ponds and streams) and beautiful large moths such as luna and cecropia moths that burned their wings in the zapper and were left flopping helplessly on the ground.

Ironically, bug zappers do little or nothing to decrease mosquito or gypsy moth populations. So zappers have no place near your garden—or anywhere else!

DID YOU KNOW? Lacewings have a funny-looking relative known as the "antlion" or "doodlebug" (family *Myrmeleontidae*). Adult antlions are about 1½ inches long and resemble dragonflies. The bug's whimsical name may be due to the appearance of the larvae, which have an oversized head, short legs, and a bristly body. They also walk backward. This fellow is not funny to an ant, however, as its long spiny jaws are lethal. Antlions make pits in the sand, where they lie in wait for ants or ticks. When the ants pass by or fall in, the antlion consumes them. They are found mainly in dry, sandy soil in sheltered spots in the southern and southwestern United States.

GREEN LACEWINGS (Chrysopidae)

ADULT
Actual size =

Distinctive features: These pale green to bright green insects have transparent wings, which they hold upright over their small bodies. They also have golden or copper-colored eyes. The larvae have prominent pincers, and their bodies are patterned in pinkish brown and cream spots. Adults are ⅜ to ⅝ inch long.

Life cycle: From spring into summer, females lay eggs on leaves near aphids. When the larvae emerge, they eat anything in reach. After two to three weeks, they pupate in round silken cocoons attached under leaves. New adults emerge one to two weeks later. Most overwinter as adults, often in clusters, in dry, dark, protected places. There are two or three generations per year.

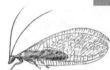

LARVA

Where to find them: You may spot green lacewings flying about in the evening in late spring or late summer, especially around meadows or forest edges. Try looking in your corn patch, too. You will recognize the creamy pinhead-sized eggs the moment you see them—with the help of a magnifying glass. Each egg is suspended on a delicate filament attached to a leaf or twig. Lacewings supplement their insect diet with nectar, so you may also find them on yarrow, angelica, Queen-Anne's-lace, sunflowers, and scented geraniums. Green lacewings occur throughout North America.

How they help you: Some research counts show that lacewing larvae eat 100 to 600 aphids before reaching the adult stage. They eat thrips, mites, whiteflies, and eggs of many pests, including leafhoppers, cabbage loopers, Colorado potato beetles, and asparagus beetles. They also eat small caterpillars and beetle larvae. They are used commercially in greenhouses, vineyards, and fields.

Special notes: There are pros and cons to aggressive predators like the lacewing larvae. For one thing, they emerge from their eggs ready to eat everything—including each other. That must be why Mother Nature designed lacewing eggs on isolated filaments. It gives each nymph a chance to eat some aphids before a "sibling" gobbles him up! For commercial sale, each lacewing egg is packed in an isolated cell to prevent cannibalism if the eggs hatch en route.

FLIES

Swatting flies may be fine in your kitchen, but don't kill any flies in your garden! With the exception of a few biters like horseflies, deerflies, and mosquitoes, most garden flies are either valuable pollinators, predators, or parasitoids—and several are all of the above. Flies have only two wings (one pair). Their life cycle includes egg, larval, pupal, and adult stages. Predatory flies have piercing mouthparts for attacking their prey and feeding on their body fluids.

APHID MIDGES (Cecidomyiidae)

ADULT
Actual size = •

Distinctive features: These tiny flies, also called gallflies, resemble mosquitoes. They have long spindly legs, long antennae, and fragile bodies. The larvae are bright orange. Adults are $1/16$ inch long.

Life cycle: Aphid midges overwinter as larvae in little cocoons in soil, emerging in late spring to search for aphids. Female midges lay up to 250 tiny orange eggs on leaf surfaces near aphids. There are several generations per year.

How they help you: One species of aphid midge (*Aphidoletes aphidimyza*) is widely used in the greenhouse industry in Europe, Canada, and parts of the United States to combat many kinds of aphids. One larva alone can eat 10 to 80 aphids before pupating. In gardens, aphid-midge larvae eat cabbage aphids and many others. Related species also attack mites, mealybugs, and other soft-bodied insects.

Where to find them: Look for tiny, bright orange larvae all over the flowers that aphids like most, including roses, especially in mid- to late summer. The adults fly at night, perhaps seeking pollen and nectar, so go searching for them with a flashlight. You may even catch a glimpse of "the mating dance," which looks like a tight little cluster of bodies just suspended in midair. Aphid midges occur throughout North America.

Special notes: Since there are many generations of aphid midges in a season, you must keep the "honeydew" coming. Choose a variety of long-flowering herbs and flowers, including Queen-Anne's-lace, dill, thyme, and wild mustard. The pupae need undisturbed soil or groundcovers, so provide permanent plantings such as wildflowers, perennials and shrubs. Aphid midges thrive in high humidity and temperatures from 60° to 80°F.

HOVERFLIES (Syrphidae)

ADULT
Actual size =

Distinctive features: These flies are often mistaken for bees because they have black- and yellow- or white-striped bodies. You can tell the difference by the pattern of movement; hoverflies hover outside of flowers and dart quickly in and out, while bees alight on flowers and stay awhile. Larvae are pale, greenish brown, sluglike maggots. They leave a dark, oily excrement behind. Hoverflies are also called flower flies or syrphid flies. Adult hoverflies are $1/2$ to $5/8$ inch long.

Life cycle: Hoverflies overwinter as pupae, attached to plants or hidden in soil. The female hoverfly lays individual eggs on leaves near aphid colonies. Larvae emerge about three days later. There may be five to seven generations per year, depending upon availability of aphids.

Where to find them: You can find the sluglike larvae wherever aphids are abundant. Hoverfly adults require nectar and pollen and are attracted to a variety of flowering plants and herbs, such as yarrow, Queen-Anne's-lace, wild mustard, horseradish, and feverfew. Hoverflies occur throughout North America.

How they help you: The adults are important pollinators, and the larvae are effective predators of aphids, leafhoppers, scale, mealybugs, thrips, corn borers, and corn earworms. One larva can consume aphids at a rate of 1 per minute, or up to 400 aphids in its larval stage, depending upon the species.

Special notes: Hoverfly larvae may be scavengers, parasites, or plant eaters. One type, the narcissus bulb fly (*Merodon equestris*), produces larvae that damage spring bulbs. However, the rest of the family make up for this troublesome relative. Larvae of the American hoverfly (*M. americanus*) and the flower fly (*Toxomerus* spp.) are probably as important as lady beetles in controlling aphids.

ROBBER FLIES (Asilidae)

Distinctive features: Some species of robber flies resemble bumblebees, and others look like damselflies. All have strong legs with which to hold their prey. They also have bearded faces with a hollowed-out area between the eyes. Many are grey and very bristly or hairy. The long, cylindrical larvae taper at each end. Adults are ½ to ¾ inch long.

ADULT
Actual size =

Life cycle: Robber flies overwinter as larvae. The larvae pupate in the soil. When the adults emerge, they must feed on both nectar and insects before they can reproduce. There is one generation per year.

Where to find them: Check in decaying wood or in the soil for robber fly larvae. When you're working in your garden, watch for flying insects that drop down on other insects from above—they're robbers! Robber flies are found throughout North America.

How they help you: Robber flies are aggressive predators of all kinds of insects, including beneficial ones. They attack butterflies, grasshoppers, wasps, bees, and flies. Larvae in the soil attack grubs, root maggots, and insect eggs.

Special notes: Robber flies were surely named by somebody under the influence of old Robin Hood stories who imagined the flies as daring, bearded robbers leaping down on unsuspecting passersby. These flies really look like robbers! Some are short and stocky, and others are thin with narrow "waists"—and they all have that hairy-looking face. The indentation between the eyes (they have *three*) definitely gives them a villainous look. Add to that the tendency to jump on their victims, and you indeed have a drama with a well-cast robber—only *we* know he's good!

DID YOU KNOW? Even if you never studied entomology in school, you can figure out lots of things about insects and their behavior just by taking a close look. For example, some predatory flies (especially hoverflies) look rather like bees because they have black-and-yellow stripes. But it's easy to separate the flies from the bees by counting their wings.

Flies have only two wings, while bees and wasps have two *pairs* of wings. (Counting the number of wings on a flying insect is tough when the insect's in flight but quite easy when it's resting on a leaf or flower.)

As for insect behaviors, I think one of the most interesting beneficials to watch in action is a tachinid fly. I often spot these flies searching for a host on which to lay eggs—walking rapidly, and with what seems like great determination, over soil and plants. When the fly spots its target, the fly signals its intent by hopping and circling around its prey.

The caterpillars and beetles that the fly attacks also enact their individual dramas clearly. They make agitated movements to try to avoid the fly's attack and will also try to remove fly eggs by wiping their legs along their bodies.

TACHINID FLIES (Tachinidae)

Distinctive features: Flies from this large family are usually stocky, with coarse bristles around the abdomen. They resemble large houseflies with mottled black, grayish, tan, or reddish brown bodies. Adults are ⅓ to ½ inch long.

Life cycle: Adults lay eggs on the bodies of other insects. The larvae feed inside the host insects, usually killing them. The larvae then drop to the soil to pupate. (Some pupate inside a host body.) Adults feed on nectar and usually fly from late spring to late summer. There may be several generations per year.

Where to find them: Look for white eggs on caterpillars or true bugs; these eggs are a clue that tachinid flies or other parasitoids have been there. You'll often spot adult tachinid flies on wildflowers and herbs in meadows and fields. I've seen them on tansy and Queen-Anne's-lace in my garden. Tachinid flies occur throughout North America.

How they help you: Many kinds of tachinid flies are effective parasitoids of vegetable crop pests, including European corn borers, corn earworms, imported cabbageworms, cabbage loopers, cutworms, armyworms, Colorado potato beetles, stink bugs, squash bugs, tarnished plant bugs, and cucumber beetles.

Special notes: Some tachinid flies are fairly general in their choices of targets, while others have specific hosts. Studies on pest control using tachinid flies show varying success rates. As with many efforts at natural pest control, one beneficial insect or pest-management strategy may not be enough—but collectively, tachinids are part of a winning team.

ADULT
Actual size =

MANTIDS

There are 11 species of mantids in North America, and 1,800 around the world, but we are most familiar with the praying mantis. All mantids have long bodies and "praying" forelegs with spines that help to capture prey. Mantids have necks that seem to rotate so that the insect can look behind itself. They can be as small as ⅜ inch or as large as 6 inches.

PRAYING MANTIS (*Mantis religiosa*)

ADULT

EGG CASE

Shown ½ actual size

Distinctive features: These familiar garden insects get their name from their tendency to hold their forelegs up "in prayer." They are about 2 inches long, are green or tan, and fly very well. They are experts at camouflage, often matching their choice of habitat plant to their bodies.

Life cycle: Females attach flat egg masses, which resemble papier mâché, to twigs or fence posts, where they overwinter. Up to 200 nymphs hatch in the late spring and proceed to eat everything in sight—including each other! The lucky ones blow off on a breeze and take over a new territory, which they dominate for their one-year life cycles.

Where to find them: Since they are territorial, you won't usually see more than one praying mantis in your garden. I've spotted a praying mantis on borage and goldenrod, but they may choose any garden or meadow plants as hunting grounds. Praying mantids are found in the southern and eastern United States and north into Ontario.

How they help you: Mantids are voracious hunters and truly undiscriminating predators of anything they can catch in their powerful forelegs. While you can buy praying mantis egg cases, I think they're a dubious purchase. However, naturally occuring mantids probably help to control pests in the garden, especially if there's a serious outbreak and the pest is abundant.

Special notes: The common praying mantis is from Europe, accidentally introduced in 1899 on nursery stock. The Chinese mantis was also introduced in 1896, and is found in the eastern United States. The narrow-winged mantis was brought in from southern Asia in 1933 and has naturalized in Delaware and Maryland. All are considered beneficial.

 **DID YOU KNOW?** Mantids would surely win gold ribbons in the Insect Olympics. A praying mantis can make two strikes with its forelegs in a *fraction* of a second. A mantis's jaws are strong enough to crack the hard shells of most insects. Some mantis species have even captured small frogs, lizards, and hummingbirds! Luckily, those are not the species you'll find in your garden. In the United States, the biggest mantis is the Chinese mantis—*only* about 3 inches! By the way, although mantids won't wrestle us to the ground, they will nip—so proceed with appreciative respect!

MITES

Mites are not insects, but they are another type of tiny creature that plays important roles in the garden. Some are plant pests, but many are also important predators of garden pests. Mites are eight-legged, flat-bodied organisms that look somewhat like very small spiders. There are about 30,000 named species of mites in the world—and lots more still to be named! One way to tell a spider from a mite is that the spider appears to have a "waist"—actually a division between the upper body and abdomen. With mites, you can't distinguish the two body parts.

PREDATORY MITES (Phytoseiidae)

Distinctive features: Predatory mites are nearly invisible to the naked eye. Even with a magnifying glass, all you'll see are tear-shaped, pale or reddish brown dots.

Life cycle: Adult mites hibernate in debris or under bark. Predatory mite species complete their entire life cycle in only a few days, so there are many generations per year.

Where to find them: You probably won't see mites around your garden because they're so small. Pollen-rich plants may help to maintain some predatory mites, and one study shows that bell peppers (which have pollen-rich flowers) maintained one species.

How they help you: Predatory mites attack spider mites, thrips, or fungus gnats. They may attack adults, nymphs, larvae, or eggs. Predatory mites are found throughout North America.

Special notes: Several kinds of predatory mites are sold for pest control. One success story is *Amblyseius fallacis*. This all-purpose mite preys on many harmful spider mites and can be released in strawberries, raspberries, orchards, bedding plants, and in ornamental plantings. If you buy garden plants at a greenhouse this year, ask the manager if she has worked with any "mighty mites" lately.

DID YOU KNOW?

In the fall, thinking about pest control is usually low on our list of priorities. Your attitude may be "what's done is done," and you'll tackle next year's pest problems next year. But fall garden cleanup can make a big difference in next year's pests. I'm not just talking about raking and cleaning up garden debris. This time, I mean hiring—actually *buying*—some beneficial mites to do the job for you.

If you've had problems with spider mites in your garden, especially in your strawberries, you can get help from *Amblyseius fallacis*, a beneficial mite that is used widely in commercial crops. When released in the fall, the mite will also wipe out mites in your home garden. It will overwinter, too, and become active in spring.

DID YOU KNOW? Spiders are remarkably ingenious at spinning webs suited to their style of hunting and self-protection. Sheet-web weavers (Linyphiidae) make flat or dome-shaped "sheets." One species is called a hammock spider because it stretches its sheet between fence posts or branches. Funnel web weavers (Agelenidae) make webs that "funnel" the prey down to the hungry spider at its base. No matter the style, if you see a web, just let it be—you have a garden helper somewhere nearby.

SPIDERS

Many people are scared of spiders, but in the garden, they're nothing to fear—unless you're an insect looking for plants to munch on! Spiders belong to a group of organisms called arachnids, having eight legs and two body parts. Most spiders have eight simple eyes. There are about 3,000 species of spiders in North America. Studies of spiders in agricultural crops show their pest-control value in crops as diverse as potatoes, rice, and cotton. Home gardeners can encourage them by providing mulch—especially straw—and a diversity of flowers. Although they have jaws, very few spiders bite people. In fact, even the most dreaded spiders, such as tarantulas and black widows, attempt to avoid and escape from humans rather than attack.

CRAB SPIDERS (Thomisidae)

**ADULT
Size varies
with species**

Distinctive features: These small spiders skitter sideways, backward, or forward, like crabs. They are usually short and wide, with the second pair of legs longer than the others (also giving that "crab-claw" appearance). There are 200 North American species, so crab spiders come in many colors, many of them camouflaged to match their preferred plant hiding places. Adults are ½ inch long.

Life cycle: Crab spiders don't spin webs. Instead, they search out their prey on plants, both day and night. They usually wait for prey on flower heads. The female produces eggs in silken sacs, which she protects until she dies, usually before the spiderlings emerge.

Where to find them: These spiders often hide in flower heads, waiting for flying insects. Many species prefer yellow and white flowers, such as cosmos, daisies, and goldenrod. Crab spiders are found throughout North America.

How they help you: Crab spiders are generalists and will capture any insect that passes by them.

Special notes: Some crab spiders are named for their looks. The goldenrod spider (*Misumena vatia*, sometimes called "flower spider" or "red-spotted crab spider") often hides out on goldenrod or daisies, changing its color to yellow for camouflage. The thrice-banded crab spider (*Xysticus triguttatus*) is brown, black, and white, with dashed lines across its lower abdomen.

ORB WEAVERS (Araneidae)

**ADULT
Size varies
with species**

Distinctive features: Orb weavers may be various shades of brown and orange, with dark brown bands and markings. They hang head downward in large webs (up to 20 inches across). They often have a cross-shaped mark on the abdomen, inspiring the common name "cross spider." Orb weavers have eight eyes in two horizontal rows with four eyes in each row. Adults are ¹⁄₁₆ to 1⅛ inches long.

Life cycle: Orb weavers make symmetrical five- or six-sided webs every night, eating the remains of the previous night's web. Females attach egg masses to plants at the sides of the webs.

Where to find them: You'll find orb weavers stretching webs between plants in your garden or between foundation shrubs and your house. This huge family includes several hundred species in North America, among them our familiar garden spider (*Araneus diadematus*) of the northeastern United States.

How they help: Garden spiders and other orb weavers catch all sorts of flying and jumping insects, including grasshoppers, flies, and moths.

Special notes: Some orb weavers are recluses, hiding in caves and dark places. One of these is the barn spider (*Araneus cavaticus*), which spins its webs in barns, caves, or other shady locations. Another spider that is quick to hide is the black-and-yellow argiope (*Argiope aurantia*), which drops to the ground when disturbed. It likes sunny, quiet places with no wind. I've spotted them on warm afternoons in my sunny perennial border.

WOLF SPIDERS (Lycosidae)

Distinctive features: These brown or gray spiders are called wolf spiders because of their coloration and hunting technique. They have eight dark eyes arranged in three rows, the first row having four eyes. Depending on species, adults are from ⅛ inch to 1⅛ inches long.

Life cycle: Not web spinners, wolf spiders live mostly on the ground, some digging burrows for retreat. Females carry or drag their egg sacs or transport their young on their backs.

**ADULT
Size varies
with species**

Where to find them: I see these spiders regularly when I move mulch under flowers or vegetables. I sometimes disturb a mother with her egg sac. You will also see wolf spiders basking in the sun or sitting with egg sacs in the "doorways" of burrows. There are 200 species ranging throughout North America.

How they help you: These general predators hunt at night, eating all kinds of insects, including aphids, mites, flies, moths, and beetles.

Special notes: Thin-legged spiders (*Pardosa* spp.) are the largest group of wolf spiders (about 100 kinds in North America), and only a specialist can tell them apart. The clue to identifying a spider as a wolf spider is its long-legged, thin look, dark color, and long pale and dark stripes running from head to abdomen.

WASPS

Wasps belong to an insect group that also includes bees, ants, and sawflies. All wasps have a narrow "waist" and two pairs of membranous wings. Adult wasps have chewing mouthparts and some have tonguelike structures they use to drink nectar. Females of most species have a stinger. Their life cycle includes eggs, larvae, pupae, and adults. Most wasps are beneficial as pollinators or as predators or parasitoids of insect pests. There are thousands of species of wasps in North America, so just a *few* of these outstanding beneficials are listed here!

APHIDIID WASPS (Aphidiinae)

**ADULT
Actual size = ●**

Distinctive features: These wasps are tiny and black, with long antennae. Adults are ⅛ inch long.

Life cycle: Most species lay hundreds of eggs, each in the body of an aphid. The larvae eat the contents of the aphid and pupate inside the dead aphid's body. The new adult wasp cuts a hole in the aphid body and emerges, leaving a shell behind. Adults live one to three weeks, and there are several generations each year.

Where to find them: Aphidiid wasps show up wherever there are aphids and supplemental nectar and pollen, but they may be hard to spot. Look for the empty shells of dead aphids, called "mummies," on plant leaves—they look like beige, papery sacs. Aphidiid wasps are found throughout the United States.

How they help you: Scientists report that aphidiid wasps are effective controls for summer and fall aphid infestations, more so than early-season aphids. Females of some species can parasitize hundreds of aphids a day. Most of those aphids then die before reproducing. Studies show significant success in controlling pea, bean, melon, potato, cabbage, and green peach aphids.

Special notes: Many aphidiid wasps are sold commercially and are one of the best success stories in greenhouse organic pest management in the United States and Europe. *Aphidius colemani* and *A. matricariae* can prevent problems with up to 40 kinds of aphids. Best of all, the wasps are able to establish themselves in most regions of the United States and can overwinter. To encourage them in your garden, maintain wildflowers and perennials, including herbs of the Carrot Family such as dill, Queen-Anne's-lace, fennel, and coriander.

DID YOU KNOW?

One little wasp has really earned star billing for over 60 years of greenhouse heroism. It's *Encarsia formosa*, the terror of greenhouse whiteflies. This pinhead-sized wasp isn't native to the United States, but it's now being raised commercially and has become established in some areas of the United States. These wasps need warm, humid climates, cannot tolerate any pesticides, and require a ready supply of whiteflies—something that many greenhouses have all too often!

BRACONID WASPS (Braconidae)

**ADULT
Actual size =**

Distinctive features: These small black or brown wasps look like flying ants. The wasps have a long, tubelike protrusion beneath the body called an ovipositor (it's used to place eggs.) The cocoons look like white bumps on the bodies of parasitized caterpillars. Adults are up to ⅜ inch long.

Life cycle: Adult wasps insert eggs into a host egg, larva, pupa, or adult. The larvae develop inside the host's body and then form cocoons. The whole life cycle may be from 20 to 50 days.

Where to find them: When you see white cocoons attached to caterpillars, beetle grubs, and fly larvae, it's evidence that braconid wasps are at work in your garden. It's estimated that there are over 1,900 species of braconids in North America.

How they help you: Studies of braconid wasps in corn and cabbage crops show that they're effective against European corn borers, cabbage maggots, and diamondback moths. Other prey include tent caterpillars, gypsy moth caterpillars, tomato hornworms, and armyworms. Some species of braconids are commercially available.

Special notes: Braconid wasps benefit from flowering plants beginning in spring, such as sweet alyssum.

CHALCID WASPS (Chalcididae)

**ADULT
Actual size =**

Distinctive features: Chalcid wasps are tiny black wasps. Through a magnifying glass, they may be metallic blue, green, or yellow. The tubelike structure called an ovipositor is not visible in chalcid wasps, so that's one way you can distinguish them from braconid wasps. Some chalcid wasps "play dead" if they are disturbed. Adults are 1/16 to ⅜ inch long.

Life cycle: Female wasps lay one or two eggs in the skin of a caterpillar. The larvae feed inside the caterpillar, pupate, and emerge. Some species lay eggs that develop into up to 1,000 larvae each. Adult wasps feed on nectar or honeydew (a secretion given off by aphids and some other insects).

Where to find them: You may spot chalcid wasps anywhere around your garden or in permanent plantings. Chalcid wasps are found throughout North America.

How they help you: Chalcid wasps feed on a wide range of pests, including aphids, whiteflies, leafhoppers, caterpillars and scale.

Special notes: Some experts regard chalcid wasps as more significant controls for pests than braconid or ichneumonid wasps because chalcids can produce so many larvae from just one egg. It's an unusual asexual type of reproduction called hypermetamorphosis!

**ADULT
Size varies with
species**

ICHNEUMONID WASPS (Ichneumonidae)

Distinctive features: This is one parasitoid you can see easily! The females often have a huge, dangling, tubelike structure for laying eggs (an ovipositor) that is even longer than her long antennae and legs. Colors vary through reds and browns. Adults vary in size from ⅛ inch up to an impressive 1⅝ inches.

Life cycle: Female wasps inject eggs into hosts—usually caterpillars. The wasp larvae slowly consume the host until the adult wasps emerge.

Where to find them: I have seen ichneumonids on window screens or around the porch light on a summer evening (another good reason to ban bug zappers!). You may also find a dried-up caterpillar or cocoon with another cocoon inside. The inner cocoon harbors an ichneumonid.The adults need nectar and water. They'll frequent your bug bath as well as Parsley Family plants like tansy, lovage, dill, and sweet cicely. There are over 3,300 species in North America.

How they help you: Ichneumonids target many vegetable- and fruit-crop pests. Commercially, they're used to control pests such as diamondback moths, European corn borers, and cabbage moths.

Special notes: In nature's systems, insects are not "good" or "bad," but simply living things that have a niche and a unique way of surviving. Ichneumonid wasps may parasitize the caterpillars of some of our favorite moths and butterflies, as well as spider egg sacs. However, these wasps target so many more of our problem insects that we clearly call them "beneficial."

DID YOU KNOW? Fear of wasps is nearly paralyzing to some people. They avoid picnics, shun the porch, and invest in can after can of toxic sprays just to rid the house of a wasp nest. But most wasps are beneficial, although a few stings can make the friendliest human wary!

It may help you to know that none of the small parasitoid wasps described here sting people or pets at all. Even most large parasitoids like ichneumonid wasps are nonstinging. Their long ovipositors (egg-laying tubes) look threatening, but they're only a danger to insect pests. One species, the giant ichneumonon (*Magarhysa macrurus*), can insert its ovipositor a full inch into wood to lay an egg on its victim (which is usually an insect larva in the tree).

If you find a nest of wasps near your house where you can't tolerate it, remember this: Wasps are most likely to be agitated and sting you if they're disturbed during hot, humid weather. Remove the wasp nest only on a cool, dry, dark evening, and place it where the wasps can escape unharmed.

TRICHOGRAMMA WASPS (Trichogramma spp.)

Distinctive features: These are very tiny, about the size of a pencil point. If you viewed a *Trichogramma* wasp through a microscope, you would see a squat, yellowish or brown wasp with red eyes and short antennae. Adults are about 1/50 inch long.

Life cycle: Female wasps lay eggs in the eggs of another insect. The young pupate within the host egg, and one or several adults will emerge within a week. Several generations may develop each season. They overwinter as pupae in the host egg.

Where to find them: *Trichogramma* wasps are so small that you won't see them in your garden. However, they probably are there, frequenting plants with delicate flowers, such as Queen-Anne's-lace, tansy, coriander, and parsley. *Trichogramma* wasps are found throughout the United States.

How they help you: These wasps are one of the most widely used biological controls for commercial agriculture. They're released for control of imported cabbageworms, corn borers, corn earworms, cabbage loopers, and many other pests. They're only effective when released over a wide area, and the timing of the release has to be just right. In your home garden, rely on native *Trichogramma* wasps for pest duty.

Special notes: Biological controls like attracting or buying beneficial insects for pest control are rarely effective as single measures. (Instead, the smart gardener does several positive things at once—including arranging for many beneficials to be around at all times.) *Trichogramma* wasps are a good example: Since some of these wasp species emerge in warm weather, they're not very effective for early season pests, but growers can release them to help with pest problems later in the season.

DID YOU KNOW? Hornets are a type of wasp, and believe it or not, some hornets are beneficial insects! Many people are afraid of hornets, but the European hornet is a predator that attacks grasshoppers, horse-flies, and yellowjackets. Giant hornets and bald-faced hornets also destroy many insects. So leave hornets in peace as much as possible, both to avoid being stung and to allow then to carry out their beneficial duties.

Chapter 6

Perennials in the Pumpkins, Shrubs on the Side

Are there really perennials in my pumpkin patch? No, but I often end up with pumpkins among my perennials! I have a permanent perennial and wildflower bed in my vegetable garden, and sometimes my pumpkin vines clamber across the path into the asters and coneflowers. Perennials and shrubs are powerful plants for attracting and sheltering beneficial insects and animals, so I've found ways to include them in and around my vegetable garden. I'm also developing a small hedgerow of shrubs and perennials on the west side of my garden. In this chapter I'll share with you my suggestions for your own perennial, wildflower, and shrub plantings to complement your companion garden—whether it is located on country acres or in a city backyard.

Perennials among the Vegetables

THE PERENNIAL PLANTS in and around my garden are "health spas" for beneficial insects. The perennial flowers and shrubs offer food, water, lovely housing, and safe conditions for my six-legged and eight-legged helpers. Of course, I can't control who "checks in," and some of the spa guests are bound to be insect pests. Nevertheless, most of the time there's a natural balance that's in my favor as a gardener. In fact, my "health spa" turns out to be hazardous for insect pests!

A Perennial Paradise

I've discovered that planting perennial flowers and shrubs has other benefits besides attracting beneficial insects. In fact, shrubs and perennials are so beneficial for your vegetable garden that I think every garden should include a permanent planting area. Here are some of the reasons why.

To attract birds. Birds are a wonderful natural insect control. Certain shrubs and trees attract and help birds more than others,

WILDLIFE THAT PREYS ON INSECT PESTS

Beneficial insects and birds aren't the only kinds of beneficial animals. Several other kinds of wildlife are predators of pest insects or problem rodents. Take a few simple steps to attract and assist these helpers.

Bats. The common brown bat can eat 3,000 insects (including lots of mosquitoes) in one night. You can build houses especially for bats to roost in. They're also attracted by ponds.

Lizards and salamanders. These creatures eat vast numbers of insects and do no harm to anyone. They're attracted by cool, damp places like rock piles.

Snakes. Dangerous snakes are rare—there are only four species in the United States—and not likely to visit the garden. The ones you see control rodents, insects,

even slugs and snails! Snakes like the shelter of rocks, woodpiles, or brush near the garden.

Toads and frogs. Just one toad can consume well over 10,000 insects (slugs too!) in one year. Make a cool, dark toad shelter out of rocks or inverted clay pots that have "doors" chipped out.

Moles. Even these maligned marauders of spring lawns have a garden benefit. Moles eat huge numbers of grubs, like Japanese beetle grubs. They even cultivate parts of my garden but have moved on to deeper or damper locations by planting time! So before you act to "get rid of" any of nature's living gifts, consider the big picture—how everything relates to everything else. Maybe you'll find you have lots more friends than you knew!

but the presence of almost any type of hedge or tree—plus water—will make your garden more attractive to birds.

To shelter wildlife. If your image of wildlife is Peter Rabbit nibbling lettuce, you may think I'm crazy to say that wildlife actually helps us in the garden. If so, check out "Wildlife That Preys on Insect Pests" on the opposite page. And remember: In a diverse, naturally balanced garden, we need to work with the complex set of connections between predators and prey, hunters and hunted. I agree, you don't want Peter Rabbit and his buddies in your garden, but you *do* want to attract and shelter wild creatures like toads, frogs, and lizards. Don't worry, you can still fence your garden! Most fences that keep bunnies and woodchucks out of your garden will still allow the small beneficial animals to get in.

To block the wind. Wind strips away your mulch, tears at black plastic, and erodes any uncovered soil. Wind protection is an absolute requirement for butterflies, helps many beneficial insects, and keeps the corn from toppling! A wind block doesn't hurt the gardener, either, when chilly fall winds are blowing and there's still harvesting and cleanup to do. So planting a hedgerow of shrubs and perennials on the windward side of the garden (in most cases, the west) helps your soil, your harvest, and your comfort!

A sheltering hedgerow. The hedgerow I've planted on the western edge of my garden provides two kinds of shelter: homes for birds and beneficial insects, and protection against cold spring winds for my young vegetable plants.

To create a beautiful frame. There's a lot to be said for enhancing the beauty of your garden's surroundings. Imagine how soothing it would be to sit in the shade of a hedgerow when you take a gardening break. And after a long session of picking beans or digging potatoes, it always lifts my spirits to turn and admire my beautiful perennials. For you photographers, a hedgerow or perennial border makes a stunning backdrop for your best garden photographs.

Beautiful Possibilities

Once I decided to devote some space to perennials in my vegetable garden, I discovered that it created some great new gardening possibilities. Suddenly I had a place for brightly colored perennials like crocosmia and Maltese cross (*Lychnis chalcedonica*) that didn't blend into my perennial borders easily. I could use my vegetable garden as a testing ground for new perennials and a holding bed for others until I was ready to work them into my borders. It didn't matter whether each perennial fit perfectly into a well-planned design, because a vegetable garden changes from year to year anyway.

I've discovered that combining perennials with vegetables and herbs gave the flowers a whole new dimension. Dull gold yarrow, an unimpressive filler among perennial cousins, became a standout paired with dill or peppers. A small red coreopsis that was too short to make a strong statement in my border shone brilliantly when I paired it with the pale blue of flowering borage.

Where to Plant Perennials

There are plenty of good sites for perennials in a vegetable garden. Like me, you can plant a border of perennials and herbs on the back, front, or both sides of the garden. You'll find an example of such a perennial border on page 119.

You can plant a circle or triangle of perennials right in the middle of your garden and let the crop neighborhoods rotate around it every year. (Check the design for a Wheel Garden on page 132.) I love the idea of having a small perennial garden with a chair and perhaps even a little table right in the middle of the garden. Then, I could actually sit and read a garden book, play with my companion-garden layout, or make notes in a garden journal!

If you want to start small with perennials, try the Welcoming Corner garden on page 117. This bed will add a cheerful, colorful accent to your garden and provide a safe

Sally Says

"To help with pest control, I'll take planting perennials over spraying and dusting to kill pests any day!"

haven for beneficials, but it doesn't take up too much space or interfere with tilling the garden.

No-Till Options

If you have raised beds or have built up your soil so that you don't have to till your garden, you can put perennials anywhere. Plant a few bright perennials, ornamental grasses, or wildflowers at the end of each garden bed. You can repeat the same plants or choose plants with a strong color theme. You can even plant perennials intermittently throughout the beds. They'll look different each season because of the different vegetables you're growing.

Choosing Perennial Companions

I choose perennial companions for my vegetable garden the same way I select annuals and herbs. First, I make sure I select some long-blooming varieties from the Aster and Carrot Families. I also include some low-growing plants because they provide shelter for ground-dwelling beneficial insects. And I strive to have something in bloom continuously from early spring into late fall.

To be a true haven for beneficials, your perennial bed should not have bare soil or much unplanted space between plants. A few "bug shelters," such as little

rock clusters, boards, and leaf mulch, are helpful, too. Remember, you want to meet all your guests' needs—and that means providing water, food, shelter, and breeding places.

SALLY'S HELPFUL HINTS

My Favorite Perennials

Over the years, I've settled on several favorite perennial flowers and herbs for the vegetable garden. Here are my top recommendations by bloom season. Even if your garden is too small to include a separate perennial bed, try planting one or two of these perennials at each corner of your garden. If you'd like a greater range of choices, you'll find a complete list of perennials, annuals, herbs, and more that attract good bugs in "Plants for Beneficial Insects" on pages 247–257.

Spring Bloomers

Chives	Pinks
English daisies	Rock cress
Lavender	Rugosa roses

Summer Bloomers

Black-eyed Susans	Helianthus
Coreopsis	Shasta daisies
Cranesbills	Tansy
Coneflowers	Yarrows

Fall Bloomers

Asters	Goldenrods
Boltonia	Joe-Pye weeds
Chrysanthemums	

Perennial Gardens for Beneficials

I'VE DESIGNED three perennial beds that will work well for nearly any vegetable garden. These beds include many of my favorite perennial companions—both for their looks and their good-bug–attracting power. In all three gardens you'll spot a bird-bath or bug bath to supply water for the beneficial visitors.

The Welcoming Corner is designed to fit at an outside corner of a vegetable garden. The Central Perennial Bed is an oval bed that can be the center-piece of a garden, with veg-etable beds all around it. The Perennial Border is a long, narrow bed that can be planted along the edge of a square or rectangular garden.

A Welcoming Corner garden. In late summer, this corner perennial garden is filled with lush flowers, and it's alive with birds and beneficial insects. You'll find the plan for this garden on the opposite page.

Design for a Welcoming Corner

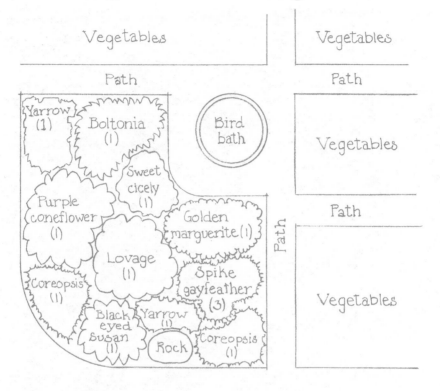

This cheerful corner bed welcomes guests to your garden—both human and insect (the good guys!). The garden stresses long bloom and variety in a small space, so I've designed it to have a single plant of several different perennials, plus a few herbs like lovage and sweet cicely.

You can let certain "weeds" like Queen-Anne's-lace and wild daisies that attract beneficial insects spring up in perennial beds like this one. The perennials I've selected are tough enough to compete with the weeds. Be sure to put small rocks in the birdbath as landing sites for beneficials.

Plants for a Welcoming Corner

Black-eyed Susan
  (*Rudbeckia fulgida* 'Goldsturm')
Boltonia
  (*Boltonia asteroides*)
Coreopsis
  (*Coreopsis verticillata* 'Moonbeam')
Golden marguerite
  (*Anthemis tinctoria*)
Lovage
  (*Levisticum officinale*)
Purple coneflower
  (*Echinacea purpurea*)
Spike gayfeather
  (*Liatris spicata*)
Sweet cicely (*Myrrhis odorata*)
Yarrow
  (*Achillea* 'Coronation Gold')

Design for a Central Perennial Bed

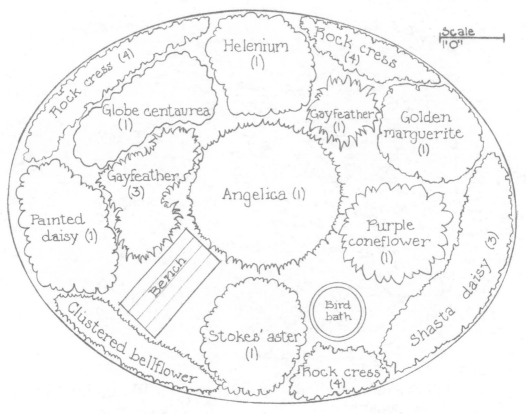

Plants for a Central Perennial Bed

I designed this perennial cluster to be the focal point of a vegetable garden. Plant it at the center of your garden and surround it with vegetable beds. This garden includes many proven good-bug attractors. It's heaven to rest on the bench between chores, surrounded by flowers and drifting butterflies. The angelica can grow up to 8 feet tall, so the chair will be shaded in the late afternoon. On the plan, I've included the number of plants you'll need to plant in parentheses following the names of the plants.

Angelica (*Angelica archangelica*)

Clustered bellflower
  (*Campanula glomerata* 'Joan Elliot')

Gayfeather (*Liatris* sp.)

Globe centaurea
  (*Centaurea macrocephala*)

Golden marguerite (*Anthemis tinctoria*)

Helenium (*Helenium autumnale*)

Painted daisy (*Chrysanthemum coccineum*)

Purple coneflower (*Echinacea purpurea*)

Rock cress (*Arabis caucasica*)

Shasta daisy
  (*Chrysanthemum* × *superbum*)

Stokes' aster (*Stokesia laevis*)

Design for a Perennial Border

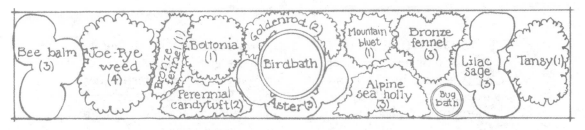

Scale
3'0"

KEY
Bf · Bronze fennel   G · Goldenrod
B · Bugbath   M · Mountain bluet

The romantic in me would love to frame my entire vegetable garden with beds of perennials. But my practical side probably wouldn't allow me to sacrifice so much of my garden space for flowers!

As a compromise, I created this design for a perennial border to frame one side of a vegetable garden. The border is 16 feet long, but if your garden is more than 16 feet long, you can extend the border by repeating some of the plants in the design. If your garden is less then 16 feet long, plant part of the border along one side of the garden and the other part along a second side. If you plant this perennial border on the south side of your garden, keep in mind that some of the tall perennials will cast shade. You can take advantage of that shade to extend the growing season for cool-season crops like lettuce and broccoli. On the plan, I've included the number of plants you'll need to plant in parentheses following the plant names.

Plants for a Perennial Border

Alpine sea holly
(*Eryngium alpinum*)

Aster
(*Aster novae-angliae* or
A. novi-belgii)

Bee balm
(*Monarda didyma*
'Croftway Pink')

Boltonia (*Boltonia asteroides*)

Bronze fennel
(*Foeniculum vulgare*
var. *purpureum*)

Perennial candytuft
(*Iberis sempervirens*)

Goldenrods
(*Solidago* spp.)

Joe-Pye weed
(*Eupatorium maculatum*
or *E. purpureum*)

Mountain bluet
(*Centaurea montana*)

Lilac sage
(*Salvia verticillata*
'Purple Rain')

Tansy
(*Tanacetum vulgare*)

Attracting Birds and Wildlife

FROM THE VIEWPOINT of an organic gardener, the more birds around the garden, the better. Birds eat Colorado potato beetles, Mexican bean beetles, cabbage loopers, tomato hornworms, Japanese-beetle grubs, flea beetles, and mosquitoes—just to name a few! While birds are gobbling up insect pests, they may also eat some beneficial insects and earthworms. Certain kinds of birds also tend to nibble tender lettuce and pea leaves, but that's easy to remedy by covering the plants with floating row covers. In the overall balance, birds definitely do more good than harm.

Many of the same techniques that help beneficial insects also help beneficial wildlife, but there are some differences and extras, too. Here's a rundown on how to attract beneficial animals.

Provide water. Creating a garden pond or even a small water garden will attract birds. If your yard includes an area with wet soil, don't struggle to maintain it as lawn or turn it into a traditional garden. Instead, work with the wetness and plant moisture-loving bog perennials. And don't forget to

PLANTS FOR THE BIRDS

There are entire books devoted to plants that attract birds, and if you become interested in backyard birdwatching, I'd encourage you to investigate the best choices for your area. Here's just a sampling of some tried-and-true plant choices for birds.

American holly (*Ilex opaca*)

Arrowwood viburnum
 (*Viburnum dentatum*)

Bayberry (*Myrica pensylvanica*)

Cherries (*Prunus* spp.)

Cornelian cherry (*Cornus mas*)

Cotoneaster
 (*Cotoneaster adpressus* var. *praecox*)

Crabapples (*Malus* spp.)

Dogwoods (*Cornus* spp.)

Eastern red cedar (*Juniperus virginiana*)

Eastern white pine (*Pinus strobus*)

Firethorns (*Pyracantha* spp.)

Hawthorns (*Crataegus* spp.)

Highbush blueberry
 (*Vaccinium corymbosum*)

Highbush cranberry (*Viburnum trilobum*)

Honeysuckles (*Lonicera* spp.)

Sargent crabapple (*Malus sargentii*)

Serviceberries (*Amelanchier* spp.)

Sumac (*Rhus* spp.)

Winterberry (*Ilex verticillata*)

keep birdbaths and ground-level water dishes filled with clean water throughout the year.

Grow a variety of plants. There are many plants that attract birds because of their berries, cones, or seeds or because they offer good sites for nesting. I've included some of the best trees, shrubs, and groundcovers in "Plants for the Birds" on the opposite page.

Let some lawn go natural. Only a few birds like areas of open lawn. When you convert a lawn area into a wildflower meadow, you'll create a great bird habitat. Birds also love mixed plantings of native shrubs and groundcovers.

Leave a bit of wildness. This can be anything from a small meadow to a shady corner under trees or even just a patch of weeds! To the extent that your neighborhood allows, avoid large, bare, cultivated areas. (Teach your neighbors what wildlife needs to thrive and maybe they'll get a bit "wilder," too!)

Plant a hedgerow. A strip of mixed trees, shrubs, wildflowers, perennials, and grasses is a wonderful wildlife shelter. You can create a hedgerow between sections of your property, at the edge of your backyard, or right beside your vegetable garden. (See my hedgerow design on page 123.)

A backyard wildlife habitat. Even if you don't live near the woods, you can create a lovely woodsy retreat for birds and beneficial wildlife by combining a small tree with several shrubs, groundcover, and perennials.

Don't apply pesticides.
This goes without saying in your vegetable garden, but it applies to the rest of your yard, too. Also, be careful with the toxic nongardening products— including antifreeze—that you use around your property.

Feed the birds. Simple bird feeders are a great draw for birds. (And while they're visiting your feeders, they'll eat some insects, too.) Some naturalists even plant a "food patch" for birds that includes millet, sunflowers, and zinnias.

Create lots of *edges*. Edges are the areas where one kind of planting blends into another kind of planting, such as a forest blending into a meadow. These edges, often the home for low-growing and fruitful native shrubs, are ideal habitats for many birds and other animals. Even in a small yard, you can create edge areas for wildlife by planting a mixed grouping of shrubs, perennials, and groundcovers like the one shown on page 124.

Make brush piles. To make a brush pile, heap up tree prunings, yard waste, and used Christmas trees. (If you build the pile on a base of small logs, you'll provide food and shelter for large birds, such as pheasants and wild turkeys, as well as small animals.) Site this discreetly so it won't be an eyesore.

Protect natural habitats. In many areas of our country, we've driven wildlife out of their habitats by developing land. We can help make up for loss of habitat by welcoming wild garden helpers in our own yards. Also whenever possible, we should encourage forest and wetland protection.

Plantings for Birds and Wildlife

ATTRACTING WILDLIFE was my primary goal when I planted a hedgerow about 6 feet away from my companion garden along the west side. (The plan for this hedgerow is shown at right.) I had a wonderful time researching and selecting trees, shrubs, and groundcovers that would attract or help beneficial insects and birds. I also called on the expertise of a local landscaper, and I'd encourage you to do the same before you try a project of this scale.

Make sure that the plants you choose are easy to care for and suit the site and soil conditions as is—without amending the pH or the drainage. And be sure you choose plants that tolerate animal damage. After all, you don't want to have to build deer and rabbit barriers in your wildlife shrub border!

If you're not ready to tackle a full-scale hedgerow project, you may want to try a smaller planting of trees and shrubs like the one shown on page 124.

Design for a Hedgerow for the Birds

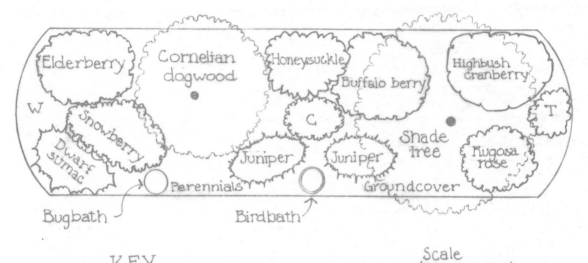

Elderberry
Cornelian dogwood
Honeysuckle
Buffalo berry
Highbush cranberry
W
C
T
Snowberry
Dwarf sumac
Juniper
Juniper
Shade tree
Rugosa rose
Perennials
Groundcover
Bugbath
Birdbath

KEY
W · Wildflowers
C · Cotoneaster
T · Tansy

Scale
8'0"

I designed this small hedgerow around an existing tulip tree (*Liriodendron tulipifera*). If you don't have an existing tree, I'd recommend planting an amur maple (*Acer ginnala)* because it is very hardy (to Zone 2) and has fragrant, early flowers and seeds that attract birds.

In the area marked "Perennials" on the plan, plant a mix of perennial flowers with proven good-bug–attracting qualities. In the area marked "Wildflowers," plant wildflowers like milkweed, asters, buttercups, and goldenrods, or let them spring up naturally. Two beautiful groundcovers I recommend are bunchberry (*Cornus canadensis*) and bearberry (*Arctostaphylos uva-ursi*).

Plant List for a Hedgerow for the Birds

Buffalo berry (*Shepherdia argentea*)
Cornelian cherry (*Cornus mas*)
Cotoneaster (*Cotoneaster* 'Firebird')
Fragrant sumac (*Rhus aromatica* 'Gro-Low')
Juniper (*Juniperus virginiana* 'Gray Owl')
Elderberry (*Sambucus canadensis*)
Groundcovers
Highbush cranberry (*Viburnum trilobum*)
Honeysuckle (*Lonicera* 'Freedom')
Perennials
Rugosa rose (*Rosa rugosa*)
Shade tree
Snowberry (*Symphoricarpos albus*)
Tansy (*Tanacetum vulgare*)
Wildflowers

Design for a Sheltered Retreat

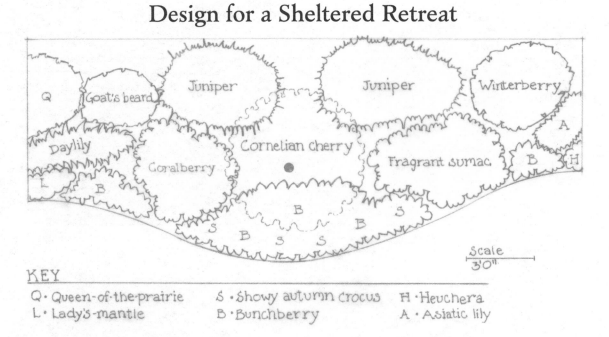

KEY

Q · Queen-of-the-prairie	S · Showy autumn crocus	H · Heuchera
L · Lady's-mantle	B · Bunchberry	A · Asiatic lily

Tackling a full-scale hedgerow isn't for every gardener. You can provide a habitat for beneficials on a smaller scale by planting a Cornelian cherry tree (which is related to flowering dogwood) in a grouping of shrubs and perennials. To establish the bunchberry groundcover, start by planting plants 1 to 2 feet apart. This planting is about half the size of my hedgerow but offers the same benefits for wildlife.

When you create an area in your yard for beneficial wildlife, don't worry about keeping it too neat. Remember that fallen branches, leaf litter, and even weeds offer cover and possibly food for beneficial insects and animals, so let the area stay as natural as possible.

Plant List for a Sheltered Retreat

Asiatic lily (*Lilium* Asiatic hybrids)

Showy autumn crocus
  (*Colchicum speciosum*)

Bunchberry (*Cornus canadensis*)

Coralberry
  (*Symphoricarpos* × *chenaultii* 'Hancock')

Cornelian cherry (*Cornus mas*)

Daylilies (*Hemerocallis* hybrids)

Goat's beard (*Aruncus dioicus*)

Heuchera (*Heuchera* 'Palace Purple')

Juniper
  (*Juniperus virginiana* 'Gray Owl')

Lady's-mantle (*Alchemilla mollis*)

Queen-of-the-prairie
  (*Filipendula rubra*)

Fragrant sumac
  (*Rhus aromatica* 'Gro-Low')

Winterberry
  (*Ilex verticillata* 'Winter Red')

Chapter 7

Having Fun with Companion Gardening

It's no secret that gardening can be fun. After all, gardening is the fastest growing hobby in the United States! Still, there are times when gardening feels like a chore—when the weeds are winning, when our tough soil just gobbles up the compost and is still hard to dig, or when it's just too hot to get out and water. That's the time to say, "Lighten up! Let's get back to the fun!"

In this chapter, that's just what I do. I share some tips and techniques that are more playful than practical. You'll find some whimsical garden designs, plus a few neat growing techniques that may solve some of your garden problems. I hope they'll inspire you to dream up some great fun ideas all your own. So before you turn the page, answer this question: Are you having fun yet?

The Fun Starts Here

Sally Says

"*Toss your traditional rectangular garden plan out the window. Just for fun, why not try a garden that's a circle, or even a triangle?*"

IT'S EASY TO HAVE FUN with a companion garden. After all, you're not just planting vegetables. You're also planting fragrant herbs and colorful flowers, and you're attracting birds, butterflies, and other wild friends to double the fun! As you've learned, the herbs and flowers do serve a serious purpose. But once you've done the work of grouping your crops and choosing plant friends for them, designing your garden layout and watching your garden grow can be a real pleasure.

Simple garden projects can add new zip and excitement to your garden. Try projects that are both fun and practical, like a toad shelter or a homemade trellis for growing gourds or flowering vines. Fix up a colorful and creative scarecrow. Even if it doesn't scare any animal pests, it will make you smile!

Dream Up a Garden Theme

There are so many ways to play with companion gardens. I like to create gardens with exciting color schemes, just as if I were designing a perennial bed or border. You can also give a garden a regional theme or use lots of trellises and supports to make a vegetable jungle. Once you start, you're bound to come across some great new ideas. Here are a few suggestions to get you started.

A chili-sauce garden. My grandma made a terrific sweet/hot chili sauce, and even in a tough gardening year, I always grow the ingredients for the chili, including onions, sweet peppers, chili peppers, and tomatoes. You may have your own family heirloom chili recipe begging for garden-fresh ingredients. If not, do a little experimenting, and create your own!

A cool cabbage combo. I like to end the gardening season in style with some bright, bold color in my garden. For a great mix of red, blue, and purple, plant red cabbages in a 3-2-3 pattern (as shown on page 78), and substitute dainty blue cupflowers (*Nierembergia* spp.), love-in-a-mist (*Nigella damascena*), and rocket larkspur (*Consolida ambigua*) for some of the heads of cabbage. At each end of the bed, plant purple garden mums. I don't know whether all the flowers in this combination are helpful companions, but they certainly help lift my spirits on a sunny fall day!

Stir-fry flair. Chinese vegetables are mostly cool-weather crops, so you can create a bed just for fall and early winter salads, stir-fry, or Chinese specialties. Some of the Chinese vegetables to try include Chinese cabbage, celery cabbage, daikon radish, Chinese broccoli, mizuna, and Chinese spinach.

Some like it hot! There are some wonderful hot colors in both flowers and vegetables that you can combine to make a sizzling "hot garden." Try planting a bed of tomatoes and peppers with bright red salvias, Mexican sunflowers, and tall, red-orange marigolds. Scatter tall red cosmos throughout. Mix in some red cabbage, red basil, and scarlet runner beans. Then give it all a border of bright red petunias.

A festive fence of beans. Grow a multicolored bean fence using a combination of dry beans, purple beans, and yellow wax beans. Just plant each seed in sequence, spacing them 7 inches apart along a fence or trellis. If you use varieties that have a similar number of days to maturity, you can harvest your own colorful three-bean salad all at once!

For the child in all of us. Whether you have children or not, a special secluded spot in the garden is a wonderful place to sit and listen to birds, read a book, or just watch the gourds grow.

Some Gardens Just for Fun

THERE'S NO LIMIT to the sizes, shapes, and combinations you can create in companion gardens. To help inspire you, I've designed three very different and delightful companion gardens.

Three Fun and Fanciful Designs

I think vegetables have as much right to be in the front yard as any other kind of garden, so one of my designs is for a salad garden to highlight the foundation and front walkway of a suburban home.

Vegetable gardens can be very pretty, especially when we mix in flowers to create companion gardens. And successful vegetable gardeners want to show off what they've grown (especially if the garden says "Look what you can grow organically!"). Plus, the front yard is often the place with the right sun or soil for a vegetable garden.

The garden includes all the vegetables and herbs you need for a terrific salad, and even the flowers in it are edible.

Just one note when you're planting edibles in your front yard. Keep them away from the edges of driveways or streets where they can be contaminated by road salts or automobile exhaust.

The second design is a circular garden that I've called the wheel garden because the plan looks like an old-fashioned wagon wheel with paths for spokes. Between the spokes, there are wonderful combinations of vegetables, herbs, and flowers.

My third special garden design is a great choice for gardeners with limited space. I call it the Small TALL Garden because it uses lots of trellises, arbors, and towers to maximize production in small beds.

All of these gardens meet the basic definition of companion gardens: The crops are grouped in families, the garden includes lots of flowers and herbs, and everything's intensively planted in raised beds. I did make some concessions, perhaps adding a few more flowers than I would have in a garden where production was the primary goal. And in some cases, rotating crops is a bit harder. But making these adjustments is worth it to me for the extra excitement these gardens provide.

Choosing Varieties

In most cases, I haven't specified what varieties of crops or flowers to grow, except for a few specific varieties that have special qualities. For example, 'Siam Queen' basil has lovely purple flowers that add

Sally Says

"With companion gardening, there are hundreds of ways to combine crops and flowers. No two gardens will ever look exactly alike!"

excitement, and 'Purple Wave' petunias have a spreading habit that makes them a wonderful groundcover. For the vegetable crops, it's important for you to choose varieties that grow well in your local area and that have flavors you like! Don't be afraid to substitute for crops that you wouldn't eat. For example, I frequently use Swiss chard in my gardens because I really like it. But I know lots of people who'll politely pass it by at the table. If you're in the "no Swiss chard" crowd, just substitute another leafy crop that you enjoy eating.

A front-yard salad garden. If you have a sunny lawn in your front yard, liven it up with raised beds full of salad fixings, including edible flowers. You'll find a plan for this garden on pages 130–131.

Design for a Front-Yard Salad Garden

KEY

G · Gladioli
S · Spinach/New Zealand Spinach
Ct · Cherry tomato
B · Borage
SQ · 'Siam Queen' basil
J · Johnny jump-ups
H · Hollyhocks
R · Radishes
Sb · Salad burnet
Rℓ · Romaine lettuce
Lℓ · Leaf lettuce

Scale
3'0"

Here's the layout for my front-yard salad garden. The garden has four beds, each 3 feet wide and 20 feet long (the equivalent of a conventional 15- by 20-foot garden). Here, they're arranged to flank a pathway leading to the front door. You can arrange the beds in any way that suits your front yard. For example, if you have a curving walkway that leads from your driveway to your front door, you can lay out the beds on either side or both sides of the walk.

To make this garden extra-special, I used *only* edible flowers, so anybody can go out to harvest supper. The edible flowers include pansies, violets, petunias, and daylilies. (In this garden, we *do* eat the daisies!)

Planting the Garden

In the plant list on the opposite page, numbers in parentheses indicate how many transplants, bulbs, or sets to plant. Plant other crops from seed; one packet should be plenty.

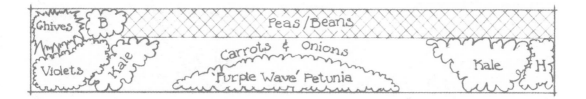

Plants for a Front-Yard Salad Garden

Vegetables	Herbs and Edible Flowers
Beans (pole varieties)	Basil (3)
Carrots	'Siam Queen' basil (3)
Cherry tomato (1)	Bee balm (1)
Cucumber (1)	Borage (2)
Kale	Calendulas (10)
Leaf lettuce	Chives (2)
Mesclun (mixed salad greens)	Daylilies (2)
New Zealand spinach	Dill
Onions (24 to 36)	Gladioli (6 to 12 bulbs)
Peas (tall varieties)	Hollyhocks (5)
Radishes	Johnny-jump-ups (12)
Romaine lettuce	Garden mums (2)
Spinach	Nasturtiums
Swiss chard	Pansies (20)
Tomatoes (4)	Parsley (2)
Zucchini (1)	'Purple Wave' petunias (2)
	Rose, 'The Fairy' or other shrub type (2)
	Salad burnet (1)
	Sweet William (8)
	Violets (9)

Design for a Wheel Garden

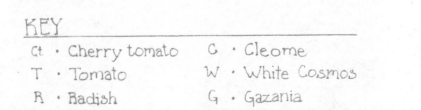

Yellow cosmos
Swiss chard
Buckwheat

Zinnias
Dill
Bush beans
Potatoes

Path

Potatoes

Path

Nasturtiums

Path

Cucumbers
Summer squash
Zucchini
Cucumbers

Pole beans and peas

Lettuce and spinach

Calendulas

Path

Path

Peppers
Basil
W
T
T
T
T
Siam Queen' basil

Kale
C
Broccoli underplanted
with sweet alyssum
Ornamental kale

Scale
4'0"

KEY

Ct · Cherry tomato   C · Cleome

T · Tomato   W · White Cosmos

R · Radish   G · Gazania

Any round garden is a perfect place to practice crop rotation. In this case, I've planted a circular garden 20 feet in diameter with a 4-foot-wide "hub" or center circle. The garden is divided into six wedge-shaped beds with 18-inch-wide paths in between. To reduce or enlarge the garden, just make the beds shorter or longer.

Managing the garden. The best management strategy for this garden will be to work the soil well before you first shape the beds and not to till after that. Keep the soil covered with mulch or cover crops, and create permanent wood-chip paths between the beds. You can till the garden by tilling in a spiral from the center out, but only if you use a temporary path covering like grass clippings or straw. Even in a fanciful garden like this, I suggest planting a cover crop like buckwheat every few years to rebuild the soil.

The garden hub. Your round garden doesn't have to have a plain circle of grass or mulch at its hub. Use the space for a fun garden project. I can picture a comfortable lawn chair next to a birdbath or a tall ornamental grass like maiden grass (*Miscanthus sinensis*). You could even plant a small apple tree for shade.

Other possible "centerpieces" include a water garden in a tub or a large pot of Jerusalem artichokes surrounded by mint. (Let the plants tussle for space while you breathe in the mint scent and harvest some crunchy tubers.) Just be sure to leave enough space around the center planting for weeding, watering, and harvesting.

Planting the garden. In the plant list below, numbers in parentheses indicate how many transplants or sets to plant. Plant other crops from seed; one packet should be plenty.

Plants for a Wheel Garden

Vegetables

Beans (bush variety and pole variety)	Potatoes (16)
	Radishes
Broccoli (9)	Spinach
Cucumber (2)	Summer squash (1)
Kale	Swiss chard
Lettuce (leaf variety)	Tomatoes (4)
Peas (tall variety)	Cherry tomato (1)
Peppers (12)	Zucchini (1)

Herbs

Basil (12)	Dill
'Siam Queen' basil (8)	

Flowers

Buckwheat	Gazanias (2)
Calendulas (10)	Ornamental kale (7)
Cleome (3)	
Cosmos (3)	Nasturtiums (5)
Yellow cosmos (5)	Sweet alyssum (12)
	Zinnias (9)

Design for a Small TALL Garden

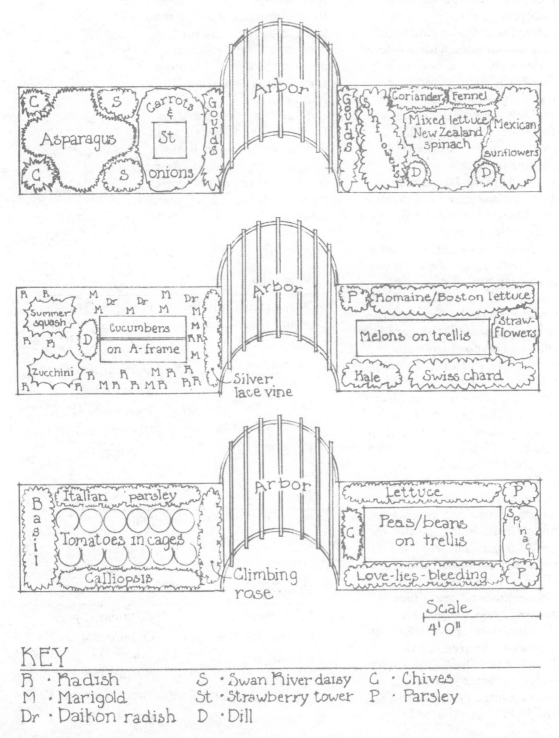

Scale
4' 0"

KEY

R · Radish	S · Swan River daisy	C · Chives
M · Marigold	St · Strawberry tower	P · Parsley
Dr · Daikon radish	D · Dill	

If you read gardening magazines, you've probably noticed that it's often city gardeners who have the most creative small gardens in their tiny yards or on their balconies and rooftops. I lived in New York City many years ago, and I remember how small city lots can be. So I designed a small-space companion garden to grow maximum crops in a minimal space. The design includes lots of trellises and arbors (that's why I call it the Small TALL Garden). It's great for anyone who wants lots of production in a small space, whether in the city, suburbs, or country.

There are six beds, each 3½ by 7 feet. Arching arbors connect pairs of beds across a center path. (You'll find building instructions for PVC pipe arches on pages 154–155.) The center path is 4 feet wide (but you can adjust the width to suit whatever arbors you build or buy).

Plant supports. You can use many kinds of cages, trellises, or fences to grow pole beans, tomatoes, and vine crops like cucumbers and winter squash. In this design, the vine crops grow over a "tent" made of heavy wire mesh that is nailed over a hinged frame.

You'll also notice a strawberry tower in one bed. I think the price of the tower is worth it for the luxury of harvesting fresh strawberries from a small garden!

Planting the garden. In the plant list at right, numbers in parentheses indicate how many transplants, crowns, or sets to plant. Plant other crops from seed; one packet should be plenty.

Plants for a Small TALL Garden

Vegetables

Asparagus (5)	Onions (24 to 36)
Beans (pole varieties)	Peas (tall varieties)
Carrots	Radishes
Cucumbers (3)	Spinach
Daikon radishes	Summer squash (1)
Gourds (4)	Strawberries (16 to 20)
Kale	Swiss chard
Lettuces (mixed varieties)	Tomatoes (3)
Melons (3)	Zucchini (1)
New Zealand spinach	

Herbs

Basil (7)	Fennel (3)
Chives (2)	Parsley (2)
Coriander (3)	Italian parsley (6)
Dill (3)	

Flowers

Calliopsis (6)	Mexican sunflowers (5)
Love-lies-bleeding (3)	Sunflowers
Marigolds (5 to 9)	Swan River daisies (2)

Ornamental Climbers

Climbing rose	Silver lace vine (*Polygonum aubertii*)

Two Special Climbers

The Small TALL Garden on page 134 includes two special flowering ornamentals, a climbing rose and silver lace vine. Both of the plants are beautiful and easy to grow.

Climbing roses. When I look for a climbing rose, I want one that's disease tolerant, pest-free, and hardy to the colder side of Zone 5 (preferably Zone 4). Not too many roses fill the bill. I've selected 'Henry Kelsey' as one of those few, reported by many rosarians as the best climbing rose for northern areas. It produces vigorous shoots laden with blooms that have deep red petals and contrasting gold stamens. 'Henry Kelsey' blooms from summer through the first frosts.

Other candidates for this situation are 'William Baffin' (deep pink, hardy to Zone 3), 'Leverkusen' (medium yellow, hardy to Zone 4 or 5), and 'John Cabot' (medium red, hardy to Zone 3).

Silver lace vine. If you plant silver lace vine, you may end up with a vine 25 to 30 feet long by the end of the summer. In areas with cold winters, silver lace vine may die back in winter and "only" grow 15 feet the following year. This vigorous vine likes full sun or partial shade and prefers dry, well-drained soil.

If silver lace vine sounds too aggressive for your taste, there are other easy climbers to try. Dutchman's pipe (*Aristolochia macrophylla*) can grow to 15 to 20 feet but is easy to control by cutting back each winter. It sports huge heart-shaped leaves and delicate, 3-inch, tubular, yellow flowers. Everblooming or climbing honeysuckle (*Lonicera sempervirens*) is fragrant and long-flowering and likes rich, well-drained soil and full sun or partial shade.

Creating Your Own Designs

I hope my fun designs and ideas trigger your creativity. Just remember, you don't have to make huge changes in your gardens all at once. You can start with something as simple as planting one bed in a new location or in a new shape. Try an oval or triangular bed. Or create a small companion-garden bed as a highlight in your front lawn. Why not, when you're mixing so many colorful flowers and herbs among the vegetables!

Chapter 8

The Four Fundamentals of Companion Gardening

I confess: I'm a compulsive composter. I scheme for new sources of compost materials, and during prime times for gathering them, I keep my car stocked with buckets, shovels, and plastic bags in the trunk. Leaves and pine needles that other people consider trash are a treasure to me. While I'm delighted to find these compost ingredients on the side of the road, it still amazes me that people throw them away. That's because turning organic materials into compost and using them as mulch are fundamental in my garden. Composting, mulching, and cover cropping all build great soil, and that means a healthy, productive garden. Plus, using mulch and cover crops means less weeding and watering, and that's a big bonus for a busy gardener like me!

Your Garden Needs Organic Matter

MIXING VEGETABLES with flowers and herbs is the special secret of companion gardens. But there are four organic gardening fundamentals that are just as important as setting up garden beds with a companionable mix of plants. These four fundamentals—gathering organic materials, making compost, applying mulch, and sowing cover crops—all relate to protecting and improving the soil.

Taking care of the soil is about half the work of gardening and the reason for almost all gardening success. Building the soil has some great side benefits—it will save you time and energy on tasks like fertilizing, weeding, controlling pests, tilling, and even watering.

Being a Garden Gatherer

I garden organically, and that means I need a constant supply of organic matter to build my soil. I gather organic materials all year long for making compost, for mulching, and for filling new garden beds. In the fall, I act a lot like a squirrel. That is, while the squirrels are busily gathering, carrying, and burying nuts, I'm carting leaves, picking up sticks, making piles of this and that, and burying kitchen scraps.

Gathering Good Materials

In spring and fall, I often stop my car along the roadside to pick up bags or piles of leaves, grass clippings, or—my favorite!—pine needles. I'm all in favor of gathering materials I can find easily and cheaply, and my roadside finds meet those requirements. I can collect bags of leaves by the hundred from the curbside in my local area, and with a little scouting, I'll bet you can, too.

Grass clippings, pulled weeds, and kitchen scraps are easy for most gardeners to gather. Does

The family shredder. Put a chair near the garden for grandparents, kids, or other family or friends. While they keep you company, they can help out by shredding newspaper into strips. Most people can tear about six sheets at once; I like strips about 1 inch wide.

anyone in your household work in an office building? If so, ask him or her to take a plastic bucket to work and gather the coffee grounds from the office coffeepot each day. You can add them to compost or use them as a fertilizer around your plants.

Newspaper is a great organic material. I have a friend who stockpiles the newspapers from her office. Just one week's worth of the *New York Times* is enough to lay the ground layer for a new garden bed. And shredded newspaper is a terrific compost ingredient that's available year-round. I stick with regular newspaper, not the coated magazine-style paper that's used in insert sections.

Check for specialized sources of free or cheap organic materials in your area. Gardeners who live near a cider mill should ask if they can haul away pomace (the crushed apple pulp left after cider making). If you live near a stable, you may be able to get free horse manure. One organic farmer in central New York State arranged to have lake weeds delivered—by the *ton*— whenever the lake bottom was dredged.

Many municipalities are getting into the act and stockpiling grass clippings, leaves, and other organic materials at local recycling centers, where residents can haul off the raw materials or even pick up finished compost for free.

Stockpiling Materials

Once you've gathered organic materials, where can you keep them? Some kinds are easy to store. Bags of leaves can sit in a corner of the yard indefinitely, and so can tree and shrub trimmings. It's best to spread grass clippings as mulch or compost them quickly, because they'll turn slimy and sour if you leave them piled in a large heap for more than a few days.

There are some organic materials that shouldn't be stockpiled or used as mulch because they can spread pest, disease, and weed problems. These include weeds that have gone to seed, diseased plants and garden waste, garden debris that may harbor insect eggs or larvae, and hay (because it's full of seeds). It's best to put these materials into an active compost pile as soon as you've gathered them.

Sally Says

"A friend of mine says I should have a bumper sticker that reads, 'I brake for pine needles!'"

Collecting organic stuff. My stockpile of organic materials for compost and mulch includes leaves, brush, shredded newspapers, kitchen scraps (kept frozen in milk containers through the winter), and bedding from the horse stalls.

Love Your Compost Pile

COMPOST IS THE BEST natural fertilizer for your plants. Compost happens when you mix a variety of organic materials together and let them decompose. It's important to include materials that are high in nitrogen, like manure, and materials that are high in carbon, like dried leaves.

You can speed the composting process by turning the materials. Keeping the pile at the right moisture content also aids decomposition.

I start every gardening session delivering kitchen scraps, garden debris, or some fresh manure to the compost pile. It's the best warm-up—physically and mentally—for gardening.

How to Make Compost

Composting styles are as individual as gardeners. Some gardeners just heap up any organic materials they have in a corner of the yard and let them sit. Others turn their pile every week to keep the composting process happening fast. You may prefer using a commercial compost bin or tumbler. It's not the style of composting that counts— it's the results!

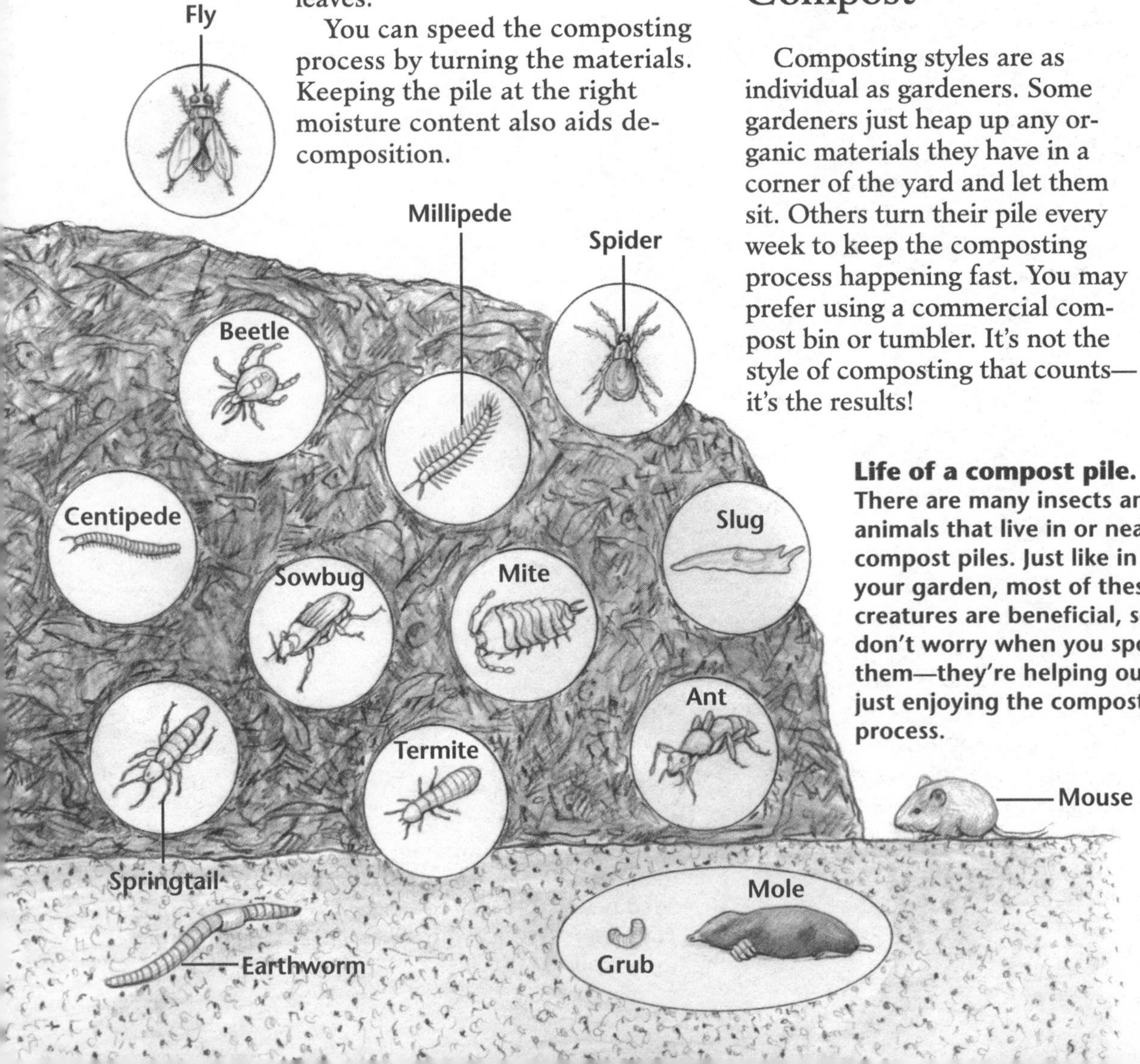

Life of a compost pile. There are many insects and animals that live in or near compost piles. Just like in your garden, most of these creatures are beneficial, so don't worry when you spot them—they're helping out or just enjoying the composting process.

Fly

Millipede

Spider

Beetle

Centipede

Sowbug

Mite

Slug

Ant

Termite

Springtail

Mouse

Earthworm

Grub

Mole

I make compost in three bins built from salvaged wooden pallets. If I need more room, I set up temporary wire fence enclosures about 4 feet in diameter. Sometimes I even make a compost pile right in the garden so the magical stuff is in place the following season. I generally make new compost piles in the fall and spring and use each one six to eight months later.

Starting a New Pile

To start a new pile in the fall, I lay a base of some coarse brush, tree trimmings, or corn stalks, and then plant a perforated PVC pipe upright in the center of the pile. (The pipe helps get air into the center of the pile.) Next, I add 6 inches of leaves and top them with 1 to 2 inches of kitchen scraps (no meat or fat!) and coffee grounds. I also toss in some weeds that have soil clinging to the roots.

The final layer is about 3 inches of fresh horse manure. Then I repeat the layering until I've used up all the materials and the pile is about 5 feet high.

Ideally, a compost pile should be as moist as a wrung-out sponge. If a pile is too dry, I wet it with the hose. If the pile seems too wet, I turn it a little and add leaves or even some shredded newspaper. Once my piles' moisture levels are under control, I cover each pile with a tarp, and I don't turn it; I just let it cook. If I had a better back or more time, or if I were in a rush, I would turn the pile after the first flush of heat occurs (in four or five days), and maybe weekly thereafter.

By spring, the fall pile is ready to use—at least the bottom half. I pull out the "unfinished" pieces and use them as my starter for a new pile. I build the spring pile the same way, using leaves and yard waste, adding 2 inches of grass clippings on the leaves whenever I can. I keep the grass layers less than 3 inches thick—otherwise they turn slimy and smelly! If you have a treasure trove of grass clippings, just alternate them with layers of shredded newspaper, dry leaves, and a little soil. Your pile will heat up quickly. You can even make a pile by alternating 4-inch-thick layers of leaves with 2-inch layers of grass, adding a few handfuls of soil to each leaf layer.

The great cover-up. I spread compost materials over empty garden beds in the fall and cover them with whatever I have at hand, like an old shower curtain. Then I spread straw over the top to hide the less attractive covering. By spring, I have new compost to plant my crops in!

Mulch for Moisture and More

MULCH RETAINS soil moisture, prevents erosion, blocks weeds, and promotes a steady soil temperature. Soil organisms are very happy in those moist, protected conditions and do an even better job of aerating the soil, breaking down organic matter, and producing nutrients for plant roots to absorb.

Choosing Mulches

I like to spread mulch a few inches deep around all my crops. Life is just too short for infinite weeding, and my clay soil will always need maximum soil-building assistance!

Over the years, I've come to have favorite uses for each kind of mulch; here's a rundown of how I use them.

Straw. Studies prove that straw mulch around potatoes thwarts the Colorado potato beetle's effort to emerge from the soil. Straw is a great mulch to use around raised beds and cold frames because it retains heat, helping to warm the crops. Straw also makes a fine pathway mulch because it decomposes so nicely when it's tilled into the soil. Be sure to mulch with straw, not hay. They look similar, but hay contains seeds and can create serious weed problems if you mulch with it.

Grass clippings. Fine-textured grass clippings are easy to sprinkle between close-growing crops like lettuce and carrots. I also use grass clippings around heavy feeders like peppers to add some nitrogen.

Newspaper. I use sheets of newspaper four to six sheets thick to mulch crops that I plant as transplants, as shown on the opposite page. Newspapers also work well as a mulch for Squash Family crops.

Leaves. Leaves fill the bill for mulching large, open areas around young squash, pumpkins, or other sprawling crops. I have lots of leaves to spare, since I gather plenty each fall, so I also use them to disguise newspaper mulch when I want to make the garden look a little prettier.

Living mulch. Living mulches like clover can cover lots of ground and keep down weeds, so I use them under corn and tomatoes, which are widely spaced at planting. Living mulches also make beautiful, soft coverings for pathways.

Pine needles. Pine needles acidify the soil slightly, which helps potatoes, strawberries, and raspberries grow better. I also use pine needles to mulch asaparagus and as a delicate mulch around flowers. I have a ready source of pine needles because my neighbor likes to rake his yard—which is

Sally Says

"I find earthworms in droves under newspaper mulch. Somehow, newspapers are to earthworms what potato chips are to teenagers!"

surrounded by 75-foot white pines! In some parts of the country, people have caused serious harm by "harvesting" fallen pine needles from forests, and I don't recommend gathering pine needles from wild areas.

A Place for Plastic?

Black plastic is a common mulch in commercial agriculture, but some gardeners feel that black plastic has no place in an organic garden because it is synthetic and rather ugly. I love black plastic—in its place—and use it in several ways. I agree, it's not pretty, but it's easy to cover plastic with nice-looking mulch, such as pine needles, grass clippings, or leaves.

There is nothing like black plastic for suppressing weeds. In my garden, I wrestle with barnyard grass, quackgrass, and creeping Charlie at every turn. Whenever the weeds are getting ahead of me, I mulch. I buy heavy-grade plastic because it lasts many years.

I also lay giant sheets of plastic over whole sections of garden in the spring, when I don't have time to plant. I use black plastic over the winter to cover weedy beds. I also use black plastic around tomatoes when I want to bring on the heat, and I often cover the soil around Cabbage Family or Squash Family crops when they are under row covers.

Whenever I use black plastic, I make it do triple duty as heat collector, weed blocker, and soil improver. I stuff leaves, shredded newspaper, unfinished compost, grass, or kitchen scraps (buried a little if rodents are a worry) right under the plastic—up to 5 inches thick.

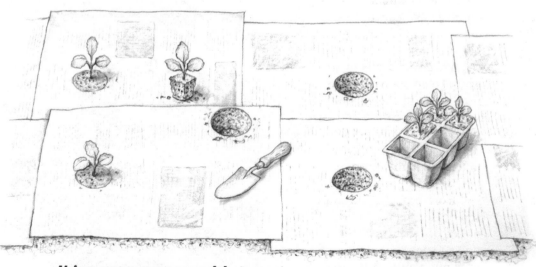

Using newspaper as mulch. I spread newspaper across a garden bed and wet it down so it won't blow away. Then I plant transplants through holes in the paper. As a finishing touch, I cover the newspaper with shredded leaves or grass clippings.

Cover Crops Do More than Cover

IT WAS EASY for me to try planting flowers in my vegetable garden, because I love flowers! (In fact, I have trouble deciding which garden is my favorite: my vegetable garden or the shady perennial garden beside my deck.) But I didn't know much about cover crops when I first planted them, and it seemed strange to give up space in my vegetable garden for a crop that I wouldn't eat and that wasn't a beautiful flower.

After I saw how much my soil improved after cover cropping and how my weed problems declined, I was sold. Plus, I learned that the flowers of some cover crops attract my friends the beneficial insects. To me, buckwheat flowers look (almost) as beautiful as the zinnias, calendulas, and asters that brighten my companion garden.

I use cover crops in several ways: to cover the soil in unused parts of the garden all summer, to protect beds over the winter, to block weeds in new beds, and as a living mulch under vegetable crops.

Cover cropping also protects soil from erosion and improves soil drainage. When you mow or cut cover crops, they provide on-the-spot organic mulches for growing plants. And cover crops preserve nutrients that might have leached out of the soil otherwise.

Planting Cover Crops

It's easy to plant cover-crop seeds. They'll germinate readily as long as the seed is of good quality. As with any seed, it's best to prepare a smooth seedbed before you plant—but I confess I've planted buckwheat in some pretty lumpy clay soil and still produced a good cover. (In fact, the clay is precisely why I needed the cover crop in the first place!)

SALLY'S HELPFUL HINTS

The No-Till Trick with Black Plastic

I've discovered an easy way to prepare cover-cropped areas for spring planting without tilling them. About three weeks before you plan to plant, cut down the cover crop, using a mower, a scythe, or hand tools. Then cover the area with solid black plastic or a tarp. In about two weeks, the cover crop will be dead and you can plant—right through the plastic if you want! This method is especially effective in small gardens or raised beds.

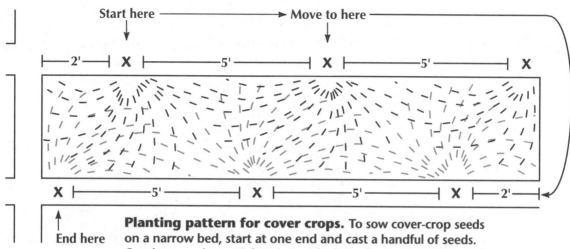

Start here ⟶ ➤ **Move to here** ⟶

├─ 2' ─┤ X ├──── 5' ────┤ X ├──── 5' ────┤ X

X ├──── 5' ────┤ X ├──── 5' ────┤ X ├─ 2' ─┤

↑
End here

Planting pattern for cover crops. To sow cover-crop seeds on a narrow bed, start at one end and cast a handful of seeds. Continue sowing at 5-foot intervals down both sides of the bed.

Lightly till or dig the garden and work in some compost if you can. Then be sure to give it a last shallow tilling or raking on planting day to kill the new crop of weeds.

My mom, who will admit to being "no spring chicken," likes sowing cover crops. It's like taking a walk with some extra arm-swinging! Just walk back and forth in the garden, holding a bag or pail of the seeds, and scatter the seeds in a wide arc. It's good to practice with peas or beans because you can see how evenly (or not) the seeds are falling. The goal is to let peas and beans fall about 3 inches apart and most other seeds about 1 to 2 inches apart. After your first pass, make a second walk through the garden at right angles to your first trip, and seed more lightly, looking carefully for any bare spots. If your sowing is uneven, it will still fill in and look lush (or you can add a few seeds later or even transplant from a crowded spot). It's okay to sow thickly—all the better to block weeds, too!

If you're just sowing a single bed in your garden, the technique is a bit different. You'll still use the same arm-swinging motion, but you'll sow at intervals along the bed, first along one side, then back along the other, as shown in the illustration above.

Sowing cover crops. Spreading cover-crop seeds is a simple job. Just take a handful of seeds, and sweep your arm in front of your body as you release the seeds.

Common Cover Crops

There are lots of cover crops to choose from, but I have a few favorites. You can contact your Cooperative Extension Service for information on the best cover crops for your area. Your choice will depend on how you plan to use the crop—to block weeds, to improve the soil, or to attract beneficials. In the listings that follow, I've included tips on some of my favorite ways to use these crops.

Alfalfa

Alfalfa is a perennial legume, so it makes soil more nutrient-rich. Alfalfa also has deep taproots that improve soil drainage and bring up nutrients from deep in the soil. Beneficial insects love alfalfa flowers.

I've discovered that woodchucks love alfalfa, so I use it to lure them *away* from my garden. Just sow a secluded plot of alfalfa far away from your garden, where the woodchucks can dine and lounge contentedly without crossing the wide, open space to reach your garden.

Plant alfalfa in spring or late summer and plan to let it grow a full year or longer. Sow ½ to 1 ounce of seed per 100 square feet of garden. Alfalfa can be a tough crop for home gardeners to handle because it's very hard to work into the soil with hand tools alone.

Annual Ryegrass

In cold regions, annual ryegrass is one of the few choices for fall planting because it can germinate and make some growth before it's killed by frost. The crop can block weeds, depending on how thick you plant it. Annual ryegrass also prevents soil erosion.

Plant annual ryegrass in early fall. Sow 3 to 5 ounces of seed per 100 square feet of garden. Be sure to till the crop or cut it down in the spring before it grows too tall for you to manage.

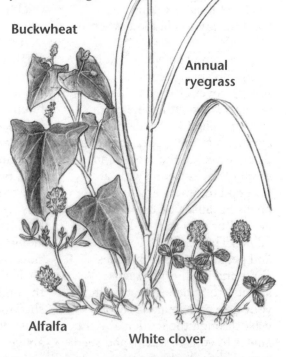

Buckwheat

Annual ryegrass

Alfalfa

White clover

Best cover-crop companions. There are more than a dozen cover crops to choose from, but four of the most widely used are alfalfa, buckwheat, annual ryegrass, and white clover.

Buckwheat

Buckwheat is my favorite cover crop, and it's the beneficial insects' favorite, too! Buckwheat is inexpensive, easy to plant, and beautiful. It flowers in about seven weeks, blocks weeds, and is easy to turn into the soil by hand. It won't survive frost, so don't use it as a winter cover crop.

I plant borders of buckwheat around the edge of my garden and use it as a cover crop on beds that are empty part of the season.

Plant buckwheat in spring or summer, sowing 3 to 5 ounces of seed per 100 square feet of garden. If you don't want the crop to self-sow, turn it under a couple of days after it flowers. Buckwheat has shallow roots, so it's fairly easy to hoe or pull if it regrows where it's not wanted.

Clovers

There are several kinds of clovers, and they all fix nitrogen, attract and protect beneficial insects, and prevent erosion. Plant them in spring or late summer—most will survive over the winter. You can kill clover by mowing it at flowering time. I sometimes let clover overwinter and start regrowing, and I just dig holes among the clover to plant my vegetables. My weed control is built in!

White clover. White clover is the best choice for paths or living mulch under short or medium-sized garden vegetables. The clover doesn't compete noticeably for nutrients, but it surely blocks weeds, attracts bees and other beneficials, and enriches the soil when you turn it under at the end of the season. Plant it in spring or August. Sow ½ to 1 ounce per 100 square feet.

Red clover and sweet clover. The deep taproots of red clover and sweet clover help improve soil drainage. Plant them between rows of tall crops like corn about one month after sowing the corn or when the corn is about 1 foot tall. Sow ½ to ¾ ounce per 100 square feet of garden.

Crimson clover. Crimson clover is killed by temperatures of 0°F, so it's a good choice if you live in a cold climate and you want a crop you can turn under easily in the spring. Sow ¾ to 1½ ounces per 100 square feet of garden.

Hairy Vetch

Another legume, hairy vetch, provides nitrogen and other nutrients, blocks weeds, and attracts beneficials. But it's difficult to manage with a tiller or hand tools, and if you let it set seed it can become a weed.

Plant hairy vetch in August, and mow or turn it under in the spring. Sow 1½ to 3 ounces per 100 square feet of garden. If you mow hairy vetch when it's in flower, it will die back and form a good mulch.

Sally Says

"Planting cover crops is one of the most valuable— and underused— techniques for imroving your soil. So try it!"

Oats

Oats add a lot of bulk to the soil, so they improve soil structure. This makes oats a good choice for improving heavy soil, but they can be hard to work into the soil, even with a tiller.

Plant oats in early spring or in August. Sow 3 to 5 ounces per 100 square feet of garden. The oats will die over the winter. Turn the crop under in early summer.

Winter Rye

Winter rye is very useful in cold regions because you can plant it late—in September, or even into October. Winter rye blocks weeds well, adds lots of organic matter to the soil, and prevents erosion. If you mow it down in April or May, it will form a wonderful mulch.

Plant winter rye in the fall, sowing 3 to 5 ounces per 100 square feet of garden. The crop can be heavy to handle with hand toolers or a tiller and can sometimes regrow after it's been turned under.

There are many other cover crops that organic farmers use successfully. They may be more difficult for you to find in stores, or have special growing needs, or require larger equipment to turn under. But if you want to experiment, you may want to try some, including triticale, bromegrass, Japanese millet, Sudan grass, lupines, and winter wheat. Remember, any cover is better than no cover!

Results You Can See

When you practice the four fundamentals of companion gardening, you'll begin to see the benefits right away. Compared to unmulched crops, crops surrounded by mulch will grow faster and yield better in the very first season. You'll see other benefits, like fewer weeds and soil that's easier to dig and needs less watering, within a year or two. Eventually, you'll have a garden routine that's centered around gathering organic material and getting it into the soil. The timing takes a while to master, but you'll find tips on what to do when for my fundamentals and much more in the next chapter, "Seasonal Care."

Chapter 9

Seasonal Care

Wouldn't you like to be a little bird peeking over the fence at the way other people garden? Then you could see their tricks and techniques for planting, watering, and all the other gardening chores! I certainly have plenty of quirks, shortcuts, and odd habits that are the real way I get things accomplished in my garden. Some of my methods aren't much like the directions I've read in gardening books, especially the books where the gardeners look so well-dressed and *clean*! I also know that lots of us garden with limited budgets and would rather make or find something rather than buy it. So I'll share an honest peek with you at how I care for my garden from winter on through the whole busy year—plus I'll add a lot of tips I've learned from some other "cleaned-up" gardeners that may make things easier for you.

Gardening through the Year

Sally Says

"Remember this—with gardening there's no one right way or wrong way as long as the birds keep singing and the tomatoes grow!"

DECIDING WHEN the gardening year starts is a bit like deciding which came first, the chicken or the egg. Perhaps it starts when you plant seeds and plants in the spring. But perhaps it starts in the fall, since many fall activities, such as preparing compost piles and tilling the soil, are really the groundwork for next season's garden.

I'm one of those gardeners who can't get the garden out of my thoughts, even when the soil is buried under 2 feet of snow (which happens quite often here in the shadow of Lake Erie!). For me, the gardening year starts in January with indoor tasks like ordering seeds and cleaning tools, and "ends" (at least briefly) in late fall when I harvest the last of the carrots and greens.

Five Seasons of Gardening

I divide the gardening year into five seasons: winter, early spring, late spring, summer, and fall. When those seasons start and end varies according to where you live and according to the weather. For me, late spring can be mid-May, but in a cold year, it's closer to mid-June! And for a gardener in North Carolina, late spring may be late

April. You'll need to decide for yourself when these seasons fall on your calendar.

In this chapter, you'll find a to-do list for each season that summarizes the garden tasks for that time of the year. I've described some of these tasks in detail in other parts of the book. When that's the case, I note in the to-do lists where you can find the complete lowdown on, for example, composting or making a garden plan.

As you browse through this chapter, keep in mind that you can't always garden "according to plan." We gardeners are often at the mercy of the weather. For example, on the day when the soil is just right for tilling, you may not be able to borrow a tiller, and rain will be forecast for the rest of the week. In cases like this, you won't be able to garden according to your perfect plan, but perhaps you can figure out a strategy that's good enough to get you through—like hiring the teenager next door to help dig part of the garden by hand so you accomplish some planting before the downpour.

Remember, gardening is and always should be fun, so don't let my to-do lists increase your stress level. Heaven knows, I don't always have my garden in tip-top shape, but I still get a good harvest each year—of produce and of satisfaction.

Gardening in Winter

WINTER IS THE TIME for make-it-yourself garden projects and tasks that you'll be too busy to accomplish once the weather turns nice. It's also the season for reading gardening books like this one and for dreaming over all those tempting catalogs while you make your seed and plant lists.

Shopping from Catalogs

Run to the mailbox and grab your pen! The arrival of garden catalogs in January creates great bursts of excitement at Wonderland Farm. But I've learned to be careful about catalog fever, because it's easy to overspend. So here are some tips for smart catalog shopping.

Read between the lines. Catalogs are sales tools, so naturally they only mention a plant's strong points. Look for what's *not* said. For example, if a tomato is billed as a "great keeper," but its flavor isn't mentioned, it may be pretty bland!

Compare prices. Even if you buy your seeds and plants locally, use catalogs to check typical price ranges, and watch for early- and late-season bargains on supplies.

Use regional sources. Companies that raise their plants and seeds in a climate similar to yours are more likely to sell varieties and species suited for your garden.

Order early. To be sure you get the choices you want, place your order before winter ends. Reputable companies will wait to ship your plants at an appropriate time for planting.

Making Garden Equipment

Make-it-yourself projects appeal to me because they save money, they let me turn trash and recyclables into useful items, and they're fun! You probably have your own special make-it-yourself items for the garden. Tomato cages and plant stakes are some of my favorites.

WINTER TO-DO LIST

- Order seeds and plants from mail-order catalog companies.
- Make homemade gardening props.
- Shred ahead—tear newspaper into strips as I suggested in Chapter 8.
- Clean, oil, and sharpen your tools.
- Fine-tune your garden plan following my guidelines in Chapter 4.

Step-by-Step Tomato Cages

I like sturdy tomato cages at least 4 feet tall. I haven't found commercial cages that really satisfy me, so I make my own out of wire fencing. I use fencing made from 14- or 16-gauge wire that has 4- by 6-inch openings. The fencing is available in 30-foot rolls, which is enough to make six or seven cages. Here's how I fashion the cages.

Step 1. Unroll the wire fencing on the floor, and use wire cutters to cut a 4-foot section of fence for each cage you want to make. Cut through the horizontal fence wires just beside one of the vertical wires.

Step 2. Line up the midpoint of the section of fence with an 8-foot-long wooden stake. Use a staple gun to fasten the wire to the stake. The pointed end of the stake should extend 18 inches below the edge of the fence.

Step 3. Bend the edges of the fencing together to form a cylinder. Wrap the cut ends of the horizontal wires around the vertical wire. Wear gloves to protect your hands from the sharp points of the wire.

Step 1

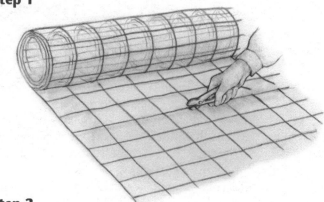

Step 2

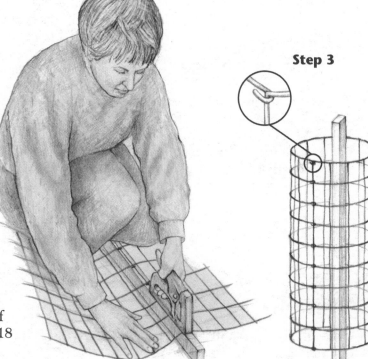

Step 3

These cages will support any type of tomato, even vigorous beefsteak varieties. The cages last six years or longer, depending on how heavy the fencing is and whether you store the cages inside during the winter.

John's Cheap Stakes

My friends and I like to make our own garden stakes and markers. For example, Master Gardener John Holnbeck recycles wooden shingles into inexpensive row markers by breaking them lengthwise into pieces about 1½ inches wide and 12 inches long. He then cuts strips from white plastic bleach bottles; each strip is about 3 inches long and ¾ inch wide. He staples the strips to the stakes and uses a waterproof pen to write on the strips. They are really "cheap stakes."

I make row markers out of chopsticks that I save from my monthly excursion to my favorite Chinese restaurant. I dip the chopsticks in paint or mark them with crayons to make color-coded markers. Or you can write on the wide end with a waterproof pen.

You can also fashion plant labels by cutting up yogurt containers, detergent bottles, and plastic orange-juice containers.

Tuning Up Your Tools

I don't have enough time to take good care of my tools during the active garden season, so I work hard to clean and sharpen them well each winter.

When you bring your dull and dirty tools inside for clean-up day, first spread out newspapers or a sheet—it saves you from having to clean your floor when you're through with the tools! Using a dry steel brush, brush any dry soil off the tool blades. Then set to work with soap and water and steel wool. Next, dry the tools, and apply linseed or tung oil to the wooden handles.

The final step is sharpening. I use a #10 bastard file to sharpen my garden tools. To sharpen the edge of a hoe, shovel, or trowel, push the file hard across the blade, using the full length of the file on each pass. Be sure to sharpen the beveled side of the blade.

Black plastic

Metal file

Trowel

Magnifying glass

Seeds

Pen

Row markers

Scuffle hoe

Garden scissors

Pruners

A great tool organizer. One of the nicest gardening gifts I've received is my trusty tool bucket. During my winter tool clean-up session, I reorganize my tools and supplies so come spring, all I have to do is grab my tool bucket and go!

Gardening in Early Spring

IF YOU LIVE in the southern United States, you may not yearn for the change from winter and early spring to late spring. But for northern gardeners, early spring is a distinct and sometimes frustratingly long time of year. It's finally warm enough to work outside, but the soil's still too wet to dig, and there's too much danger of frost to plant most of your crops. But I manage to find plenty of early-spring fix-up projects to satisfy my need to get outside.

Building Trellises

Early spring is a good time to set up trellises for crops you want to grow vertically, like pole beans, peas, and gourds. I often use teepees for beans, and chicken-wire trellises for peas.

My friend Mary Giambra, a Master Gardener from Marilla, New York, designed a sturdy structure from PVC pipe that has several possible uses, including an arching trellis. You can also add sections to make a series of arches in order to build the framework for a hoop house. To make these arches, you'll need 36 feet of PVC pipe, six T-joints, and eight elbow joints.

Step-by-Step PVC Arches

To make a trellis out of PVC arches, prepare by using a hacksaw to cut eight 2½-foot pieces, seven 2-foot pieces and four 6-inch pieces of PVC pipe.

Step 1. Make two arches, connecting the lengths of pipe as shown below.

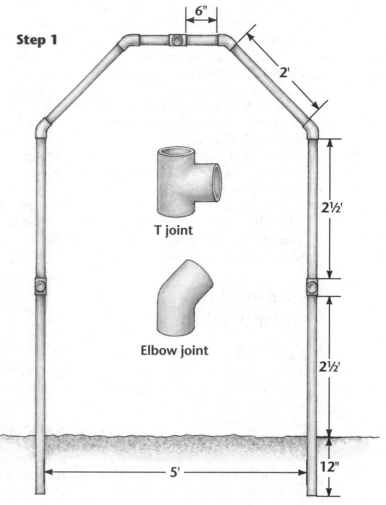

Step 1

T joint

Elbow joint

6"

2'

2½'

2½'

12"

5'

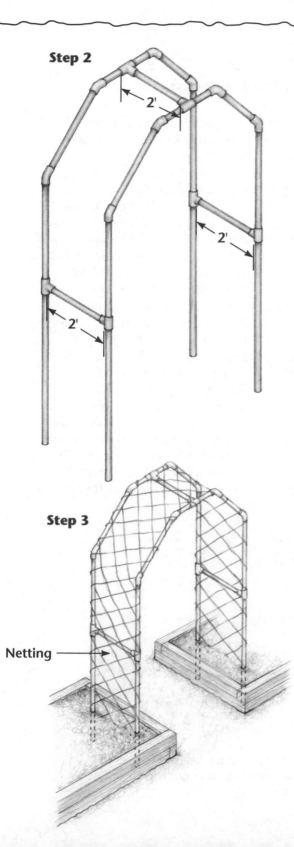

Step 2

2'

2'

2'

Step 3

Netting

Step 2. Connect the arches by inserting three 2-foot sections of pipe as crosspieces in the open fittings in the T-joints.

Step 3. Sink the feet of the arches into the soil of your garden or raised beds, inserting about 1 foot of pipe into the soil. The PVC is too slippery for some plants to cling to, so cover the trellis with pea netting, or weave rough twine in a zigzag pattern back and forth between the two arches.

Unmulching

Pulling mulch off your beds on sunny spring days helps warm and dry the soil. You can re-mulch after planting (you'll have to hoe lightly to kill surface weeds before you plant). In areas with poor drainage or heavy clay, it's important to cover unmulched areas with a solid cover like plastic or a tarp when it rains to keep the soil from becoming saturated.

I don't unmulch the perennial clusters or the beds where I plan to plant hot-weather vegetables like peppers, pumpkins, and basil. The soil will warm naturally under the mulch by the time air temperatures are suitable for planting these crops, so unmulching will just lead to weed problems.

When you unmulch, leave some mulch in place at the ends or sides of beds to shelter spiders, ground beetles, and other good bugs that overwinter under mulch.

Cold-Weather Weeding

On days when your first thought is "It's too cold for gardening," try some weeding. It's good exercise, and it will help free your garden of any tough weeds later. Pull weeds whenever the ground is unfrozen but damp. The weeds usually pull out quite easily. As long as they haven't gone to seed, put the pulled weeds in a stockpile for composting.

One special warning about early weeding: Don't pull out the companion plants you'll be looking for later! Your garden beds may include many weed, wildflower, and volunteer seedlings from last season's annuals and herbs. Learn to recognise the useful plants in their infancy. Check the illustrations below, which show some of the most common seedlings.

Grooming Perennials

To help your perennials bloom longer in summer, take time to care for them in spring. If you left seedheads in place for the birds to feed on or for winter interest, cut them back now. Remove old leaves or plant debris, too. Remember, go lightly: Birds, beneficials, and other wild things like it wild!

When you work in your perennial beds, keep in mind that some perennials don't start to regrow until late spring. Don't dig them up in your impatience to fill the vacancy! Butterfly weed (*Asclepias tuberosa*), balloon flowers (*Platycodon* spp.), and butterfly bushes (*Buddleia* spp.) are slow starters. It's too easy to destroy the crowns of these plants by digging before the new foliage starts to emerge.

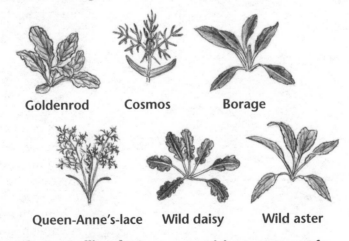

Goldenrod   Cosmos   Borage

Queen-Anne's-lace   Wild daisy   Wild aster

Save these seedlings! When you weed, keep an eye out for these seedlings, and let some remain in your garden. Their flowers will help attract beneficial insects.

Using Simple Cold Frames

Cold frames are great for extending the growing season in spring and fall. They can help you start some crops early, harden off your trays of seedlings and transplants before planting day, and carry lots of crops into the late fall. If you don't plan to build or buy a permanent cold frame, try setting up a temporary cold frame. One method is to buy bales of straw, set them up in a rectangle, and place window glass or clear plastic across the top to form a tiny greenhouse. I rigged a protected area for trays of seedlings by suspending old storm-door glass panes across the path between two raised beds. Even an old storm window propped against your house can provide short-term protection and give you a small jump on the season.

Starting Vegetables from Seed

Many home gardeners get great satisfaction from starting their own seeds under lights. On the other hand, lots of people try it and end up frustrated, with poor results after a lot of fuss. My advice: Only start seeds indoors if you plan to set up indoor lights. (Windowsills just don't provide enough light, at least in the Northeast.) There are many great references on seed starting—one of my favorites is Nancy Bubel's *The New Seed-Starter's Handbook.*

I'm lucky to live near some great nurseries that produce high-quality transplants, so most years, I don't take time to start seeds indoors. When I do, I concentrate on the easiest seeds for indoor starting, the Cabbage Family and Squash Family crops. You can also start tomatoes, peppers, and eggplant from seeds, but they require some extra care. If you enjoy the process and have the setup, great!

EARLY SPRING TO-DO LIST

- Prepare trellises and arbors.
- Build framed beds like the ones shown in Chapter 3.
- On sunny days, warm the soil by unmulching.
- Weed often and early, without stepping on the soil.
- Cut back and clean up perennials and hedgerows.
- Start some early crops in raised beds and in temporary cold frames.
- Start seeds indoors.
- Scrounge for compost materials, and make a new compost pile; see Chapter 8 for the method I use.
- Set up your watering system and hoses—check my "hose rules" in Chapter 3.

Gardening in Late Spring

ALTHOUGH THE DATES you call "late spring" may vary from year to year, you know when it's arrived: Late spring is the time you can actually work the soil and do some serious gardening!

Working the Soil

To tell when your soil is ready to be worked without damaging its structure, squeeze some in your hand. If the soil crumbles, it's ready for digging. If it cakes or forms a patty, it's too wet, and you'll have to wait.

Whether you work your soil with a rotary tiller or by hand, don't overdo it. Till or fluff the soil no deeper than 7 inches about two weeks before your estimated planting day. Your purpose is simply to break the soil crust, kill the surface weed seedlings, and expose weed seeds and grubs to the birds. Then on planting day, work the surface again, no deeper than 2 inches, to kill off any new weed seedlings.

Transplanting Tips

Now's the time to set out transplants for many crops, whether you've grown them yourself or bought them at a garden center. Remember these guidelines for successful transplanting.

- Harden off your transplants for one to two weeks before planting by putting them outside during the day. At night, bring them inside, or keep them inside a cold frame.

LATE SPRING TO-DO LIST

- Till or dig the soil.

- Get planting! It's now safe to plant everything except very tender crops like eggplant, peppers, basil, squash, and pumpkins. Directions for planting specific crops are in Chapter 10.

- Mulch every bit of soil that is not planted—see my specific recommendations in Chapter 8 and Chapter 10.

- To prevent pest problems, cover some crops with floating row covers.

- Trap and handpick slugs.

- Set up water dishes and baths for insects and birds, toad houses and rock piles for toads and frogs, and tall bird perches for birds.

- Plant seeds for summer cover crops, following my instructions in Chapter 8.

- Transplant on an overcast, cool day—not the first hot, sunny day you have.

- Keep transplants out of the wind while you're transplanting.

- Moisten seedlings thoroughly before you plant, and water well afterward.

- Pull or cut circling or matted roots apart before you plant.

- If frost, heavy wind, or hard rain threatens, protect newly planted transplants by covering them with baskets, tin cans, milk cartons, or sheets draped over short stakes.

Preventing Pest Problems

Now is the time to start stopping pests—before they hurt your plants. In a companion garden, your most important pest-prevention tactic is in the planting. But there are some other techniques you can try in late spring that may prevent problems later on.

Using Row Covers

Floating row covers are sheets of lightweight synthetic fabric that let air and water through but keep pests out. When you drape row covers over your crops, as shown at right, you'll prevent problems with common

pests like flea beetles, imported cabbageworms, cabbage loopers, and squash bugs.

Several brands of floating row covers are available at garden centers and from mail-order garden suppliers. I recommend that you buy row cover fabric in 5- or 6-foot widths so that you can cover your beds and still have excess fabric to bury at the edges. Choose one of the heavier-grade fabrics that don't tear easily, because your row covers can't have holes for those little pests to sneak through.

I sometimes keep crops like broccoli and cabbage covered from transplanting to harvest. I also cover vine crops like squash to keep out squash bugs. If you do this, remember to allow for pollination, or there will be no squash or pumpkins! Just remove the row covers when you see the plants in full flower.

Plant and cover. To protect crops like broccoli that are targeted by cabbage loopers and flea beetles, make hoops out of 4-foot sections of heavy wire to support floating row covers. Space the hoops 6 feet apart along the bed, and bury the row-cover edges under soil, rocks, or path coverings.

Stopping Slugs

I don't know of any companion plant that repels slugs, but I wish I did. Slugs can be a real problem, especially when there's a wet spring. They eat a wide variety of garden crops, especially lettuce, spinach, and Cabbage Family crops.

You can fight back by hand-picking and killing the slugs. It's not a fun job, but it really helps. Slugs gather under the boards that I use as garden pathways. During the day, I flip the boards over and offer the slugs as a meal for the birds. I also sink shallow dishes into the soil and fill the dishes with yeasty beer or a solution of water and yeast. The beer and yeast attract the slugs. When the slimy critters crawl into the dishes to drink, they drown.

Welcoming the Helpers

In a companion garden, spring is the season to put out the welcome mat for garden helpers. Here's a list of reminders about how to attract beneficial insects, birds, and other beneficial animals to your yard.

- Stick a tall bird perch or two in the garden, where birds can land, rest, and look around. A perch can be just a tall stake with a small crosspiece attached.

- Set up birdbaths with lots of pebbles in them.

- Allow some dandelions to bloom to provide early nectar for lady beetles, then pull the plants before they go to seed.

Uncovering slugs. During the day, slugs will congregate under boards or overturned melon rinds. Put out these slug havens, and then collect the slugs and dump them in a bucket of soapy water.

❧ To supply nectar early, sink pots of annuals into the soil, and remove them for use elsewhere when your garden has other flowers to offer.

❧ Make toad houses from inverted clay pots with chipped holes for doorways. Or simply pile up some rocks to provide a cool hiding spot.

Gardening in Summer

IT SEEMS TO ME that we spend weeks yearning for summer, but when summer gets here it's too hot to enjoy being outdoors! When summer heats up, I garden in the early morning and in the evening to beat the heat.

Watering

Even the best mulchers have to water sometimes. We don't want to use more water than necessary, but we don't want to wait until our plants have wilted to tell us they're thirsty. Here are some quick rules of thumb to help you decide when and how to water.

How often? Water when the soil feels dry to your finger about 2 inches down.

How much? Water vegetables and most flowers until the soil is damp at least 4 to 5 inches down.

What time of day? Watering in the morning is best. I avoid evening watering because it promotes fungal growth and creates perfect conditions for slugs. I avoid midday watering because the water evaporates fast, and it's not efficient. However, if the

plants are stressed, *water them!* Sometimes you can't fit in watering in the morning, so it's better to water when you can than not to water at all.

We've all heard that our gardens should get 1 inch of water per week, and believe me, that's more water than you'd think. For example, it takes about 120 gallons of water to supply one inch of water for a 10- by 20-foot garden. Just one full-size tomato or pumpkin plant needs 2 to 3 gallons of water a week.

Fixing Hoses on Short Notice

If someone accidentally runs over your hose with the lawn mower, or if your hose just springs a leak, it's wise to know how to repair it fast. You can repair your hose with a simple repair kit, available at your hardware store or garden center. (It's guaranteed that hoses always rip on holidays, when the stores are closed, so I keep a basket of hose repair supplies, complete with sharp knife and all the ends and connectors I may ever need.)

Step-by-Step Hose Repair

Here's my technique for fixing failing hoses:

Step 1. Use a sharp knife to cut out the leaky or damaged section of hose. Be sure to cut straight across the hose. If the weather's cold, bring the hose inside. It's hard to cut through a cold, brittle hose.

Step 2. Insert the repair coupling into the opening at the end of the intact hose and push it firmly into place. Repair couplings can be made of either metal or plastic; both types work well. Again, it's easier to do this when the hose is warm.

Step 3. Use a screwdriver to tighten the clamp in place next to the coupling. Discard the damaged section of hose.

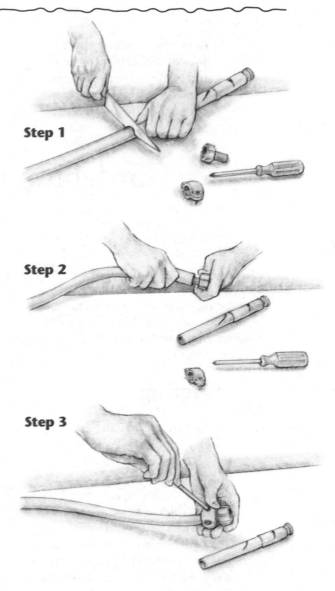

Step 1

Step 2

Step 3

Patrolling for Pests

In your companion garden, you should have very few serious pest problems, but it's still well worth it to inspect your plants for signs of trouble.

Walk through your garden and inspect each plant up close. Look on the undersides of leaves, at the growing tips, and down near the base of the stem—all likely spots for pests to hide and disease symptoms to show. If you find pests and don't know what they are, turn to the "Preventing Pest Problems" chart on pages 260–265, which will help you identify the pests and decide how to combat them.

You may spot signs of disease here and there in your garden, but don't panic. A few discolored leaves don't mean a crop will be ruined. But if you find a plant that's seriously diseased, pull it up and throw it away—

you wouldn't get a worthwhile harvest from it, and it would only spread the disease throughout more of your garden.

Fertilizing

Adding fertilizer as a *side dressing* or *top dressing* isn't essential, but at times it can really help your crop. This simply means putting a little organic fertilizer on or into the soil near the plant roots. I side-dress most crops when the plants have just begun to produce fruit, tubers, or whatever I'm planning to harvest.

I use compost or alfalfa meal for side-dressing crops. I spread the material in a circle beneath the outer canopy of leaves for plants like broccoli, brussels sprouts, and tomatoes. For corn, I sprinkle the fertilizer all along a row of plants. For crops like onions that I plant in blocks, I sprinkle the fertilizer as evenly as I can around the plants.

One alternative to side dressing is to spray plants with a solution of fish emulsion or seaweed extract. These products are rich in a wide range of nutrients. They may cost more than other fertilizers, but for a small garden it may be well worth your investment. Apply the spray diluted according to the directions on the package.

I don't bother fertilizing peas, beans, most root crops, or greens like lettuce and spinach, because it doesn't seem to increase their yields. You'll find specific fertilizer recommendations in the crop entries in Chapter 10, "Sally's Top Crops and Companion-Garden Secrets."

Planting for Fall

After all the work of preparing fertile garden beds, I certainly don't want to let them sit empty. So as soon as I finish harvesting a crop, I plant something else in its place. This creates a whole new set of crops to harvest in the fall.

There are some real advantages to fall gardening. For one thing, I'm not as busy as I am in the summer, so it's easier to find time to care for the garden. There are many fewer pests to contend with. It's also a second chance for success with crops that didn't do well the first time around.

SUMMER TO-DO LIST

- Check soil moisture frequently, and water as needed.
- Stay on the alert for serious diseases or pest buildup.
- Fertilize or side-dress heavy-feeding crops.
- Start a fall garden now.
- Harvest thoroughly and often to keep your crops producing. You'll find harvesting tips for specific crops in Chapter 10.

Harvesting

You've probably been harvesting since late spring, but a lot more harvesting happens quickly at the end of summer. If you're lucky, you have friends and family to help gather, store, prepare, freeze, or can your treasures. The gardener's job is to keep the harvest going.

Remember to keep things picked: Letting fruits stay on the vine can signal the crop to stop producing.

It's okay to let a few herb, broccoli, lettuce, and spinach plants go to seed, because some of them provide just the right nectar at the right time to keep our beneficial insect friends around the garden.

Gardening in Fall

IN THE FALL, we clean up the vegetable garden and cover the soil for the winter. It's also the time to set up safe havens for beneficial insects, birds, and helpful wildlife.

Helping Beneficials and Birds

Many beneficial insects overwinter right in the garden. Cover crops and mulch protect these overwintering beneficials. Leave the water dishes in your garden filled right up until freezing weather so beneficials have a source of water. Leaving boards, stones, or cardboard in place also protects ground beetles over the winter.

Birds require water and food, either to survive in your local area or during migration, so learn about bird feeding, and keep feeders filled through the winter. In the garden, leaving the seedheads of perennials, cover crops, and weeds in place will attract many birds.

Brussels sprout stems

Log

Twiggy brush

Making a brush pile. To help birds and beneficial animals survive the winter, make a layered brush pile in a corner of your yard. Crisscross thick logs or wide pipes, lay brussels sprout stems or corn stalks over them, and top the pile off with twiggy prunings from shrubs and trees.

Garden Cleanup

Garden cleanup is a bit different than usual in a companion garden. You won't just make a clean sweep, because your garden neighborhoods will finish at different times. And you'll treat each bed differently, depending on which crop family

---

FALL TO-DO LIST

🐦 Prune back garden perennials, but let seedheads remain for the birds.

🐦 If you were not doing so already, start a bird-feeding program, and provide water to help your wild friends all winter.

🐦 Make a brush pile for the wildlife.

🐦 Plant the last of the cover crops according to my directions in Chapter 8.

🐦 Clean up plant debris and work the soil.

🐦 Build a big compost pile to overwinter. I describe my method in Chapter 8.

🐦 Make sheet compost on beds where you want to build fertility.

🐦 Scrounge for organic materials like straw, leaves, and aged wood chips.

🐦 Protect crops that you want to harvest during the fall.

🐦 Bring your garden journal up to date. Write a final entry in your garden journal to sum up the garden season.

---

and plant friends will move into the bed next spring. In some beds, you'll sow a cover crop as soon as you finish harvesting. In others you'll continue to harvest right through fall, so after clearing out the crop, you'll work the soil and then cover it with organic mulch, plastic, or a tarp. In beds where you want optimum nutrition next season, you'll sheet compost by spreading a layer of manure or other high-nitrogen organic matter over the soil surface.

As you clean up, watch for annual weeds, like ragweed, lamb's-quarters, and pigweed, that have gone to seed around your garden. Snip off the stems, gather the seedheads, and discard them with your household trash.

Where Cleanup Counts

Some kinds of garden cleanup are vital. If any sections of your garden suffered insect or disease problems, the damaged plants must be pulled, roots and all, in the fall. I always remove the remains of cucumbers, melons, squash, pumpkins, and all Cabbage Family crops from my garden. I burn the remains, but if burning isn't allowed where you live, dispose of them in your trash.

It's also important to harvest potatoes and tomatoes thoroughly, and if you compost the plant remains, make sure they're in an active compost pile. Late blight, a serious fungal disease, and several other disease organisms can overwinter in garden debris and reappear in volunteer plants that sprout from unharvested fruits and tubers. So it is especially important to resist the temptation to take advantage of those "freebies." Instead, destroy them.

Overwintering Garden Favorites

I don't get fancy with hoop houses and cold frames, but there are a couple of simple tricks that extend my harvest of carrots and greens until Christmas.

Carrots get sweeter and sweeter as the temperature drops, so cover them with a thick straw mulch, and you can harvest a snack any time you happen to be skiing by!

Lettuce, spinach, and most greens—including Chinese cabbage and Swiss chard—will tolerate several frosts. Keep them going by placing straw bales around the plants and covering the bales with a discarded storm window or a piece of heavyweight, clear plastic. You can also use the hoops that held up your row covers to support clear plastic to make a minigreenhouse. (In warm spells, be sure to lift up the sides to avoid "cooking" the plants.)

Summing Up the Garden Year

If you ever write in a garden journal, fall is the most important time for making notes. Record the names of what you grew, what looked great, what had problems, what was too close or too far apart, and which companions worked best.

Whatever the season, remember that the less factual but more personal notes are also very important to include in your garden journal. After all, gardening is a passion for many of us—but still a hobby and not a *job*! So add comments on what you did and didn't enjoy doing and what was pleasing or frustrating during the season. (My notes always include "mulch more and weed less!") You may want to try drawing sketches of your garden in your journal or taping some photos of your garden to the pages. The more fun your journal is, the more likely you'll use it in all seasons.

How My Companion Garden Works

My garden is full of life, with a diverse mix of plants, insects, birds, and other animals. And I'm not shy about inviting you in for a glimpse at it—weeds and all. In this section, you'll see my crop neighborhoods, framed raised beds (including construction day), perennial cluster, favorite insects, frog pond, and some dear pets and people that are part of my garden "wonderland." I hope the visit encourages you to develop your own personal companion garden using some of my special techniques and tips. Thanks for stopping by!

To protect the soil structure ▶
in my garden, I build raised
beds before I plant. Then I lay
old boards in the pathways to
mark them clearly. That way,
everybody (even the dogs)
walks where I want them to!

It's easy to spot the different
crop neighborhoods in my
garden. My Cabbage Family
neighborhood includes
brussels sprouts, broccoli,
cauliflower with dill, and a
buckwheat border. Across
the way is the Tomato Family
neighborhood.
▼

▲
Strawflowers line the edge of
the Tomato Family neighborhood.
This section of the garden
includes peppers, eggplants, and
tomatoes with parsley, coriander,
and flowers, of course.

The Squash Family neighborhood includes
'Turk's Turban' and butternut squash,
summer squash, and pumpkins. Black
plastic mulch under the crops keep weeds
in bounds, and the calendulas, dill, and
nasturtiums help keep the crops pest-free.
▼

If you decide to build framed raised beds, get help from family and friends on construction day. My brother-in-law Craig Vogel led the bed-building effort in my garden. We used hemlock landscape timbers to create beds 3½ feet wide and 12 feet long.

◀ Even though hemlock is rot-resistant, it will eventually break down. So for extra protection, we lined the beds with heavy builders' plastic before filling them.

You can fill framed raised beds with purchased topsoil, but it's cheaper to create your own soil using a mix of organic materials. We loaded my beds with sticks, shredded paper, weeds, manure, straw, and grass clippings.

If you make soil "from scratch," it's best to let the materials decompose and settle before you plant. My daughter, Alice, was impatient (me, too) so we planted some perennials and garlic in one bed the first fall. The mix was far from decomposed—but the plants grew anyway.

Gardening in framed raised beds gives you an early spring start, especially if your garden has clay soil that dries out slowly. My beds allow me a full month's jump on the season for planting cool-season crops like peas, spinach, onions, and potatoes. Naturally I also plant companions: These onions share the bed with pinks and parsley.

The potato–bean duo (*above*) is an absolute must in a companion garden because planting them together outwits two nasty pests— the Mexican bean beetle and Colorado potato beetle.

In midsummer I'm harvesting potatoes just as the beans start coming (*left*).

No, it's not a jigsaw puzzle; it's a tiny, improvised raised bed! I used wood scraps to fashion a 12- by 24-inch block, where I grew a surprising number of long, straight carrots.

Don't overlook the potential of corners and edges in your garden beds. I seeded mixed lettuce around the edges of the mini–raised bed. You can harvest the lettuce by snipping the tops with scissors, and it will regrow over and over, as long as the weather stays cool.

It's easy to make a compost bin out of wooden pallets, which are sometimes free at feed or home-supply stores. An iron pipe with holes lets air into the center of the pile, and the compost thermometer tells me if the pile is really "cooking."

With its lovely white flowers, buckwheat is my favorite cover crop. Buckwheat is easy to grow and has great soil-improving power. Plus it attracts many kinds of beneficial insects, particularly parasitic wasps, hoverflies, and honeybees. I often use it as a border around the garden.

Our horse Becky is a gentle companion. And, not to be indelicate, she's also the best manure maker I know! Manure is a great high-nitrogen jump start for the compost pile.

To make a new bed ▶ without digging, I spread black plastic and tuck a lot of organic material, like shredded paper or leaves, under it. Earthworms will find the material quickly and start to break it down. I spread straw over the plastic for looks and also to encourage pest-gobbling spiders.

To keep beneficial insects happy, you must supply water in the garden—both at ground level and birdbath level. The birds like it, too! The rocks and pebbles give insects a place to land without drowning (*left*). My birdbath sits in the center of a perennial and wildflower cluster filled with flowers like daisies, bee balm, yarrow, goldenrod, and mums. Even my dog Moby enjoys contemplating this colorful garden cluster (*below*).

When you stroll ▶
through your com-
panion garden, take a
close look, especially
at the undersides
of leaves. You'll often
spot yellow clusters of
lady-beetle eggs—a sign
that nature's systems
are working (and that
makes aphids nervous).

Some beneficial
insects are easy to
spot. I've spied many
lacewings sipping
nectar on tansy
flowers (*above left*).
Praying mantids
(*above right*) look
like the fierce
hunters they are—
they eat anything
they can grab,
including other
mantids. And heroic
lady beetles (*right*) will
leap tall lettuces just
to capture all those
aphids!

◀ Toads and frogs consume hundreds of insects a day. Sheltered areas such as groundcovers, rock piles, or overturned pots with chipped-out "doorways" are great homes for frogs and toads. Any low basin or pool sunk into the ground delights them.

If weeds get out of control in a garden bed, try a cover-and-conquer strategy. Spread a solid black plastic covering to choke out the weeds. I added a discarded wading pool and lined it with heavy plastic to make a small pool for beneficial insects and animals, and I carefully planted a few large perennials like lovage and angelica through the plastic. Ginger the dog loves the sun-warmed plastic and straw.

▼

Birds are one of a gardener's best friends. ▶
Plant some bird-sheltering shrubs and put
up nesting boxes and houses to encourage
birds like this bluebird to set up housekeeping
near your garden. Resident birds will feed on
pest insects, especially during nesting season.

Owl the cat loves to pose and preen near me
wherever I'm working in the garden. She's
also interested in moles and mice, but she
ignores the passing parade of toads, birds,
and insects. I'm certain that the frequent
presence of my dogs and cats is one reason
why I have nearly no problems with wildlife
eating up my garden plants. I also leave a lot
of wildlife-friendly habitat untouched, so
perhaps my local wildlife find plenty to eat
without raiding my garden.
▼

Toward the end of summer my garden is beautiful—and so full of food and flowers! The russet cornstalks, the perennial cluster with its New England asters and goldenrods, and the textures of the green vegetable crops create a pleasing picture—and plenty of fresh food to harvest. This is the time of year when harvest helpers are welcome garden companions.

My daughter, Alice, is a budding gardener and a fine cook. She likes to use garden-fresh zucchini and peppers in her famous omelettes—really one of the best reasons to wake up on a Sunday morning!

My mom, Jean, helps me in lots more ways than harvesting. She's the first out with the pruner in the spring and the rake in the fall, and like all great moms, is always the first to say, "My, your garden certainly looks lovely!"

My cat Buddy, whom I rescued from the wild, is the most loving friend around. In keeping with his wild roots, he patrols my garden all summer. As for me, there's time to work in the garden and time to just observe. In fact, that's the great fun in companion gardening—watching to see just how successful your choices of crop friends and families will be.

Chapter 10

Sally's Top Crops and Companion-Garden Secrets

It's so satisfying to grow your own vegetables. You plant tiny seeds or small plants, protect them, water and feed them to help them grow, and in the end, you have delicious food to eat. It's a bit like raising a child— except for the eating part—and it's a lot faster. The results are much more predictable too, as most parents will tell you. And if something doesn't work out, there's always next year's garden!

In my companion garden, I grow the whole gamut of vegetables. Sometimes I leave out the corn, because it takes so much space. But I hope I never ever have to do without the taste of my own first-picked tomatoes or the crunchy sweetness of freshly dug carrots. The best part of it all is that special pride I feel when I bring in the harvest and say, "I grew it myself!"

Giving Each Crop Its Due

DO YOU HAVE a favorite crop? Tomatoes, beans, or perhaps peppers? I enjoy all of the crops I grow, and I like to give each one special attention. That's what this chapter is all about—the special tips and techniques that can boost yields, extend the harvest, and make gardening more fun.

Each crop has its own entry, and each entry is divided into several categories to help you find information easily. Here's a rundown of those categories.

Family unit. As you'll recall, I group vegetables into crop families. In this section I'll tell you which crops I like to grow together in the same bed or section of the garden.

Friends. For each crop you'll find some specific flower and herb friends recommended. My suggestions are not the only possible choices. I've just offered a few of my favorite combinations.

Growing basics. Soil and light requirements, timing of planting, and seed-starting information all fall in this category. Some crops, like asparagus and potatoes, require a special planting technique, and you'll find those directions also.

Spacing. I pack plants in tightly in my garden. Each entry has a spacing diagram that shows my basic spacing technique for the crop. I also describe spacing alternatives and explain how to mix companion herbs and flowers into a spacing pattern.

Feeding. I don't fertilize my crops much, because I prefer to feed my plants by enriching the soil with organic matter. But fertilizer is good insurance for a hefty harvest, so I offer my recommendations for organic fertilizers to boost yields.

Mulching. Mulch is a must in my garden, and for many crops I have particular favorite mulches. I also give advice about when and how much to water.

Problems and solutions. We all have occasional problems with our crops, and pests aren't always the culprits. Sometimes problems are caused by the weather, or poor soil, or our own mistakes. In this section I offer advice on avoiding some of the common problems that I've experienced in raising vegetables.

Harvesting. A successful harvest is our goal, so I tell you how to harvest your crops when they're at the peak of flavor.

Sally's tips and tricks. These are a varied collection of planting, harvesting, fertilizing, and pest-prevention techniques that I use in my own garden or that I've learned from my many gardening friends (especially the Master Gardeners). They're some of the best "homegrown" garden secrets I know.

Asparagus • *Asparagus officinalis* • Liliaceae

FAMILY UNIT

A healthy asparagus patch can last 30 years, so group asparagus with other long-term crops, like rhubarb. I grow asparagus in a permanent bed next to my strawberries.

FRIENDS

Your permanent asparagus bed is a great place to plant perennial Aster Family flowers like coreopsis. Annual herbs like dill or coriander and tall annual flowers like cosmos also make good companions for asparagus.

GROWING BASICS

Asparagus needs neutral soil: The pH should not be below 6.5. This crop needs six hours of sun daily or a full day of dappled sun. Good drainage is essential. If you have slow-draining or heavy clay soil, check my method for raised planting, shown at right.

Buy or order asparagus crowns in time for early spring planting in your area. For maximum production, choose an all-male variety—they have higher yields than conventional varieties.

To plant asparagus, dig or till the top foot of soil. Then dig trenches 6 inches deep. Shape mounds of soil in the trenches and spread the crowns over the mounds. Cover the crowns with at least 2 inches of soil at planting. Add more soil over time as the asparagus spears emerge.

Spacing. Asparagus beds may be 3 to 4 feet wide, with crowns spaced 15 inches apart in a 2-1-2 pattern. Or try planting crowns in two rows down the bed, evenly spaced with a center row of a tall companion, like hollyhocks.

Feeding. At planting, enrich your soil with a generous amount of compost or rotted manure. For established plantings, top-dress with compost after harvest. In fall I add additional compost as well as aged leaves.

Asparagus

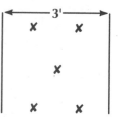

Space crowns 15" apart in a 2-1-2 pattern

Sally's TIPS & TRICKS

Crowns on Compost

Asparagus crowns tend to rot away if they're buried in heavy or wet soil. So if you have poorly drained soil, just plant your asparagus on top! Make mounds of compost topped with 2 inches of soil on the surface of a prepared garden bed. Drape the roots of an asparagus crown over each mound. Then heap at least 3 inches of good topsoil over the entire bed.

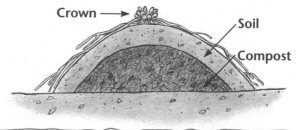

Crown → Soil Compost

Mulching. Any fine mulch will help control weeds. Try grass clippings, finely shredded paper, or pine needles. Heavy mulches may prevent spears from emerging properly. Water well whenever the soil is dry 4 inches below the soil surface, especially during the first year of growth.

PROBLEMS AND SOLUTIONS

Chewed stems with brown blotches. Asparagus beetles are the most common asparagus pest, but you can minimize problems by cutting down the fronds in the fall and destroying them. Use a dandelion fork to cultivate the soil between plants in the fall before you put down the winter mulch. If you have a severe problem, cover the crop with row covers from early spring until harvest is complete.

Reddish brown streaks and spots on stems. Asparagus rust can make the plants look unsightly. Try to encourage better air circulation around your plants. If you have severe problems, start a new patch in a location with good drainage, using a rust-resistant variety.

HARVESTING

Asparagus requires careful planting and initial patience, but then it pays you back almost forever. My harvest rule of thumb is: Year One, take none. Year Two, cut a few. Year Three, lots for me! Cut as much as you like in the spring, but after six to eight weeks, let some spears mature into fluffy fronds.

Beans • *Phaseolus vulgaris* • Fabaceae

FAMILY UNIT

Versatile beans work well in many kinds of crop families. Research studies and my own experience show that pairing beans with potatoes reduces problems with these crops' archenemies: Mexican bean beetles and Colorado potato beetles. Beans also make a family with squash and corn—the traditional Three Sisters grouping. I grow pole beans on teepees to shade salad greens, and on trellises between sections of lettuce, mesclun, or other short crops.

FRIENDS

Savory, French tarragon, basil, and dill are good plant friends for beans. I plant salvias or snapdragons with beans and like to have tansy growing nearby.

GROWING BASICS

Beans need full sun but aren't fussy about soil conditions. They are tender, so don't plant them until danger of frost is past. For an early start, try sprouting seeds indoors, as shown on the opposite page. Beans are legumes, so to ensure best production, use

Snap beans

3'

x x x x x x
x x x x x x
x x x x x x

Space seeds 5"– 6" apart in all directions

an inoculant when you plant them. Inoculant is a powder containing bacteria that help the legume fix nitrogen.

Spacing. For large intensive plantings of bush beans, broadcast the seed lightly over the planting area, aiming to have seeds 5 to 6 inches apart. Then I broadcast soil over the seeds to cover them. If you're a serious bean eater, sow successive plots every two to three weeks through the summer until seven weeks before your first average fall frost date. For instructions on interplanting beans and potatoes, see pages 223–225.

To plant pole beans around a teepee, sow about seven seeds around each pole, and then thin to three or four plants per pole. To plant pole beans as part of a Three Sisters grouping, see the planting diagrams on pages 79–80.

Feeding. Bush beans don't need fertilizing, but boosting pole beans with a little compost halfway through their growing season ensures the best yields.

Mulching. Fast-growing beans provide their own soil covering when grown in wide rows. When I plant pole beans, I surround them with greens (lettuce or New Zealand spinach). Use straw or grass to cover any bare spots. Once beans are in flower, keep them well watered.

Sally's TIPS & TRICKS

Presprout Your Beans

In cold soil, beans germinate slowly—or not at all. To get your crop off to a fast start, presprout your beans indoors. Just spread some beans on a piece of damp paper towel, and roll them up in the towel. Stick the towel in a jar, and sprinkle it regularly with water to keep it damp (not sopping) until you see little sprouts poking through the outer layer of the paper. Then carefully remove the towel from the jar, unroll it, and plant the sprouted beans outdoors in your garden. This technique can give you as much as a two-week jump on harvesting.

Bean seeds

Paper towel

KENTUCKY WONDER 5/5

Roots of presprouted seeds

PROBLEMS AND SOLUTIONS

Seeds don't germinate. Frost may kill beans planted too early in the spring, or the seeds may rot in cold, wet soils.

Reddish brown blisters on leaf undersides. Bean rust causes these blisters on the leaf undersides. Increasing air circulation can help reduce problems, so try thinning your stand, and for future crops, plant at wider spacings. Don't work among bean plants when they're wet from dew or rain, because this can spread disease problems.

Skeletonized leaves. Leaf "skeletons" are the classic sign of Mexican bean beetles. Handpick any beetles, larvae, and eggs you find. If you've had past serious problems with bean beetles, plant early-maturing varieties, and cover your bean crop with row covers to keep the beetles out. Interplanting beans with potatoes and other plant companions usually attracts predatory insects and keeps the pests in check.

HARVESTING

Pick snap beans when they're slim and tender, and harvest every few days to catch the beans at their best. If you're growing a crop for dry beans, pick the bean pods after they turn brown and you can hear the beans rattling inside the pods when you shake them. Store the dry beans in an airtight jar in a cool, dry place.

Sally Says

"If you grow too many beans, just till some under—they'll improve the soil."

Beets • *Beta vulgaris* • Chenopodiaceae

FAMILY UNIT

Beets grow well with other root crops. If you have raised beds, beets and other root crops deserve first place. I interplant beets and onions as early in the spring as I can. Later, I add carrots where there is room.

Beets also mix well with salad greens, because you can harvest beet greens using the "cut-and-come-again" technique shown for lettuce on page 215.

FRIENDS

Beets have few pest problems, so they don't need too many friends to help them get along. Try putting pots of catnip or mint near your beets to repel flea beetles. Combining the edible with the ornamental, beets and chives make a pretty border around roses.

GROWING BASICS

Plant beets in well-drained, light soil or in raised beds. Choose a site in full sun or light shade. Beets do poorly in temperatures higher than 85°F, so use shade cloth, or wait and grow beets as a fall crop. Beets are likely to become tough

Beet

Space transplants 3"– 4" apart in all directions

without even soil moisture. Soil pH should be from 6.0 to 7.5; more acidic soils often lead to a boron deficiency.

Sow beet seeds 1 inch deep, up to a month before the last frost date. Beets are one of the few root crops that grow well from transplants, so you can buy transplants from a nursery if you have a late start.

Spacing. Whether alone or mixed with friends, plant beets 3 to 4 inches apart in all directions. If you sow closer, use the thinnings in stir-fry or salads.

Feeding. Beets are light feeders, and I don't bother fertilizing them.

Mulching. If you plant beet seeds in spring and have a sudden hot spell, spread 1 inch of finely chopped leaves or compost over the plot, and keep the area watered. The extra coolness may save the crop. If your beets are closely spaced with their plant friends, there won't be any room for mulch. For more loosely spaced beets, you can use any fine organic mulch, such as grass clippings.

PROBLEMS AND SOLUTIONS

Tough, flavorless roots. Hot weather can ruin beet roots, so keep the plants moist and cool.

Holes or tunnels in leaves. Flea beetles chew tiny holes in leaves, and leafminer larvae leave serpentine tunnels as they feed under the leaf surface.

This damage usually doesn't hurt yields. If you want to prevent it, place row covers over the crop at planting.

Spots on leaves. Leaf-spot diseases are prevented by rotations; avoid locations where beets, spinach, or Swiss chard were grown for a year or two. You can also try planting disease-resistant varieties.

HARVESTING

Harvest greens anytime with the "cut-and-come-again" approach, and keep at it so they don't get tough. Pull baby beets when they are over 1 inch in diameter to cook with their stems. Harvest larger beets before severe heat spells, leaving 1 to 2 inches of the stems attached to prevent "bleeding" and staining.

For fall crops, gather all your beets after a hard frost, cut off the tops near the roots, and keep the beets in sand in a cool place, such as a root cellar.

Sally Says

"Keep beets cool! Protect germinating seeds with mulch, shade growing plants, and keep the water coming."

Sally's TIPS & TRICKS

Better Beets

If your memory of beets is your mom making you eat them ("they're good for you!"), you probably haven't tried any lately. Beets have evolved! There are golden beets, striped beets like 'Chioggia', and baby burgundy-colored beauties like 'Action' and 'Pronto'—and they're still full of iron. So try planting a colorful beet medley, and maybe the next generation of kids will think of beets as a treat.

Broccoli • *Brassica oleracea*, Botrytis Group • Brassicaceae

Broccoli

FAMILY UNIT

Botanically speaking, broccoli is part of the Cabbage Family, which also includes cabbage, brussels sprouts, cauliflower, kale, and Chinese cabbage. I grow these crops together because of their common cultural needs and problems.

FRIENDS

Broccoli mixes well with many Aster Family plants, like zinnias, asters, and marigolds, as well as parsley, for fall plantings. Plant these friends so they'll flower continuously near your broccoli, especially if you aren't using row covers.

Underplant broccoli with a thick seeding of sweet alyssum—the alyssum will block weeds and attract beneficials.

GROWING BASICS

Plant broccoli in rich soil, well blended with compost and aged manure to a depth of at least 12 inches. Grow it in full sun; it can also take light shade but will produce smaller heads.

Soil temperature should be over 60°F at planting. Broccoli is a cool-weather crop and can even tolerate light frosts; however, broccoli can "button" (make tiny heads) if it's forced to endure air temperatures of 40°F for longer than ten days. Ideal growing temperature is 60°F to 65°F. Soil pH should be close to 7.2 in order to

avoid the fungal disease called clubroot.

To start broccoli from seeds, sow seeds indoors about two months before the last spring frost, and set transplants out about a month later. If you buy transplants, check the roots, and don't buy pot-bound plants—they will form small heads.

Spacing. Space broccoli in wide rows in a 2-1-2 pattern, about 15 inches apart in all directions. Plant companion flowers and herbs in the spaces on both sides of the single broccoli plants.

Feeding. These heavy feeders need good soil to form large leaves and big roots—so give them your best. I side-dress with compost about three weeks after planting. If your plants have pale green or yellowish leaves, they may be suffering from too little nitrogen. Spray plants with fish emulsion to give them a boost, but don't overfeed, or your plants may end up with hollow stems. The bottom line: Soil building up front really counts!

Mulching. I mulch my spring broccoli with straw. Then I cover the plants with row covers and leave them covered until they're nearly ready to harvest. Keep broccoli well watered, because lack of water causes small heads or premature bolting.

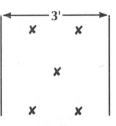

Space transplants 15" apart in a 2-1-2 pattern

PROBLEMS AND SOLUTIONS

Poor production. Heat is enemy number one for broccoli, especially too much too soon. If your spring broccoli yield is poor, try summer planting, as described in "Fall Broccoli," below.

Holes in leaves. Broccoli's number two enemies are the cabbage looper and imported cabbageworm. Once you find damage, just handpick the caterpillars off the plants. To prevent future problems, cover plants with row covers at planting and leave on until harvest.

Seedlings cut off at the base. Cutworms chew through stems near the soil. To prevent damage, place cardboard tubes or tuna cans around the transplants at planting.

Tiny holes in leaves. Row covers will keep flea beetles from damaging your plants. Mixed plantings may confuse flea beetles. Large transplants can withstand some damage.

Hollow stems. If your broccoli has hollow stems, it's a result of too much nitrogen. The plants have a rapid burst of growth after a feeding of high-nitrogen fertilizer. The broccoli heads may also develop unevenly. You can still eat plants with hollow stems. To avoid the problem with future crops, use mature compost when you side-dress.

HARVESTING

Some varieties of broccoli produce a large primary head and few sideshoots, while others produce lots of sideshoots. Cut stems on a slant, 4 to 6 inches below the heads when the heads are full but before they begin to loosen and turn yellowish. Cut sideshoots off at the main stem.

Sally's
TIPS & TRICKS

Fall Broccoli

Planting broccoli in summer for a fall harvest can be much easier than raising spring broccoli. Most broccoli pests are gone by late summer, and you'll have fewer problems with heat causing your broccoli to bolt. So force yourself to start a new crop even in the heat of July and August!

When planting a fall crop, add an extra week or two when you calculate planting time, because your crop will mature more slowly in cool fall weather. For broccoli (and also cabbage, and cauliflower) that means starting seedlings 12 weeks before your first average fall frost date and transplanting them 8 weeks before. Mulch your crop with straw or newspaper several sheets thick. Keep extra mulch on hand to pile up around the plants when frost threatens.

Brussels Sprouts:
- *Brassica oleracea*, Gemmifera Group
- Brassicaceae

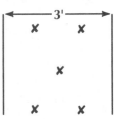

Brussels sprouts

FAMILY UNIT

Brussels sprouts are in the Cabbage Family, and they fit in well with the rest of the family, including broccoli, cabbage, and cauliflower.

FRIENDS

Try interplanting brussels sprouts with tall herbs from the Carrot Family, such as fennel, dill, or coriander. You can also try underplanting sweet alyssum or surrounding your brussels sprouts with asters or zinnias.

GROWING BASICS

Plant brussels sprouts in full sun in rich soil with a pH of 5.5 to 6.8. Brussels sprouts take about four months from seed to harvest. I suggest starting them from seed indoors about six weeks before the last expected spring frost and setting transplants outdoors in early May for a September harvest. You can also plant them in June or July for a fall crop that lasts well into November.

Spacing. Plant brussels sprouts 15 inches apart in a 2-1-2 pattern. Plant companion flowers and herbs in the spaces on either side of the single brussels sprout plants. You can also plant brussels sprouts in a single row, as shown below.

Feeding. Brussels sprouts are heavy feeders, so plant

Space transplants 15" apart in a 2-1-2 pattern

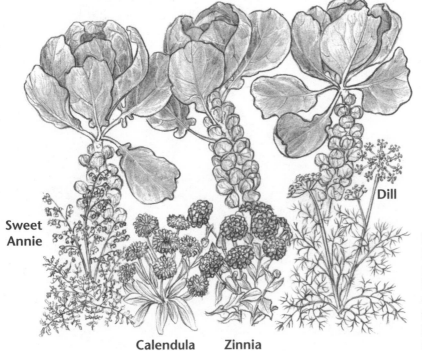

Sweet Annie

Calendula   Zinnia

Dill

Brussels sprout buddies. You can plant brussels sprouts in single file down the center of a bed with flowering companions like dill, sweet Annie, and zinnias alongside.

them in soil that has had well-rotted manure or compost worked into it. Spray plants monthly with fish emulsion.

Mulching. Because brussels sprouts occupy a bed for a long time, it's important not to let weed roots get entrenched among the crop roots. Use a solid mulch like newspapers spread six or seven sheets thick over the entire bed. You can also spread grass clippings or chopped leaves several inches thick. Avoid straw because it creates favorable conditions for slugs, which can be a problem for brussels sprouts.

PROBLEMS AND SOLUTIONS

Sprouts don't form. If you have lots of leaves but no sprouts or very loose, straggly sprouts, the temperatures were probably too warm. Brussels sprouts require cool weather to form their sprouts; temperatures above 75°F inhibit sprout production. Try planting later next time so sprouts can form in cool fall conditions.

Large, ragged holes in leaves. Slugs or imported cabbageworms are the culprits. You can trap slugs under boards or melon rinds, or in shallow dishes of beer set out in the garden. You can also hand-pick them and dispose of them in soapy water. Hand-picking also helps control imported cabbageworms, but the best bet is prevention by covering crops with row covers.

Healthy-looking plants wilt. Wilting is a sign that cabbage maggots are chewing on the plant roots. If you find infested plants, it's best to pull and destroy them. To prevent future problems, put a square of tar paper around the base of each seedling at planting.

HARVESTING

Pick a few brussels sprouts as soon as they are big enough to snap off the stems, always starting at the bottom of the stalk. Sometimes you can prolong the harvest by early and continuous picking, removing the leaves as you go. Brussels sprout plants get very tall, so mound up soil around the stems as you harvest to keep the plants from keeling over.

Brussels sprouts tolerate a few frosts, and many people believe that the sprouts taste even better after being nipped by a moderate frost.

Sally Says

"I've even harvested brussels sprouts through the snow to serve with Christmas dinner!"

Sally's
TIPS&TRICKS

Plumped-Up Brussels Sprouts

I harvest my brussels sprouts over a long season, starting from the bottom of the plants. Halfway through the harvest period, I also remove most of the plants' leaves. The plants look rather like ostriches, with long bare necks and "plumes" at the top! But my technique helps the plants channel all their energy into the remaining sprouts, so they'll be as plump as possible for serving with Thanksgiving dinner.

Cabbage • *Brassica oleracea*, Capitata Group • Brassicaceae

Cabbage

FAMILY UNIT

Grow cabbage with other Cabbage Family members like broccoli, cauliflower, brussels sprouts, and kale.

FRIENDS

Plant flowers and herbs from the Aster and Carrot Families near your cabbages. These friends, including calendulas, chrysanthemums, dill, and Queen-Anne's-lace, attract a wide variety of beneficial insects to help control many cabbage pests.

GROWING BASICS

Cabbage tolerates many kinds of soil but must have good drainage, a pH of 6.0 to 6.8, and lots of fertility. It grows best in full sun.

Cabbage is a cool-weather crop, so grow it in spring or fall. You can start cabbage seeds indoors about eight weeks before your last spring frost date, and set out transplants when they're about four weeks old. If cabbage plants are exposed to several weeks of 40° to 50°F air temperatures, they may form multiple heads or go to seed early. If your area has cool spring temperatures, you may want to grow cabbage in the fall instead, starting by sowing seed outdoors in the garden in July.

Spacing. Plant cabbage transplants in a 3-2-3 pattern about 10 to 12 inches apart. You can substitute flowering companions for the center plant in each set of three in the pattern.

Feeding. At planting, enrich your soil with lots of aged manure or compost. One month after planting, spray plants with a fish emulsion solution. Mix a slightly weaker solution than the standard formula described on the fish emulsion package label.

Mulching. Closely spaced plantings nearly cover the soil as the plants mature, but spread newspaper, straw, or lawn clippings between plants to stop early weeds.

PROBLEMS AND SOLUTIONS

Stunted or split heads. Planting cabbages outside too early leads to stunted heads. Planting late may expose maturing heads to warm weather, which causes plants to produce

Space transplants 10"–12" apart in a 3-2-3 pattern

Sally's TIPS & TRICKS

Colorful Cabbage

For colorful combinations with red cabbage, try planting flowers like bachelor's buttons (*Centaurea cyanus*), love-in-a-mist (*Nigella damascena* spp.), or blue pansies. In fall, add cupflowers (*Nierembergia* spp.) framed with rust, pink, or dark red chrysanthemums. But beware: They'll be almost too pretty to harvest!

seed stalks that split the heads as they emerge. Keep notes about these types of problems so you can refine your planting dates for subsequent crops.

If you spot heads that are starting to look pointed (a sign that a seed stalk is forming), you can prevent the heads from cracking by slowing down the plant's maturing process. To do this, use a sharp spade to make a cut on one side of the cabbage stalk about 2 inches below the head. This severs some roots and slows growth.

Holes in leaves. Cabbage loopers and imported cabbageworms chew on cabbage leaves. Handpick the caterpillars. To prevent them from damaging crops, cover plants with row covers at planting.

Wilting plants. Plants may wilt because cabbage maggots or root-knot nematodes have damaged the roots. It's best to remove and destroy these plants to keep the problem from spreading. To prevent future damage, cover crops with row covers at planting to keep the cabbage maggot flies from laying eggs. Growing a crop of French marigolds and turning them under can suppress root-knot nematodes.

HARVESTING

Cut cabbage heads when they are firm and well rounded. For a fall crop, harvest all heads before the first hard frost. The best way to store cabbages is to pack them in dry straw in a cold cellar with their roots still attached.

Sally Says

"Reacting to the effects of weather is the biggest challenge in growing cabbage."

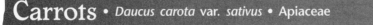

Carrots • *Daucus carota* var. *sativus* • Apiaceae

FAMILY UNIT

Grow carrots with other root crops and with salad greens. A typical bed for this family unit may have a 4-foot section of interplanted onions and beets, a 4-foot section of carrots with radishes interspersed, and a 4-foot section of lettuces. You can repeat this sequence as many times as needed.

FRIENDS

Traditional companion-planting lore suggests using onions and related crops near

and among carrots to confuse or repel the carrot rust fly. So grow onions near your carrots, and plant chives at the end of every other bed in the root-crops-and-greens section of your garden.

Also plant Carrot Family herbs such as caraway or coriander near your carrots, along with calendulas, chamomile, and Swan River daisies.

GROWING BASICS

Carrots need deep, loose, well-drained soil. If your soil is

Carrot

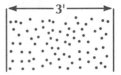

Scatter seeds across full width of bed

less than ideal, you can grow carrots in raised beds, or choose short, round, or baby carrot varieties. Carrots like soil pH of 6.3 to 6.8. Carrots grown in more acidic soils may have poor flavor and dull color. Grow carrots in full sun and don't overwater, or the roots may rot.

Carrots must be direct-seeded in the garden, and they can take up to three weeks to germinate. You can plant seeds in early spring, but if you live in a region with heavy spring rains, you may want to wait until late May to plant. That way you'll avoid having your delicate seedlings washed away by spring downpours. You can also plant carrots in mid-summer for a fall/winter crop.

After planting, I cover my carrot patch with a board or black plastic to keep the soil moist and block weeds. I remove the board or plastic after two weeks.

Spacing. The fastest way to plant carrot seeds is to mix them half and half with sand and scatter the mixture randomly across the bed. After germination, thin the plants to 2 to 3 inches apart in all directions. If you're patient, you can sow the seeds 2 inches apart in all directions, saving the task of thinning later on. You can also interplant carrots with other root crops, as shown in the illustration at right.

Feeding. Carrots are light feeders, and overfeeding causes hairy roots and other problems. Prepare your soil by adding composted manure and other soil amendments the season prior, and don't fertilize your carrots after planting.

Mulching. Once carrot seeds have sprouted (and after thinning if it's needed), sprinkle a fine mulch such as lawn clippings between the plants.

PROBLEMS AND SOLUTIONS

Twisted, deformed, stunted carrots. Poorly shaped carrots are usually due to heavy or rocky soil or overcrowded conditions. The carrots are generally still edible, even if they're not pretty! For better crops in the future, plant carrot seeds in loose, well-worked soil.

Holes in roots. The larvae of carrot rust flies chew holes in carrot roots. To prevent problems, wait and sow seeds in June

Sally Says

"Carrots get sweeter and sweeter as the snows get deeper."

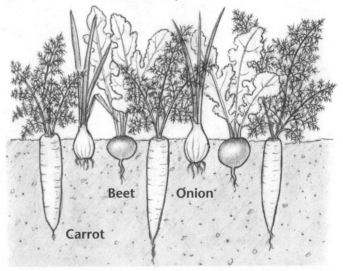

Interplanting root crops. To really mix up the crops in a bed, try interplanting onions, carrots, and beets in each crop row. Space the plants 3 to 4 inches apart in the row, and space rows 3 to 4 inches apart as well.

or cover your carrot patch with row cover right after planting.

Carrots start to flower. If the heat comes on too soon, carrots may go to seed early. To prevent, cover carrots with shade cloth in early summer.

Tops of roots turn green. Exposure to sun results in carrots with green shoulders. To prevent this, add a little fine topsoil as carrots mature and begin to peek out of their beds, especially if a heavy rain has beaten down their soil covering.

HARVESTING

Check your carrots by pulling one or two when you suspect they're ready. Once you're ready to harvest them in quantity, water the patch to make harvesting easier. Pull the carrots, brush off the soil, and cut or twist off the tops. Layer the roots in moist sand and keep in a dark, cool place.

Sally's
TIPS & TRICKS

Mini-Bed for Carrots

I often run out of garden space that has the deeply worked, loose soil that carrots need. But I love carrots, so I make mini–raised beds on the spot for them. Use 2- by 4-foot boards or 4- by 4-foot timbers to make a frame. Set the frame right on top of the existing soil in the bed where you want to plant carrots. Add some aged compost, leaf mold, and soil to fill the box, and *voilà!*—a planting bed deep enough for almost any carrot. You can get a lot of carrots in a frame just 3 by 4 feet. At 20 carrots per square foot, that's 12 dozen!

Cauliflower • *Brassica oleracea* Botrytis groups • Brassicaceae

Cauliflower

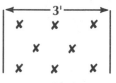

Space transplants 10"–12" apart in a 3-2-3 pattern

FAMILY UNIT

Cauliflower belongs to the Cabbage Family and grows well with other family members, including broccoli and brussels sprouts.

FRIENDS

I like to see cauliflower surrounded by bright flowers in fall, so I plant them with cherry-colored zinnias. Dill or Queen-Anne's-lace attracts beneficials, and so will volunteer goldenrods that sprout in the bed.

GROWING BASICS

Cauliflower thrives in full sun and rich soil, especially when you plant it in midsummer for a fall harvest. Plant transplants about 14 weeks before your first average fall frost.

You can also plant cauliflower in spring, but it needs soil temperatures of about 65°F to grow well. Start seeds indoors ten weeks before the last expected spring frost, and plant transplants outdoors two to three weeks before the last frost date.

Spacing. Plant cauliflower transplants in a 3-2-3 pattern 10 to 12 inches apart in all directions. You can substitute an aromatic herb or flowering companion for the center plant in each grouping of three plants. Or plant short flowers like dwarf zinnias around the outside of the bed, where they'll peek out around the cauliflower leaves.

Some sources say that closely spaced cauliflower plants yield small heads, but I don't find that's true if I fertilize my plants well. I like close spacing because it helps keep the soil covered and maintains soil moisture.

Feeding. Cauliflower is a heavy feeder, so get it off to a good start by adding a trowelful of compost in the bottom of each planting hole and then covering the compost with 3 inches of soil. That way the roots reach the rich stuff just when they need a boost. Side-dress or foliar-feed with seaweed extract or fish emulsion every three weeks, if possible.

Mulching. Mulch cauliflower with newspaper or a generous layer of grass clippings or chopped leaves. You can also underseed with sweet alyssum.

PROBLEMS AND SOLUTIONS

Plants form very small heads. This condition is called "buttoning," and you can blame it on the weather. Buttoning can happen after a hot, dry spell or when soil temperatures remain below 50°F. It may also happen when soil nitrogen is low or when there's too much weed competition. Don't give up right away when plants form button heads; sometimes they'll grow out of it. To prevent problems in the future, improve soil fertility and hope for the right weather.

Plants form yellow heads. Cauliflower heads turn yellow when they're exposed to the sun. Yellow heads are fine to eat, and they may even be more nutritious than white heads. If you want white cauliflower, you'll have to blanch it, or choose self-blanching varieties.

Plants form brown heads. Brown heads are a sign of a boron deficiency, which sometimes happens because the soil pH is wrong. (Cauliflower needs pH of 6.0 to 7.5) Try a foliar spray of liquid kelp or seaweed extract. Another short-term trick is to add some

Sally Says

"For a colorful surprise, grow purple cauliflower. But be prepared— when you cook the heads, they turn pale green."

Sally's
TIPS & TRICKS

Bright White Cauliflower

If you want white cauliflower heads, you'll have to blanch them. The simplest way is to fold some leaves over the head when it is between the size of an egg and a baseball. Fasten the leaves in place with a clothespin or rubber band. You can also fold some leaves right over the head and snap their central "rib" so they stay bent over. This technique also works to provide some frost protection in fall.

borax at the rate of 1½ teaspoons to 15 gallons of water, used over every 100 square feet of garden space. For future crops, improve soil boron content by growing cover crops like clover or hairy vetch, and add rock phosphate.

HARVESTING

Test the firmness of cauliflower heads frequently. The heads are ready to harvest when they change from rock hard to just firm. (Try it; you'll find it's easy to feel the difference.)

Check cauliflower heads often, especially if you're blanching them. Once cauliflower heads are blanched they develop quickly—from three to four days in hot weather up to two weeks in cold weather. Light frost improves their flavor, but cauliflower must be cut before a hard freeze. Cauliflower will keep up to one week in the refrigerator; wrap heads in plastic first.

Celery • *Apium graveolens* var. *dulce* • Apiaceae

Celery

FAMILY UNIT

Celery can join just about any family in your garden, depending on where you have room. I usually find a place for a row of celery in the Cabbage Family area or in the neighborhood with the salad greens, carrots, and onions. It also makes sense to grow celery with leeks, because they both need blanching.

FRIENDS

Grow celery with medium to tall flowers like cosmos, daisies, snapdragons, or zinnias. Don't grow asters with celery, because the asters may attract insects that transmit a disease called aster yellows. This disease causes the lower celery leaves to turn yellow and drop off.

GROWING BASICS

Celery needs lots of water, a long growing season, and rich soil with a pH of at least 6.5. Plant celery in full sun or very light shade.

Start celery seeds indoors about 8 weeks before the last frost date, and keep the seedlings cool (around 50°F maximum). Set transplants outside at least two weeks after danger of frost, when they are about 6 inches tall. Place celery transplants single-file in a 4-inch-deep trench. If you also grow leeks, you can alternate celery plants with leek plants in the trench. The trenches help to accumulate extra water.

Spacing. Plant celery in a single row down the center of a 3-foot-wide bed, spacing plants about 8 to 10 inches apart.

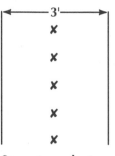

Space transplants 8"–10" apart in a single row

Feeding. Celery has a large appetite for potassium, so spray your plants monthly with fish emulsion, diluted according to instructions on the container.

Mulching. Celery is one crop I don't mulch, because the activity of blanching tends to keep weeds down. Also, slugs can be a problem with celery, and mulch tends to create good conditions for slugs.

PROBLEMS AND SOLUTIONS

Hollow, tough stalks. Hot weather or not enough water is the cause. Plant celery early in spring, and water well.

Bitter taste. Dry, hot weather can make celery bitter. To keep your celery tender and mild, blanch the stems, using boards, milk cartons, or newspaper.

Chewed leaves. Parsley-worms will feed on celery plants. It's easy to handpick these green-and-black striped caterpillars, but don't destroy them. Move them to plants where you won't mind a little damage, because they'll eventually turn into beautiful swallowtail butterflies!

HARVESTING

You can cut off individual outer stems as needed for salads or soups. To harvest whole plants, cut through the crown just above the roots. Store celery in plastic bags in the refrigerator; it will keep for several weeks.

Sally Says

"Celery has one really close friend: leeks. They both like to hunker down in trenches and get blanched."

Sally's
TIPS & TRICKS

Blanching Celery

Blanching is the process of covering or wrapping maturing stems so they remain tender and white. I start blanching celery by mounding soil around the stalks. When the plants reach 8 inches tall, I place 12-inch-wide planks on either side of the row of celery plants. I pound a few stakes into the soil to keep the planks upright. That way I don't risk squashing the plants.

I plant tall plant friends like cosmos, calendulas, and coreopsis along the sides of the bed to screen the boards from view.

Celery

Cosmos

Calendulas

Chinese Cabbages • *Brassica rapa,* Chinensis Group & Pekinensis Group • Brassicaceae

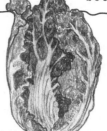
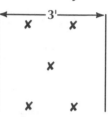

Bok Choy

FAMILY UNIT

There are two types of Chinese cabbage—bok choy (also called pak choi), which has a loose-leaved head, and pe tsai, which forms a tight head. Chinese cabbage mixes well with salad greens or with the Cabbage Family. If you grow tall crops like corn or pole beans, you can also plant Chinese cabbage beside them—it will thrive in the shade they cast.

FRIENDS

Plant low-growing flowers like sweet alyssum with Chinese cabbage in early spring. Annual dahlias, zinnias, or marigolds go well with fall plantings.

GROWING BASICS

Chinese cabbages prefer short days and cool weather, so grow them in early spring or fall to avoid bolting and bitterness. They'll grow well with partial shade from tall neighboring crops. Give them well-drained soil with lots of compost or organic matter mixed in. For more tender heads, blanch the plants, as shown at right.Use cold frames or other season extenders to lengthen your harvest into late fall.

Spacing. Space Chinese cabbage about 8 inches apart in a 2-1-2 or 3-2-3 pattern.

Feeding. Chinese cabbage usually doesn't need fertilizer. If you want to, you can side-dress monthly with compost, or spray plants with a solution of fish emulsion.

Mulching. Use grass clippings, pine needles, or compost. Avoid straw if slugs have been a problem in your lettuces or other greens.

PROBLEMS AND SOLUTIONS

Large holes in leaves. Slugs chew holes in leaves, leaving a slime trail behind them. In early spring, handpick slugs.

Space transplants 15" apart in a 2-1-2 pattern

Sally's
TIPS & TRICKS

Blanching Chinese Cabbage

One easy way to blanch Chinese cabbage is to use paper milk cartons as individual plant shelters. Just open both ends of a milk carton and slip it over the cabbage plant. Then plant bushy flowers like African daisies or cosmos along both edges of the row to hide the milk cartons from view.

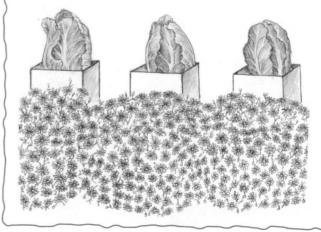

Keep mulches pulled away from plants until the soil dries out. Crops planted in raised beds with ideal drainage will have fewer slug problems. Fall crops are mostly problem-free.

HARVESTING

To harvest bok choy, cut off individual leaves 1 inch above soil level. The plants will regrow. To harvest heading types, use outer leaves as the head forms.

Corn • *Zea mays* • Poaceae

FAMILY UNIT

Native Americans have traditionally planted corn, pole beans, and squash or pumpkins together in a planting called the Three Sisters. I don't always plant beans with corn, but I do let my squash or pumpkin vines ramble among the cornstalks to cover the soil and trip up marauding raccoons.

FRIENDS

Nasturtiums are a great flowering friend for a Three Sisters planting. You can also plant clover between corn rows and buckwheat along the edges of a patch.

GROWING BASICS

Corn likes rich, well-drained soil with a pH between 5.5 and 6.8. Wait until the soil temperature is close to 70°F to plant corn. Dig trenches 4 to 5 inches deep, sow seeds in the trenches, and cover the seeds with 1 inch of soil. Fill in the trenches as the corn grows; this helps them stand tall in a windy site. Plant in blocks rather than long rows to increase pollination. Keep compost and manures away from seeds and young plants to avoid rotting.

Spacing. Space seeds about 10 inches apart in rows 30 inches apart. If the variety you're using doesn't have a high germination rate, plant two or three seeds together and snip off extra seedlings later, if needed. If you're planting corn in a Three Sisters planting, see the planting illustrations on pages 79–80.

Feeding. Corn needs lots of nutrients, especially nitrogen and phosphorus. Side-dress with compost or well-rotted manure when plants are about 9 inches tall, and again after tassels form. You can also foliar-feed with a fish-emulsion solution instead.

Mulching. Mulch well with straw, chopped leaves, or newspaper. Or plant clover as a living mulch about a month after the corn is planted. Corn crops need lots of water, especially during the development of silks, tassels, and ears, so provide a minimum of 1 inch of water each week.

Sweet corn

Space seeds 10" apart in rows 30" apart

PROBLEMS AND SOLUTIONS

Tunnels in ears; chewed kernels. European corn borer larvae and corn earworms bore into corn ears. To prevent problems with European corn borer larvae, clean up corn debris and cultivate the soil in the fall, rotate the crop, and attract parasitic wasps and tachinid flies by planting tansy and other small-flowered herbs and flowers nearby. To prevent corn earworm damage, put a drop of mineral oil in the silks just as they begin to form.

Ears aren't well filled. If your corn ears have areas where no kernels formed, the problem is poor pollination. Corn is wind-pollinated, so it's important to plant it in a block to ensure even pollination.

Seedlings are uprooted. Birds pull up corn seedlings to eat the seeds. If this happens, replant and cover corn rows with gutter guard, as shown below.

HARVEST

You can tell when corn is ready to pick by squeezing the tips of the corn ears. If they're hard and firm, they're ready to pick; if they feel soft, they're not ready. Also check the corn silks—if they're dry and brown, the corn is ripe. Or expose a few kernels, and puncture one with a fingernail. The ripe kernels should produce a milky liquid—neither watery (unripe) nor thick and creamy (overripe and tough).

Sally Says

"I have warm summer memories of the Corn Festival, complete with corn-eating contests, parades, and even a 'Miss Eden Sweet Corn.'"

Sally's TIPS & TRICKS

Crows in the Corn

Crows and other birds are often tempted by early corn seedlings, which they pluck out of the soil, seed and all. So I plant my corn in narrow trenches and cover each trench with a long roll of gutter guard. The product comes in many brands, but it's usually plastic or wire, about 5 inches wide, and covers the trench perfectly. By the time the corn hits the "ceiling," the plants are well rooted enough to resist crow attacks.

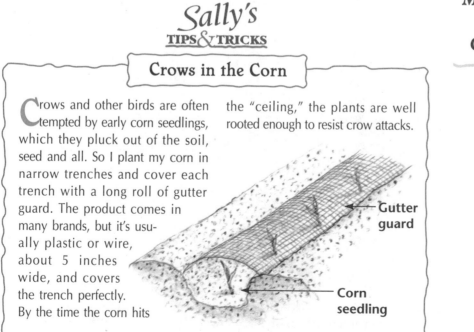

Gutter guard

Corn seedling

Cucumbers • *Cucumis sativus* • Cucurbitaceae

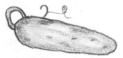

Slicing cucumber

FAMILY UNIT

Cucumbers fit right in with other Squash Family crops. You can also plant them to climb a trellis or fence in a bed with lettuce or spinach—the cukes will shade the leafy crops from summer heat. Or plant cucumbers among your Cabbage Family plants in early summer; once the broccoli and cabbage are harvested, the cucumber vines will fill in the space.

FRIENDS

Cucumbers and nasturtiums look great intertwined and provide shelter for beneficial spiders and ground beetles. Radishes and marigolds are also great companions for cucumbers.

Volunteer goldenrod plants are good plant friends to have growing among the cucumbers.

GROWING BASICS

Cucumbers need full sun and warm, well-drained soil; plant seeds or transplants outside about three weeks after your last average spring frost date. Prepare areas about 1 square foot in size by working a half-bushel of compost into the soil to make a raised hill. If you want to get a head start on growing cukes, make these hills in early spring. The raised hills will warm faster so you can plant sooner.

Spacing. Plant four cucumber seeds 1 foot apart in each hill, and space hills 4 feet

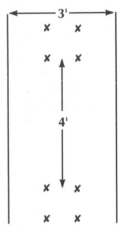

Space seeds 1' apart in hills 4' apart

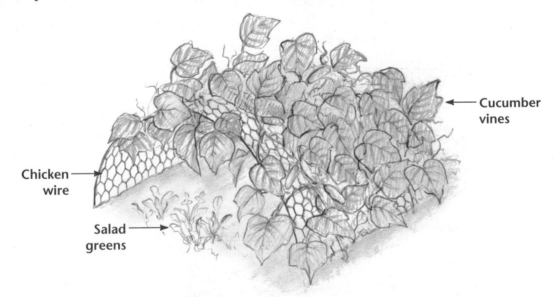

Chicken wire

Salad greens

Cucumber vines

Cucumber bridges. To grow salad greens in the shade of cucumbers, train your cucumber vines over low arches of chicken wire. Use 5-foot lengths of 3-foot-wide wire, and set them up like a series of low bridges down a bed.

apart in the row. You can plant radishes and marigolds in and around each hill, and plant nasturtiums in the row, centered between the hills.

Feeding. Give cucumbers a boost with fish emulsion, alfalfa meal, or another organic fertilizer when the vines are 1 foot long, and again a month later.

Mulching. Straw keeps cucumbers clean and dry. Spread it generously where vines will be rambling.

PROBLEMS AND SOLUTIONS

Fruits taste bitter. Bitter cucumbers result when the fruits don't get enough water while they're forming. Be sure to water cucumbers regularly as soon as flowers appear.

Plants wilt suddenly. Sudden wilting can result from infection by bacterial wilt. You can try watering the plants daily, but they may not recover. This disease is spread by cucumber beetles, so to prevent future problems, cover your cucumber patch with row cover at planting and leave the plants covered until they start to flower.

White coating on leaves. The first sign of powdery mildew is round, white spots under the leaves, so patrol early to catch it. Spray plants with a baking soda formula (use the simple recipe on page 227) every seven to ten days once you spot symptoms. Avoid overhead or evening waterings, and space vines evenly to permit good air circulation.

Wilted, shriveled leaves. Squash bugs suck the juices out of leaves, which wilt and shrivel. Pull and destroy severely infested plants. To prevent future problems, cover plants with row covers from planting until blossoming.

Yellow or brown spots on leaves. Downy mildew is a fungal disease that shows up especially in wet weather. You may find downy purple spots under the leaves. The disease spreads quickly. The wisest move is to quickly pull and destroy infected plants.

HARVESTING

Keep picking cucumbers frequently while they are small, and the vines will keep producing more. Also, once the vines reach three feet in length, keep nipping off the fuzzy growing tips of the vines so the focus is on production of cucumbers, not leaves.

Sally Says

"Don't avoid cucumbers if they make you burp. Try the burpless varieties like 'Suyo Long', and you can avoid any social problems."

Sally's
TIPS & TRICKS

A Cuke Bottle

Just for fun, try growing a cucumber in a soda bottle with a narrow neck. When the cuke is 1 to 2 inches long, insert it in the neck of the bottle. Then shade the bottle so the cuke won't cook inside. As the cucumber grows, it will fill the shape of the bottle. When the cucumber's large enough, cut it free of the plant and fill the bottle with a vinegar solution. Then get ready to answer: "How did you get that in there?"

Eggplant • *Solanum melongena* • Solanaceae

Eggplant

FAMILY UNIT

Keep eggplants together with other members of the Tomato Family. They all share many disease problems, and rotation is easier if you keep them in a single section of the garden.

FRIENDS

Plant lots of aromatic herbs and flowers around eggplants, especially red and green basil, marigolds, and dill. Cosmos also makes a beautiful companion for eggplant.

GROWING BASICS

Plant eggplant in full sun and well-drained soil. Start seeds indoors four to eight weeks before your last spring frost. Put transplants outside at least two weeks past the last spring frost date. Place a shovelful each of well-aged manure and compost in each planting hole.

Spacing. Space plants 15 inches apart in a 2-1-2 pattern. You can substitute flowering companions for some of the single plants in the pattern.

Feeding. Spray plants monthly with fish emulsion.

Mulching. Use sheets of cardboard or several thicknesses of newspaper as mulch, and plant through holes in the mulch. If you have grass clippings available, spread some clippings before you put down the mulch to provide some extra nitrogen.

PROBLEMS AND SOLUTIONS

Young stems severed. Cutworms chew through the stems of young transplants. When you replant new plants, wrap stems in foil or paper.

Tiny holes in leaves. Flea beetles are the cause of the "shot-hole" look. If these pests are a big problem in spite of your beneficial insect and bird populations, next time use row cover over the plants until they bloom.

HARVESTING

Keep picking small eggplants and the plant will keep producing. Twist the fruits to break the stem off the plant, or use a knife or pruners to cut the fruits off the plant. Pick the fruits while the skin is still glossy. Once it turns dull, the flesh may be tough.

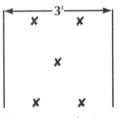

Space transplants 15" apart in a 2-1-2 pattern

Sally's
TIPS & TRICKS

Cans for Eggplant

If you've ever had cutworms wipe out your newly planted crop of eggplant, you'll want to block them for sure. Try using tuna-fish or cat-food (6½ ounce) cans with the tops and bottoms cut out. Place them over the seedlings, pushing about half the can below the soil surface. Not only do the cans block the creeping cutworm, but they also reflect a little heat and hold in a little extra water to help the young eggplant.

Garlic • *Allium sativum* • Liliaceae

Garlic

FAMILY UNIT

Garlic is part of the Onion Family, along with onions, shallots, leeks, and chives. You can grow them together as a family, or mix them into other families to help repel pests. Garlic fits well with salad greens, especially if you're planting some in fall to overwinter.

FRIENDS

I won't say garlic doesn't need friends, but it is mostly known for *being* a friend, repelling or confusing pest insects by its odoriferous presence. For a spring planting, try interplanting garlic with carrots, onions, and beets.

GROWING BASICS

Fall planting is the secret to great garlic. (Let Columbus Day, October 12, be your memory cue for planting.) Garlic needs full sun and rich soil. In fall, plant individual cloves 3 inches deep with the pointy end up; in spring, plant them 1½ to 2 inches deep. Cut off seedheads as they appear, to keep the energy going into bulb production.

Spacing. Place garlic cloves 4 inches apart in all directions.

Feeding. If you plant garlic in rich soil, it won't need any extra fertilizer. Otherwise, drench the soil around the plants with a solution of fish emulsion when garlic tops are a few inches out of the soil.

Mulching. Garlic doesn't like competing with weeds, so mulch with well-chopped leaves, pine needles, grass clippings, or straw. Watering increases garlic yield, but be sure to stop watering two to three weeks before harvest, or the bulbs may rot.

PROBLEMS AND SOLUTIONS

Small bulbs. Bulbs planted in spring are often small. Lack of sun, warm weather, nutrients, or water can also result in small bulbs. Try planting in fall, and be sure to improve the soil with compost before planting. Mulch to conserve soil moisture.

Rotten bulbs. Garlic planted in poorly drained soil may rot. For future crops, choose a

Space cloves 4" apart in all directions

Garlic Sprays

Lots of cooks wouldn't think of creating a meal without garlic, and garlic is just as fundamental for organic gardeners who want to control pests naturally. There are many formulas for garlic sprays to use as insect repellents. To make a basic garlic spray, chop a few cloves and add them to a quart of water (mix them in a blender if you have one). Let the solution sit for several hours, then strain it through cheesecloth before spraying. Lots of pests, such as Japanese beetles, don't like it. (On the other hand, your roses may not smell as sweet…!)

location with better drainage, or plant your next crop in a raised bed.

HARVESTING

When the tops of your garlic plants begin to brown and fall over, dig up one or two and check the bulbs. If they're mature, the cloves will be distinct and easy to separate. Once the crop is ready, dig up all the plants. (Don't pull from the tops, as the leaves aren't usually strong enough.) Hang plants to dry in the sun or in a warm, dry place (the top of a barn, garage, or porch). After a few weeks, you can braid the tops together, or cut them off an inch above the bulbs and store the bulbs in mesh bags. Garlic keeps for long periods in a cool, dry cellar. Do *not* refrigerate your garlic.

Gourmet Greens

FAMILY UNIT

Gourmet greens are a group of leafy crops also called *mesclun* (a French word that means "mixture"). You'll find mesclun served in gourmet restaurants and sold in specialty shops in cities all over the country.

The specific crops included in these mixtures of gourmet greens vary. They generally include some type of lettuce, along with kale, endive, Oriental greens, chicory, escarole, and corn salad. Mesclun can also include spicy greens like arugula and mustard greens.

Grow some gourmet greens wherever you would grow lettuce. Mesclun works well with a family with root crops like carrots and onions, or you can plant gourmet greens in the shade of your trellised peas and beans.

FRIENDS

A variety of flowers and herbs can mix with mesclun, especially tall ones that offer shade, like fennel, dill, sweet Annie, cosmos, or cleome.

GROWING BASICS

Gourmet greens grow well in most soils. Many of them bolt or turn bitter in the summer heat. A shady location is fine, especially in summer. Plant the seeds directly in the garden in spring whenever the soil is workable, and again in August or September for fall salads. Prepare the top 2 inches of soil well before planting to ensure that the tiny seeds will germinate. Barely cover the seeds with a fine sprinkling of soil.

Spacing. Scatter seeds lightly over the bed. If they're crowded later, just thin the plants to about 3 inches apart, and eat the extras!

Chicory

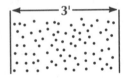

Scatter seeds across full width of bed

Feeding. Most lettuces and kin are light feeders, so extra fertilizer isn't needed.

Mulching. Gourmet greens provide their own mulch if you plant them thickly. You can sprinkle grass clippings lightly just after seeding to provide extra nitrogen and moisture, but be sure the clippings don't contain seeds, or you'll be sowing a weed problem!

PROBLEMS AND SOLUTIONS

Large, ragged holes in leaves. Slugs are the first likely culprit. Hand-picking the slugs off the plants in the early morning and collecting slugs that congregate under boards are usually sufficient for control.

Chewed leaves may also result from feeding by rabbits, wood-chucks, or other animals. I discourage them by sprinkling cayenne pepper on the ground around the plants (just be sure to wash the greens well before you eat them).

Bitter greens. Most gourmet greens will turn bitter if the weather gets too hot; to prevent this, cover the plants with shade cloth or window screens propped up on boards or rocks. Or just grow your mesclun in the shade. Watering in the midday heat helps cool the plants as well.

Leaves turn black or slimy. If your greens turn into a dark mush, chances are some type of disease is to blame. You'll have to dispose of the diseased

Sally's
TIPS & TRICKS

Forcing Belgian Endive

Belgian endive, also called witloof chicory, is a healthful but somewhat bitter green. The real gourmet delight is the forced shoot, which can be served raw or bruised. I learned this technique from a Master Gardener named Seymour Sunshine.

First, grow chicory in your garden, and dig out the roots after the first hard frost. (The leaves will be wilted.) Select roots about 8 inches long, and trim the tops, leaving a 2-inch stub. Lay the roots in sand or peat moss, and cover them with the same material. Keep them in a cool place (about 40°F) for one month.

After the month is up, it's time to start the forcing process. Trim the roots to an even length. Half-fill a bucket or box with equal parts of moist sand, loam, and peat moss (or composted manure). Put the roots upright and finish filling the container. Water them thoroughly, and cover the container with sand or damp burlap. Keep this material moist—not wet—at 50° to 60°F. In about three weeks, endive shoots will begin poking through the sand. When they reach 5 to 9 inches, harvest them by twisting or cutting. For a smaller second harvest, you can re-cover the roots and let them grow again.

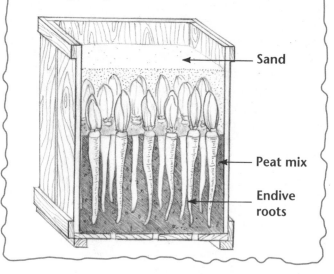

Sand

Peat mix

Endive roots

plants. For future plantings, be sure your soil is well drained, and thin plants early to prevent overcrowding. Also try repeat sowings every two weeks. Even if some succumb to disease because of wet weather conditions, other plantings should be successful.

HARVESTING

Use the cut-and-come-again method for gourmet greens, as shown on page 215, and the plants will keep producing until the weather gets too hot. Cut the leaves with garden shears 1 to 2 inches above ground level.

Kale & Collards: *Brassica oleracea,* Acephala Group
Brassicaceae

FAMILY UNIT

Both kale and collards are hardy greens that need a long growing season. Collards, also called "collard greens," thrive in the South. I group kale and collards with Cabbage Family crops. You can also group fall-planted collards with garlic, lettuce, carrots, and other late-season crops.

FRIENDS

Good companions include basil, dill, marigolds, and early-blooming flowers like dandelions or calendulas. Some research shows benefits from inter-planting collards with tomatoes to cut down on flea beetles and diamondback moths. Studies also show that using catnip as a companion reduces flea-beetle damage on collards.

GROWING BASICS

Plant kale or collard seeds outdoors four weeks before the last spring frost if you can. (The collards need the long season,

and the kale performs poorly in hot weather.) Plant kale in soil enriched with compost; collards tolerate poor soils well. Both crops do best in full sun, but kale benefits from light shade in hot climates. In the Northeast, collards only succeed if planted very early in the spring or in fall for early spring and winter harvest.

Spacing. Plant kale seeds in rows 7 to 8 inches apart in all directions. You can also sow seeds thickly in rows and harvest by trimming the tops with scissors.

Plant or thin collards to 15 inches apart in all directions, in a 2-1-2 pattern in wide rows.

Feeding. Kale is a heavy feeder; provide monthly supplemental foliar feedings of fish emulsion or seaweed extract or side dressings of compost.

Collards don't require fertilizer, but they will benefit from a side dressing with compost or a foliar feeding of fish emulsion each month.

Kale

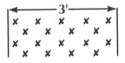

Space seeds 7"– 8" apart in all directions

Mulching. Kale can be self-mulching if planted thickly, but I sprinkle grass clippings between the small plants until they cover the soil themselves.

Collards need a heavier mulch. Plant them through sheets of newspaper, or mulch them well with chopped leaves. As fall approaches, pile lots of leaves near or between plants. Once the ground starts to freeze, cover the whole crop with several inches of leaves to protect them through the winter.

PROBLEMS AND SOLUTIONS

Holes in leaves. Cabbage loopers and imported cabbageworms are the culprits. Handpick these pests as you find them. To prevent future problems, cover crops with row covers after planting.

Wilted leaves with small black spots. The culprit here is the harlequin bug. It's a bright red and black insect, only ¼ inch long, shaped like a shield with a triangle pattern. Harlequin bugs are mostly a southern pest. Control them by handpicking early in the season and squashing the eggs, which are ringed with black and laid in neat rows.

Tiny "shotgun" holes in leaves. Flea beetles chew tiny holes in kale and collard leaves. Planting companion plants helps deter them. To prevent future problems, cover plants with row covers as soon as possible after planting.

Poor development, distorted roots. Clubroot is a serious fungal disease that lasts up to seven years in the soil, so long rotations are important. Clubroot is more prevalent in acid soil, so test your soil pH, and add lime if necessary to bring the pH closer to neutral (7.0).

Dark lesions on leaves. Some serious diseases can thwart collard production, such as black leg, black rot, leaf spot, and rhizoctonia. Destroy the infected plants quickly before the problem spreads. Kale has few disease problems.

HARVESTING

You can harvest kale any time, using the cut-and-come-again method shown on page 215. The young leaves are the most tender for cooking.

If you mulch collards with leaves, you can harvest into the winter and again in early spring. Keep cutting off the outer leaves, and the center will continue to produce.

Sally Says

"Collards taste best after the first frosts."

Sally's
TIPS & TRICKS

Blanching Collards

Although collard greens are perfectly good when they're green, you may be surprised by how tender blanched collards can be. To blanch collards, when the plants are about 1 foot tall, slip a wide rubber band around the whole plant about 8 inches from the soil. Leave the band in place until you're ready to harvest.

Leeks • *Allium porrum* • Liliaceae

FAMILY UNIT

Leeks grow well with many vegetables, so you can add them to any of your crop families. I like to plant them among onions and lettuces (the leeks repel carrot rust flies). It's convenient to interplant them with celery so that you can blanch both vegetables at the same time.

FRIENDS

Leeks have few problems; in fact, they repel or confuse many insect pests, so they don't really need flower or herb companions.

GROWING BASICS

Leeks like to grow in full sun, but they'll tolerate a little shade. They're not fussy about soil, but do best in well-drained, rich soil with a pH of 6.0 to 7.0. Start leek seeds indoors 10 to 12 weeks before the last spring frost date. Plant transplants outdoors when they are 4 to 6 inches tall and the danger of frost has passed. Dig a trench 8 inches deep, and mix compost into the bottom of the trench. Place the leeks in the trench and add about 4 inches of soil, so that only the tops of the plants show. To produce blanched stems, fill in the trench the rest of the way as the plants grow. Try to keep soil out of the juncture where the leaves meet.

If your soil is too heavy or poorly drained to plant leeks in trenches, try planting them at soil level, and mound up soil around the stems, or grow them between boards as you would with celery, as shown on page 200.

Spacing. Space leeks 4 inches apart in a single row with flowering companions along the sides. For a more intensive planting, space trenches 6 to 8 inches apart, leaving enough room in between them for the mounded soil.

Feeding. Start these hungry vegetables with a good amount of well-rotted manure or compost in the trench. For optimum size, side-dress with more compost every two to three weeks during the growing season.

Mulching. As long as you're blanching your leeks, the mounded soil acts as a mulch, and you don't need any other mulch until fall. If you want to store your leeks in the ground into the winter, mulch the whole bed with several inches of chopped leaves to keep the soil and leeks from freezing. You can continue digging the leeks as needed all the way through the winter and even the following spring.

Leeks need lots of water, so be sure to water deeply every time the soil feels dry 2 inches beneath the soil surface.

Leek

```
|<----- 3' ----->|
        X
        X
        X
        X
        X
        X
        X
        X
```

Space transplants 4" apart in a single row

PROBLEMS AND SOLUTIONS

Leeks are quite trouble-free. Hint: You can use leeks to *solve* problems for other plants. Many organic gardeners report success using a leek spray (just blend two or three leeks with 1 quart of water in a blender, and strain well) as a fungicide, since leeks contain sulfur compounds that repel pests.

HARVESTING

You can begin harvesting leeks in summer as soon as they are big enough, and continue harvesting through fall, winter, and into early spring—if you've planted enough to last you that long! Just dig under the plants with a garden fork to loosen, and wash well to remove dirt from the stems before cooking.

Sally's
TIPS & TRICKS

Planting Leek Bulblets

Once you've grown a crop of leeks, there's no need to start your next batch of plants from seed. Just let some of your leeks go to flower and set seed each year. (This happens toward fall in the South, but during the following spring in the North.) Around the base of the leeks you'll see little cloves or "bulblets." Take these off and spread them out to air-dry; plant them outdoors the following spring.

Lettuce • *Lactuca sativa* • Asteraceae

FAMILY UNIT

Lettuces grow well with onions and root crops. They also like growing with tall crops that help them keep cool. Try planting lettuce under the spreading leaves of broccoli, cauliflower, or eggplant or under bean teepees.

There are two main types of lettuce, looseleaf and heading types, but there's lots of variety within each type. The best-known heading lettuce is crisphead, or iceberg, lettuce. Romaine, or cos, lettuce grows in a compact, 9-inch-tall, tight cluster. Butterhead lettuces form loose heads and have buttery leaves. Looseleaf lettuces range from green to red or bronze in color, and some are quite heat tolerant.

FRIENDS

Since lettuce likes to grow in light shade, plant it beside some tall annual flowers. I like to use nicotiana, cleome, and Mexican sunflowers.

GROWING BASICS

Lettuce grows fine in average soil and prefers partial shade to full sun. Plant seeds in the spring several weeks before the

Romaine lettuce

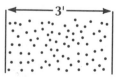

Scatter seeds across full width of bed

last spring frost date, and plant successions every two weeks for optimum production. Be sure to prepare the soil surface well so that the delicate seedlings can take hold and grow. Fall plantings can begin in late July or August and continue through September. Some varieties may survive over winter. You can also plant lettuce from transplants, starting seeds indoors as much as 12 weeks before the last spring frost date.

Spacing. The easiest way to plant lettuce is to scatter seeds across the bed. Thin looseleaf lettuce varieties to 3 inches apart. For heading types of lettuce, thin to 7 to 8 inches between plants to allow good air circulation. Remember—you can eat the thinnings, even on heading varieties.

Feeding. If you've prepared the soil in advance by adding compost or other organic matter, you shouldn't have to add fertilizer during the growing season.

Mulching. Mulching lettuce is controversial. On one hand, mulch can attract slugs, which like dark, damp places. (Pine needles may be a slug's least favorite type of mulch.) On the other hand, mulch helps minimize rot problems, especially on heading lettuces, because it keeps leaves from contacting the soil. So mulch or not, according to what you're most concerned about!

PROBLEMS AND SOLUTIONS

Large, ragged holes in leaves. Slugs like to feast on lettuce. Handpick slugs in the early morning, or place boards near lettuce to lure the slugs. Turn the boards slug side up during the day for birds to eat, or knock them off the boards into a pail of soapy water.

Rabbits may also feed on your lettuce. Discourage them by sprinkling cayenne pepper around the plants often, or use a low fence to create a barricade.

Curled, distorted leaves. Aphids suck plant juices from lettuce leaves and can really disfigure the crop. Turn a hard spray of water from the hose on the plants to wash off the aphids. In the future, plant plenty of flowering beneficials to attract aphid predators.

If young leaves are distorted or curled, the problem may also be a disease called aster yellows. Pull and destroy the infected plants. Don't plant asters near your lettuce.

HARVESTING

Harvest looseleaf lettuces often, using the cut-and-come-again method shown on the opposite page. You can continue harvesting as long as the plants keep regrowing and don't taste bitter. You can also harvest heading types in the cut-and-come-again fashion, but if you want large heads, just let the heads go uncut until they've developed sizable heads.

Sally Says

"Try tucking some lettuce under perennials or shrubs. Many kinds of lettuce are as pretty as they are tasty!"

Sally's
TIPS & TRICKS

Cut-and-Come-Again Lettuce

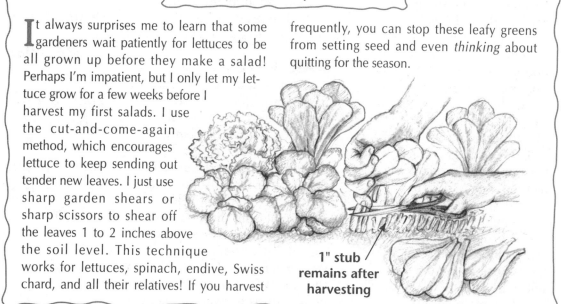

It always surprises me to learn that some gardeners wait patiently for lettuces to be all grown up before they make a salad! Perhaps I'm impatient, but I only let my lettuce grow for a few weeks before I harvest my first salads. I use the cut-and-come-again method, which encourages lettuce to keep sending out tender new leaves. I just use sharp garden shears or sharp scissors to shear off the leaves 1 to 2 inches above the soil level. This technique works for lettuces, spinach, endive, Swiss chard, and all their relatives! If you harvest frequently, you can stop these leafy greens from setting seed and even *thinking* about quitting for the season.

1" stub remains after harvesting

Melons • *Cucumis melo, Citrullus lanatus* • Cucurbitaceae

Muskmelon

FAMILY UNIT
Grow muskmelons and watermelons with other Squash Family crops, such as pumpkins, squash, cucumbers, and gourds.

FRIENDS
Plant nasturtiums along with melons, using one nasturtium plant on every second hill of melons (or one plant every third melon plant if you're planting in rows). I also like to plant radishes or marigolds around the perimeter of each hill of melons to help repel flea beetles.

GROWING BASICS
Melons like a long, warm growing season, and well-drained or sandy soil. You can plant seeds directly in the garden, but it pays to get a head start by buying transplants or starting your own. Start melon seeds indoors at about the time of your last average spring frost. Plant seeds or transplants outdoors when soil temperatures have reached 70°F (usually three or more weeks after the last spring frost). If you have heavy clay soil, add lots of organic

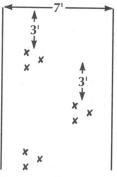

Space seeds 1' apart in hills 3' apart and offset by 3'

matter before planting. It also helps to cover the plants with hot caps (like a plastic milk jug with the bottom cut out).

Spacing. Plant three to five seeds or plants 12 inches apart in a cluster or hill, and space these hills 3 feet apart in "double-wide" rows (two 3-foot-wide beds plus the 12-inch path). The vines will spread to cover the entire area.

Feeding. Melons are heavy feeders, so add greensand, bone-meal, or rock phosphate at planting. When fruits have set, spray leaves with liquid fish emulsion; repeat two weeks later.

Mulching. If you have had past problems with squash vine borers or slugs, keep the mulch well away from the planting hills. Use black plastic or plant dwarf white clover around melons.

Water melons regularly, but lessen the amount three weeks before harvest, and stop altogether once you harvest.

PROBLEMS AND SOLUTIONS

Flavorless muskmelons. Cool summers or overwatering cause flavorless melons. Try mulching with black plastic or using other heat-attracting tricks.

Vines wilt suddenly. Bacterial wilts can cause healthy-looking plants to wilt. The disease is spread by cucumber beetles, and there's no cure. Pull up and destroy infected vines. For future crops, cover plants with row cover at planting to keep the beetles away. Remove covers in time for pollination.

Feeding by squash vine borer can also cause wilting. Be sure to clean up all plant debris in the fall to prevent borers from overwintering in your garden.

HARVESTING

About a month before your first fall frost, pinch off the tiny green melons and buds on the vines to channel the plants' energy into the enlarging fruits. Muskmelons ripen from green to yellow or tan. Also, the stems become brittle or shriveled and easily pull from the vine when ripe. For watermelons, check the tendril at the base of the stem where the plant attaches to the vine. When the tendril dries up and turns brown, the watermelon is ready to pick.

Sally Says

"I place flat rocks or short boards here and there in the melon patch as stepping stones."

Sally's
TIPS & TRICKS

Melons on a Pedestal

Save large empty cans like tomato-sauce and coffee cans to use as "thrones" to elevate your melons. Just push an empty can into the soil upside down. Set a young melon on the can. The melon will get some extra heat and will be less likely to rot than if it were sitting on damp soil.

Push can 1" into soil

Onions • *Allium cepa* • Liliaceae

FAMILY UNIT

Onions grow well with leafy greens or with other root vegetables, especially early crops in raised beds. I usually mix a few onion plants into all my crop beds because onions are helpful for discouraging or confusing many kinds of insect pests.

FRIENDS

Roses and onions are a classic companion-planting pair, with the onions serving to help keep pests away from the roses. Onions don't have many pest problems themselves, so they don't really need friends, but they do look pretty with petunias.

GROWING BASICS

Onions are easy to grow and tolerate poor soil. For best bulb size, however, work well-rotted manure or compost into the soil before planting. Choose a site in full sun, if possible.

If you plant onions from seed, be sure to prepare the soil well so the delicate seedlings can establish themselves. If you want to start onions quickly and easily, plant sets instead of seeds, planting the sets 1 inch deep as soon as you can work the soil in spring.

Spacing. Plant onions in wide rows 2 to 3 inches apart in all directions. If the seedlings become crowded, thin them out and use them in salads. If you interplant onions with beets or carrots, leave 3 to 4 inches between plants.

Feeding. When onions are about 8 inches tall (just when bulbs begin to enlarge), spray onion tops with foliar fertilizer like liquid seaweed extract or fish emulsion.

Mulching. It's hard to mulch an intensive planting of onions, except with a delicate mulch like grass clippings. Keep ahead of weeds, because onions can't tolerate weed competition. (Onions have to produce big bulbs from small roots.) Use a dandelion fork or similar tool to gently remove weeds growing among your onions.

Provide 1 inch of water per week, but stop watering once the onion tops begin to turn brown and topple.

Onion

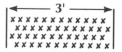

Space sets or seeds 2"–3" apart in all directions

Sally's TIPS & TRICKS

Broadcasting Onions

You can save time planting by broadcasting your onion sets—just the way you can scatter lettuce or carrot seed. Toss the sets across the bed, and try to aim so that they land about 3 inches apart in every direction. Then cover the bed with 1 inch of light soil. Nature knows which end is up!

PROBLEMS AND SOLUTIONS

Rotten onions. Onions can rot in the soil if the soil is too cold and heavy at planting. Also, there are many diseases that can cause rotting. Discard rotten onions, and plant future crops in well-drained soil that has plenty of organic matter.

Small onions. Puny onions can result from poor nutrition or weed competition. Small onions are still fine to eat. For more robust crops in the future, foliar-feed with fish emulsion, and keep ahead of the weeds!

Silvery streaks on leaves. Streaking on the leaves is a sign that thrips are feeding. You'll still get a harvest. To foil thrips on future crops, place strips of shiny aluminum foil among your onions.

Split bulbs. Onions split in half because of uneven watering, too much nitrogen late in the season, or improper storage. You can still eat split onions as long as they haven't rotted. For future crops, mulch for even soil moisture.

HARVESTING

Once onion tops start to brown and fall over, it's time to harvest. You can rush the process by bending the tops yourself. After the leaves fall or are broken, wait about a week, and then gently pull or lift the plants, leaving tops attached. (If the soil is too wet to leave them in the ground for a week, dig immediately, and let them dry in the sun.) Hang them in bunches, or put them in mesh bags, and store them in a cool, dry place.

Sally Says

"If cutting onions makes you cry, chill them first, cut them under cold water, or burn a candle. It sets a lovely mood."

Peas • *Pisum sativum* • Fabaceae

Garden peas

FAMILY UNIT

Pairing peas and beans makes sense. They belong to the same botanical family (the Legume family), and they have similar soil needs. And just as you're harvesting peas, it's time to plant beans, so you can get two crops from one garden bed. Salad greens also work well with this duo. Snow peas, snap peas (which have edible pods), and regular garden peas all have the same growing requirements.

FRIENDS

Peas have few pests. So just for fun, grow them with any flowers and herbs that flower early and look good! Low-growing spring bloomers like calendulas, marigolds, sweet alyssum, pinks, and pansies make a pretty edging for a bed of peas. I like to grow 'Purple Wave' petunias as an edging for raised beds with peas because the petunias look so pretty cascading down the sides of the beds.

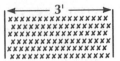

Space seeds 1"–2" apart in all directions

GROWING BASICS

Peas are easy to grow if the temperature's right. Pea seeds germinate from 40° to 75°F and like to grow in cool weather. Plant seeds as soon as you can work the soil in spring—even several weeks before the last spring frost. (Rather than dig in cold soil, use a pencil or chopstick to poke holes for the pea seeds.) Peas like full sun but will tolerate partial shade. They'll grow well in average soil but like a pH over 6.0. You can also plant peas in late July or early August for a fall harvest. The peas should develop beautifuly in cool fall weather. If prolonged cold weather is forecast, cover the plants with floating row covers.

Spacing. For a block planting of bush type peas, plant seeds 1 to 2 inches apart in all directions. For climbing peas, plant seeds 2 to 4 inches apart along the base of a trellis.

Feeding. Peas don't require much fertilizer. If you have any doubts about your soil's fertility, add some fish emulsion or another balanced organic fertilizer at blossom time. Don't use well-rotted manure because it can be too nitrogen-rich.

Mulching. Since cool soil is critical for good pea production, mulch with several sheets of newspaper or about 3 inches of straw or grass clippings. As long as temperatures stay cool, peas need only ½ inch of water per week.

PROBLEMS AND SOLUTIONS

Plants die suddenly. Hot weather can kill pea plants before they form pods. In the future, start your crop earlier

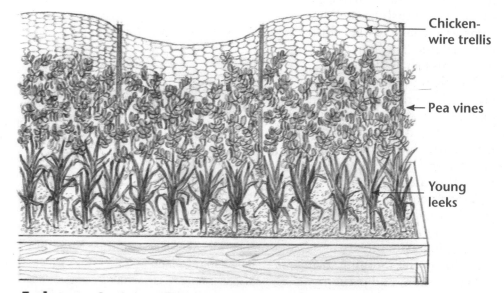

Chicken-wire trellis

Pea vines

Young leeks

Early peas. Set up a trellis in an S-curve down the center of a raised bed for early peas. Fill the rest of the bed with other cold-tolerant crops, like leeks and salad greens.

in the spring, or try a fall crop (planted 12 weeks before the first fall frost). Mulch the roots, and protect the plants from hot afternoon sun. You can shelter peas with shade netting or by planting bush types on the east side of tall crops.

Few blossoms, lots of vine. Too much soil nitrogen can cause lots of foliage without flowers. Don't plant in soil that has been recently amended with well-rotted manure or other nitrogen-rich fertilizer. Weather patterns during blossom setting can also influence blossom production. You can try to encourage blossoming by pinching back vine tips.

Blossoms but no pods. This problem can be due to lack of pollination. Peas are self-pollinating, so you can try helping them out by jostling the vines or brushing the blossoms with a fake feather duster to transfer pollen from male flowers to female flowers.

Discolored, shriveled stems. Bacterial and fungal diseases can cause these symptoms. Pull and destroy infected plants. To avoid spreading diseases, never handle pea plants when they are wet.

White coating on leaves. Powdery mildew is a common garden annoyance, but you can minimize its effects by watering in the morning, using drip irrigation, and maintaining good air circulation. If symptoms are severe, pull and destroy the infected plants.

HARVESTING

Once your pea plants develop pods, pick a few pods every day or so, and taste the pod or peas to sample quality. All types of peas become tough and lose their sweetness if you leave them on the vine too long.

Pick snow peas while they are tender and flat—once the pods start to swell, they become tough. Snap peas are sweetest when the pods fill out. Pick the pods of shelling varieties when they're still bright green and plump. Use scissors to cut the pods off the vines, because it's easy to pull the vines out of the ground if you pull the pods off by hand.

Harvest daily to keep the vines producing. Only hot weather will end pea season!

Sally Says

"My goal is to grow so many peas that I can complain, "Oh, dear, I have to sit down and shuck some more peas for dinner."

Sally's
TIPS & TRICKS

Inoculant Insurance

If you like lots of peas and beans, inoculants should be part of your gardening vocabulary. An inoculant is a special powder that contains the ideal bacteria that help legumes like peas and beans change nitrogen from the air into nitrogen compounds that plants can use. You can buy inoculant powder at some garden centers or from mail-order seed and garden-supply companies. Follow the directions on the packaging for applying the inoculant at planting. Be sure to water it well after planting. You can grow your legumes without it, but why not buy this low-cost insurance? The end result is better peas and beans—from plant size to production.

Peppers • *Capsicum annuum* var. *annuum* • Solanaceae

FAMILY UNIT

Peppers belong to the Tomato Family, and it's best to group them with other family members, like tomatoes and eggplants.

FRIENDS

Good herb companions for peppers include coriander, fennel, and basil. Marigolds, cosmos, gazanias, and short varieties of sunflowers also work well with peppers.

GROWING BASICS

Peppers like full sun, warm weather, and fertile, moist soil. You can start pepper seeds indoors six to seven weeks before the last spring frost date, but most gardeners buy plants. Gradually harden off transplants, then plant them outside in soil that's over 55°F. Peppers grow best when night air temperatures stay above 55°F; days over 90°F can cause blossom drop.

Spacing. I plant peppers 10 to 12 inches apart in all directions in a 2-1-2 or 3-2-3 pattern. This close spacing allows the leaf canopy to block weeds and keep the soil moist. Substitute flower and herb companions for some of the center plants in the pattern.

Feeding. I learned my favorite pepper fertilizer tip from my dear old Grandpa Maynard. He's passed on, but I'll always hear his gravelly voice telling me, "Put a half book of matches under every pepper!" Scatter the matches in the planting hole about 2 inches from the roots. Matches provide sulfur, which may lower the soil pH a bit, and peppers planted with them just seem to thrive.

Also at planting, put a trowelful of well-rotted manure or compost in the bottom of each planting hole, and cover it with a few inches of soil (so the plant roots won't contact the fertilizer right away). When plants blossom, spray them with a fish-emulsion solution. When you see flowers, squirt the plants with a mild solution of Epsom salts (a teaspoon to a quart of water); it provides extra magnesium to encourage fruit set.

Mulching. Mulch peppers with grass, straw, black plastic, or newspaper. Keep soil evenly moist, especially through the blossoming period, to avoid growth problems like blossom-end rot later.

PROBLEMS AND SOLUTIONS

Blossoms or young fruits drop. Blossom or fruit drop is usually due to temperature extremes, either too cold or too hot. Boron deficiency may be the problem, and it's usually a result of low soil pH—below

Bell pepper

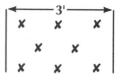

Space transplants 10"–12" apart in a 3-2-3 pattern

6.5. For a quick fix, add some borax to the soil. Mix 1 teaspoon of borax in 10 gallons of water to drench 100 square feet of soil.

Mushy areas on fruits. If peppers are exposed to direct sun, the fruits can scald. Scalded areas turn soft and will rot. To prevent sunscald, plant tall flowers around your peppers to shade the fruits.

Plants don't form fruits. Too much nitrogen fertilizer can cause plants to produce lots of foliage but no fruit. High or low temperatures can cause blossom drop, so plants can't make fruit. To remedy this problem in the future, always wait for the soil to warm before planting peppers.

Nutrient deficiencies may also be to blame. Your soil may need a phosphorus boost, so add rock phosphate, bonemeal, or greensand. To add magnesium, spray plants with a mild solution of Epsom salts, and make sure the soil pH is over 6.0.

Dark, watery spots on leaves. Dark spots on leaves and fruits may be due to anthracnose, a plant disease that thrives in wet, cool weather. Remove and destroy badly infected plants, and hope for better weather!

Dark, soft areas on bottoms of fruits. Blossom end rot shows up as mushy, shriveled bottoms on the peppers. It's caused by uneven watering early in the growing season, which leads to a calcium deficiency when the plants are in blossom. Even watering should prevent this problem.

Tiny holes in leaves. This type of damage can be due to corn borers or flea beetles. The borers are grayish pink caterpillars with dark heads. You can handpick the borers and their eggs (white), which

Sally's
TIPS&TRICKS

Ring Around the Peppers

I make my own plant shelters for peppers using empty plastic 2-liter soda bottles. It takes 12 bottles to make one shelter (ask your friends to save bottles for you). I set up the bottles in a ring and tape the bottles together with duct tape, taping around both the outside and the inside of the ring. After planting pepper transplants, I place a ring around each plant and fill the bottles with water. The water absorbs heat during the day and releases it at night, helping protect the plants on cold spring nights. Eggplants and tomatoes appreciate these plant shelters, too!

you'll find on the undersides of the pepper leaves.

If flea beetles are the culprits, protect future crops by covering them with row covers at planting.

HARVESTING

All bell peppers start out green. You can pick green peppers when they're firm and large. They'll be sweeter if you wait for them to change to red or yellow, but then pick them quickly before they turn soft. Regular harvesting encourages continued fruit production. Pick all peppers before the first fall frost.

For hot peppers, pick them while they're firm and glossy, before they turn soft. Handle hot peppers with care, and don't touch your eyes after picking hot peppers. Wearing plastic gloves is a good idea.

Potatoes • *Solanum tuberosum* • Solanaceae

Potato

FAMILY UNIT

Potatoes and beans always travel together as a family in my companion garden. The beans and potatoes share space well, and they repel or confuse some of each others' worst pest enemies.

FRIENDS

Savory, basil, parsley, and coriander are herbs of choice. Also try planting clusters of marigolds at the ends of rows, or wherever a potato didn't sprout.

GROWING BASICS

Potatoes prefer light, sandy soil, with a pH between 5.0 to 6.5. Plant seed potatoes when the soil is workable, four to six weeks before the last spring frost if you can. Cut certified seed potatoes in pieces with two or three "eyes" in each piece.

(The size doesn't matter.) Dust the seed pieces with plain sulfur (available at garden centers) to discourage fungal diseases, and let them air-dry for a few days. I plant potatoes in trenches as shown in "The Potato-Bean Duo" on page 225.

If you have heavy clay soil, you can plant potatoes in raised beds, or try planting them on top of the soil under a layer of straw. Just loosen up the soil, place the seed potatoes cut side down on the surface, and pile 8 inches of straw on top. Later, as the potato stems emerge, add another 8 to 9 inches of straw.

If slugs in the straw are a problem, use my trench method instead: Dig a 12-inch trench. Add a little compost mixed with bonemeal, then add 1 inch of soil on top of that. Place the potato pieces in the trench,

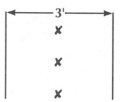

Space sets 12" apart in a single row

and cover with 4 inches of soil. When tops are up to 6 inches, nearly bury them in a mound (called "hilling"), and then bury them again when they have grown another 8 inches.

Spacing. Plant seed potato pieces about 12 inches apart in a long, single row or trench down the center of the bed. For extra-strong production, plant two seed pieces side by side at each spot.

Feeding. Potatoes don't need any extra fertilizer.

Mulching. Straw is the best mulch for potatoes. It's easy to harvest the tubers through straw mulch. Plus, straw hampers the emergence of Colorado potato-beetle larvae moving up through the soil to the plants.

PROBLEMS AND SOLUTIONS

Large holes in leaves. Colorado potato beetles and their larvae chew holes in leaves. You can handpick these critters. To prevent them, interplant potatoes with beans, and mulch the potatoes heavily with straw.

Rotten potatoes. Potatoes will rot if the weather stays too wet and the soil is too heavy. To avoid rotting with future crops, try planting on the surface or in a raised bed. Potatoes will also rot in freezing soil, so be sure to dig all potatoes once the tops die back.

Tiny or unproductive potatoes. Poor tuber production can be due to lack of

moisture, excess nitrogen, or cold nights (under 55°F). You can control the water and nitrogen for future crops, and just hope for better weather.

Green areas on tubers. If your tubers have green patches, it means they were exposed to the sun while growing or after harvest. Cut away the green parts, because they contain solanine, a mild toxin. The rest of the tubers are fine to eat.

Brownish black lesions on plants. If you see brownish black lesions on your potato leaves or stems, pay attention! These are symptoms of late blight, a serious disease that is destroying some commercial potato crops. The lesions appear first on the lower leaves, and there may be pale halos around the lesions. Destroy *all* diseased plants. Careless practices in the home garden can cause enormous damage to commercial potato fields, even 150 miles away.

To prevent late blight, buy and plant only certified seed potatoes from a reputable source. If you have any questions about late blight, contact your local Cooperative Extension office or a Master Gardener in your area.

Spotted, discolored leaves. Several diseases cause dark spots, discoloration, or mosaic patterns on leaves. It is very important to recognize them early. Your best bet is to remove and destroy diseased

Sally Says

"Keep your seed potatoes in a safe place. One year my dog ate mine, including my fancy blue potatoes!"

Sally's
TIPS&TRICKS

The Potato-Bean Duo

Potatoes and beans are my favorite set of insect-discouraging companions. After trying several planting arrangements, I've found the most logical method is planting potatoes side by side with bush beans.

1 Dig 12-inch-deep trenches 3 feet apart for the amount of potatoes you want to grow (my rule of thumb is 20 to 30 feet of row per potato eater). Stand on a board as you work to avoid compacting the soil. When the trenches are finished, put seed pieces cut side down in the trenches, 12 inches apart, and then cover them with several inches of soil.

Soil

Board

Seed potato

2 Once the potatoes have grown up through the soil in the trench, it will be time to plant beans along one side of the trench. I just push the beans into the loose soil about 4 inches apart in a band about 12 inches wide.

Potato plants

Bean seeds

Soil

3 When the potatoes have grown 4 more inches, push the rest of the loose soil up around the potato plants. Level off the area when the soil was heaped, and plant bean seeds there as you did before.

Bean seeds

Bean plants

Your second planting of beans should be ready to pick soon after your first crop finishes, just in time to eat along with your first harvest of tender new potatoes.

plants. Replant a new crop in a different part of the garden, preferably one where you haven't planted potatoes or any other Tomato Family crops (tomatoes, peppers, and eggplant) for the past three years.

Brown bumps on tubers. Scabs on tubers are a symptom of a disease called scab that looks like a scab. The scabs sometimes extend into the potato flesh. You can cut out the scabby parts and eat the rest of the tubers. Too much nitrogen in the soil increases scab problems. If you find scabby tubers, be sure to dig up and destroy all leaves, stems, and damaged tubers.

HARVESTING

Dig your first potatoes when you see some plants in flower. If you're growing potatoes with lots of straw mulch, you can just reach into the mulch with your hands to fish out some tubers. If your plants are in soil, use a garden fork to dig up the plants. Push the fork into the soil several inches away from the plants, and lever up the soil. After digging, be sure to destroy all parts of the plants to discourage the spread of disease.

Once the tops die back, it's time to harvest the remainder of the crop. Let potatoes air-dry in a shaded place, with the soil still attached (no washing!), before storing them in a cool, dry place.

Sally Says

"One of the thrills of gardening is pulling out that first potato. For a child (and the child in us), it's a miracle!"

Pumpkins & Winter Squash : Cucurbita spp / Cucurbitaceae

FAMILY UNIT

Pumpkins and winter squash are sprawling, space-hogging members of the Squash Family. Let them ramble about the base of corn plants and pole beans for a Three Sisters bed. Or keep your Squash Family plants separate as a family unto themselves. Plant radishes with squash to help ward off flea beetles.

FRIENDS

Nasturtiums are wonderful vining friends for pumpkin and squash plants. You can also try planting marigolds and sunflowers near the base of squash plants, and let volunteer goldenrod plants spring up in your pumpkin patch.

Planting buckwheat nearby will help attract pollinating insects. Planting catnip or tansy among squash vines may help to reduce squash bug numbers.

GROWING BASICS

Pumpkins and winter squash crops are heavy feeders, so provide fertile soil with a pH from 5.5 to 6.8. Plant seeds outside in warm soil after spring frosts have passed. If your growing season is very short, you can also plant trans-

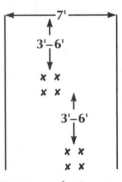

Butternut squash

Space seeds 1' apart in hills 3'–6' apart and offset by 1'–2'

plants. To start transplants, sow seeds indoors one month before you plan to plant them outdoors.

Spacing. Plant squash and pumpkins in a double-wide row—two 3-foot-wide rows plus the path in between. Space hills 3 to 6 feet apart and offset by 1 to 2 feet. You can combine squash and pumpkins in the same bed.

Plant four seeds in a hill, spacing seeds 1 foot apart. Tuck a few radish seeds around each hill. After the crop sprouts, cut off extra seedlings at ground level, leaving the two best plants in each hill. Then plant companion flowers around the edges of the hill.

Feeding. At planting, dig a big hole for each hill of seeds. Mix a bushel or two of well-rotted manure and compost into some of the excavated soil, and shovel it back into the hole to create a slightly raised hill of soil. Top things off with the remaining topsoil, and then plant the seeds.

Once a month, water with a solution of fish emulsion, or stir some compost into the soil near the base of the plants.

Mulching. Be sure to mulch the open spaces between clusters of squash plants, or the weeds will fill in for you! You can also plant dwarf white clover or buckwheat in strips among the vines. Apply 1 to 2 inches of water per week, especially during bud development and flowering.

PROBLEMS AND SOLUTIONS

Poor yield. If you don't get many pumpkins or squash, the problem may be lack of pollination. You can hand-pollinate by brushing pollen from a male flower (the one with the straight, thin stem) to a female flower (which has a slight swelling below the petals where the fruit develops). In the future, plant more flowering companions that attract pollinating insects like bees and beneficial flies.

Withered vines. Squash bugs are one possible culprit when vines wither. These shield-shaped gray-brown bugs suck juices from the leaves. Squash bugs are hard to hand-pick. To prevent them on future crops, cover plants with row covers from planting until pollination time.

Sally's
TIPS&TRICKS

Fighting Squash Diseases

Pumpkins and winter squash have a long growing season, typically 80 to 95 days. But they're prone to powdery mildew, and it often hurts the crops enough to really reduce yields. So I'm delighted that there's a simple and safe homemade solution that helps fight this disease. Just mix 1 teaspoon of baking soda and 2 teaspoons of horticultural oil (even vegetable oil will do) in 1 quart of water. Spray plants with this mixture every seven to ten days or after each rain. Research tests show that this solution is effective against powdery mildew, rusts, black spot on roses, and other fungal diseases.

Squash vine borers may also be to blame for withered vines, especially when plants wilt suddenly. You may find yellow stuff that looks like sawdust (called frass) at the base of the stems. If you neatly slit the vine, you can destroy the grub or borer inside. Then patch the slit (I have actually used small adhesive bandages!), or bury that portion of the stem. This method may or may not save your crop. For future crops, cover plants with row covers from planting to pollination.

White coating on leaves. Powdery mildew causes the powdery coating on leaves. Cut out the mildewy vines. You can fight powdery mildew by applying the simple baking soda solution described on page 227. To prevent the spread of the disease, don't handle plants when they're wet, and maintain good air circulation between vines.

HARVESTING

Pumpkins and winter squash are ready for harvest when the stems are dry and shriveled. Cut the stems with pruners or a sharp knife, leaving 2 to 3 inches of stem attached to the fruit. Protect harvested fruits by covering them with sheets, or bring them indoors before the first fall frost. Cure winter squash by spreading them out and letting them air-dry in a warm place for a week or two.

Radishes • *Raphanus sativus* • Cruciferae

Radish

FAMILY UNIT

Radishes are in the Cabbage Family, so if you're growing them in quantity, plant them with your cabbage and broccoli. I don't eat that many radishes, so I plant radishes here and there as pest repellants with my Squash Family crops and among my lettuce.

FRIENDS

Radishes are good friends to other plants, reported to repel striped cucumber beetles and squash borers, but they need friends, too. Tests showed a decrease in flea beetles when radishes were grown with mustard and nasturtiums. I plant radishes among the vine crops with nasturtiums, marigolds, and an occasional Queen-Anne's-lace.

GROWING BASICS

Radishes will grow in most soils and in full sun to partial shade. Plant radishes as early as you can, and continue planting into early summer. Water radishes frequently and generously or they'll turn woody and bitter quickly in summer heat. Plant radishes again in late summer for a fall crop.

```
◄———— 3' ————►
xxxxxxxxxxxxxxx
 xxxxxxxxxxxxxxx
xxxxxxxxxxxxxxx
 xxxxxxxxxxxxxxx
xxxxxxxxxxxxxxx
 xxxxxxxxxxxxxxx
```

Space seeds 1"–2" apart in all directions

Spacing. If you're planting a plot of radishes, sow seeds 1 to 2 inches apart in all directions. When you're planting them as a companion to other crops, just tuck seeds into the soil randomly.

Feeding. Radishes don't need any extra fertilizer.

Mulching. A bed of radishes quickly forms its own little canopy, but I start out by spreading a thin layer of grass clippings after planting the radish seeds.

PROBLEMS AND SOLUTIONS

Woody or pithy radishes. Radishes turn woody when the soil is too dry, so keep watering, especially when it's hot outside. If your radishes are pithy, try harvesting them while the roots are still quite small.

Cracked radishes. During a soggy summer, radishes can crack from too much moisture. Generally, they're still edible, even if they're not pretty.

Hairy roots. Radishes sprout lots of side roots when they're overcrowded or when they're growing in heavy soil. Next time add more organic matter to the soil, and thin radishes to 2 to 3 inches apart.

Holes in roots. Cabbage root maggots tunnel into the roots of radishes, leaving tunnels through the roots. Covering plants with row covers at planting will help prevent damage. If you've had lots of maggot problems, don't plant radishes where any Cabbage Family crops have been for at least three years. For a short-term solution, drench the soil with a lime solution (1 cup lime to 1 quart water) or stir in some wood ashes around the plants.

Tiny holes in leaves. Some gardeners use radishes as a trap to catch all the flea beetles, so you can expect to see some flea-beetle damage on your radishes! In a big radish planting they can hurt production, so row covers are essential. But in a mixed planting, the damage usually isn't severe enough to harm yields.

HARVESTING

Just sample your radishes once the roots start to enlarge, and you'll know when the flavor is right. Harvest all radishes before frost, or keep them covered along with your lettuces to stretch the salad season.

Sally Says

"For a sweet, crunchy experience, try growing the long, white Daikon radishes."

Sally's
TIPS & TRICKS

Children and Radishes

Children like fast results, but in many cases, gardening requires patience and a long wait for harvest. Radishes are a rewarding crop for young gardeners because they come up fast. I take advantage of their quick sprouting, and use them as living row markers to show the division between blocks of lettuces and other salad greens. But my daughter, Alice, just likes radishes because they give her early evidence that her gardening efforts will pay off!

Rhubarb • *Rheum rhabarbarum* • Polygonaceae

Rhubarb

FAMILY UNIT

Rhubarb is a permanent fixture in your garden, and I have known people who maintained a rhubarb patch over two generations. Rhubarb belongs in a long-term crop bed along with asparagus, strawberries, and horseradish.

FRIENDS

As far as I know, no one's studied which flower and herb companions will attract beneficials that help rhubarb in particular. In my companion garden, rhubarb is near horseradish and a bed of perennial flowers. I planted strawflowers between the rhubarb plants when they were small and switched to tall companions like dill, hollyhocks, or fennel once the plants were mature.

GROWING BASICS

Rhubarb likes full sun, cool weather, and moist, well-drained soil. You can plant rhubarb crowns or divisions in the spring as soon as you can work the soil. Plant rhubarb roots so that the crown is buried 2 to 3 inches. Rhubarb is hardy and in fact needs a cold winter to produce.

Spacing. Plant rhubarb crowns 3 feet apart in a single row down the center of the bed.

Feeding. In spring, side-dress plants with compost or well-rotted manure. An occasional spray with seaweed extract will increase productivity.

Mulching. Use any organic mulch. I like to use straw, pine needles, or newspaper covered with grass clippings.

PROBLEMS AND SOLUTIONS

Stippled yellow leaves. Stippling is a sign of infestation by spider mites. You can knock down a lot of spider mites by spraying plants with a strong stream of water from the hose. (In fact, this can be doubly effective because the predatory mites who attack the pests really like it wet, while the pest mites don't like water!)

Small holes in stalks. Rhubarb curculios are black beetles that puncture rhubarb stalks. The beetle larvae bore down into the crown. If you are observant, you can handpick the beetles before they damage plants. Also, thoroughly weed out any dock plants around your garden, because this weed harbors the curculios.

Thin stalks. When a mature plant starts producing thin stalks, it's a sign that the plant needs dividing. After harvest, divide and replant the crowns.

HARVESTING

You will have to wait out the first year after planting rhubarb without harvesting, and pull only a few stalks the second year.

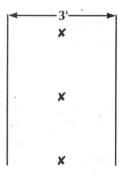

Space crowns 3' apart in a single row

From then on, you can harvest half the plant each season. It's important to *pull,* not cut, the stalk, as leaving a stub encourages diseases. (Simply feel the base of the stalk with one hand, and try to pull it from that point with the other.)

Take note: Rhubarb stems are delicious, but rhubarb leaves contain oxalic acid and are poisonous!

Sally's
TIPS & TRICKS

Rhubarb Mulch

Rhubarb leaves aren't edible, but they can be useful. When you harvest your rhubarb, cut the leaves off the stems while you're still in the garden. Spread the leaves around your rhubarb plants and other garden plants for an extra layer of tough mulch.

Spinach • *Spinacia oleracea* • Chenupodiaceae

Spinach

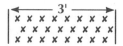

Space seeds 4" apart in all directions

FAMILY UNIT

I usually plant spinach with salad greens in the early spring or late fall. But spinach also fits fine under taller plants that will provide shade, like pole beans or peas, cauliflower, broccoli, or peppers.

FRIENDS

Radishes are a trap crop for spinach leafminers. Good flowering companions include low groundcovers like sweet alyssum, English daisies, or Swan River daisies.

GROWING BASICS

Spinach needs cool, moist conditions and grows well in partial shade. It likes moist, fertile soil but needs good drainage. Plant spinach seeds as soon as you can work the soil in spring (about a month before the last frost, if possible). I never grew good spinach until I planted some early in a well-drained raised bed. Try successive plantings every two weeks, and put some of the spinach where it will be shaded.

You can overwinter fall spinach by covering the plants with leaves or straw when the soil freezes. (Or make a little cold frame out of storm windows or plastic.) You can remove the mulch gradually in early spring, and harvest a little spinach every time you check!

Spacing. Plant seeds 4 inches apart in all directions. Or scatter the seeds more thickly, and thin them to the correct spacing. Use the thinnings for salad.

Feeding. Spinach is undemanding. If you mix some compost into your soil at planting, it probably won't need supplemental fertilizer. If you have any doubts, give it a boost by foliar-feeding with fish emulsion.

Mulching. If you plant spinach and its leafy friends closely together, they provide their own mulch. When the seedlings first emerge, I sprinkle some grass clippings among the plants. While spinach needs cool conditions, it doesn't need lots of water. Half an inch per week should be enough.

PROBLEMS AND SOLUTIONS

Seeds don't come up. Poor germination may result when the weather is hot or when seeds are planted too deeply or in heavy soil. Try again, and presprout the seeds by wrapping them in damp paper towels and storing them in a plastic bag in the refrigerator for a few days. Keep in mind that old spinach seeds don't

Sally's
TIPS & TRICKS

Shading Spinach

You can create perfect partial shade for spinach and salad greens by planting patches of the leafy greens between vertical trellises that support first peas, then beans. Set up trellises made of 1- by 1-inch wooden stakes in early spring. Wind twine vertically on the trellis to support the climbing crops. Plant spinach, lettuce, or other greens in the spaces between the trellises, and plant pea seeds along the trellises. The peas will provide spring shade. Once the soil warms and the pea crop is maturing, plant bean seeds along the trellises. The bean plants will continue shading the greens through the summer. This trick works best if you orient your trellises from east to west.

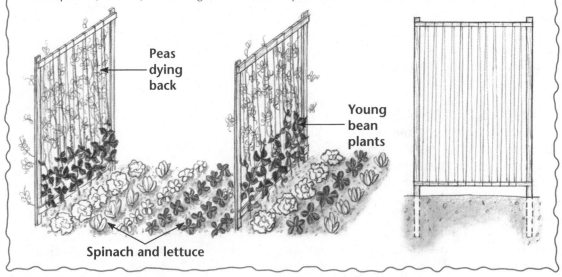

Peas dying back

Young bean plants

Spinach and lettuce

germinate very dependably, so be sure to use fresh seeds.

Leaves are bitter. Heat is probably to blame, because heat at critical times in the crop's development causes bolting, which makes plants bitter. Give up on these plants, but keep a succession of plantings going, and some are sure to succeed.

Yellow leaves. Yellowing leaves on a healthy plant signal a nutrient deficiency. Spray plants with fish emulsion and check the soil pH. (If the pH is over 7.5, the plants cannot absorb manganese, so correct the pH.)

Yellow leaves can also be a sign of disease. Get a definite diagnosis by taking plant samples to your local Cooperative Extension office, or simply destroy the affected plants, and replant in another part of your garden.

Blotchy areas in leaves. Blotches and tunnels in the leaves from leafminers are a common spinach problem. Cut off the damaged leaves as soon as you spot them. (You can eat the good parts.) Plant radishes or lamb's-quarters nearby as a trap crop, and destroy the trap plants when you see leafminer damage on them. If you've had severe leafminer problems, try covering the plants with row covers at planting.

HARVESTING

Keep cutting spinach back in cut-and-come-again style as shown on page 215, and it will continue producing until the weather is too hot. Once you see the plants start to stretch out, turn yellow, and form seedheads, they have "bolted" and are ready to compost.

Sally Says

"If spinach season ends too soon, grow heat-tolerant New Zealand spinach. It's my husband's favorite."

Summer Squash • *Cucurbita pepo* • Cucurbitaceae

FAMILY UNIT

Summer squash includes zucchini, crookneck squash, and scallop, or pattypan, squash. Summer squash belong to the same botanical family as winter squash, pumpkins, cucumbers, and melons. They don't grow long vines as enthusiastically as their relatives do, but I still group them together in my garden. Sometimes I tuck an occasional zucchini in with the salad greens after I've

harvested lettuce or spinach. Any squash can be part of a Three Sisters planting, and summer squash will do fine planted in the spaces between hills of corn and beans.

FRIENDS

Plant radishes, nasturtiums, marigolds, and basil among your summer squash. Sweet alyssum or low-growing thyme makes a nice underplanting and attracts lots of beneficials.

Crookneck squash

Space seeds 10"–16" apart in a single row

GROWING BASICS

Plant summer squash in full sun after the soil is really warm—about 75°F. Summer squash is easy to start from seeds outdoors. If you have a short growing season, you can also buy transplants or start seeds indoors around the time of your last spring frost. To plant, dig a sizable hole for each seed or transplant. Mix a half-bushel of well-rotted manure or compost into the soil you removed from the hole. Then refill the hole with the enriched soil, and plant into this soil.

Spacing. Space summer squash and zucchini 10 to 16 inches apart in a single row, and thin seedlings to 2 to 3 feet apart. If you're starting with transplants, set the transplants 2 to 3 feet apart.

Feeding. If you improve the soil at planting as I describe above, you probably won't need to fertilize your squash plants as they grow. I like to have some insurance, so I drench the soil around the plants with a fish emulsion solution at blossom time and again about three weeks later.

Mulching. It's hard to weed under prickly summer-squash leaves, so I like to mulch young plants with newspaper eight sheets thick. I just cut holes in the newspaper and slip it over the young seedlings after I thin out the extras. You can also mulch with straw, grass clippings, or black plastic.

PROBLEMS AND SOLUTIONS

Seeds don't sprout. Summer squash seeds don't germinate well in cold soil. Try replanting when the soil has reached 75°F.

Many flowers, few fruits. If your plants look healthy but won't produce fruit, the problem may be lack of pollination. If you covered plants with row covers, be sure to look under the row cover every day or so, and remove it when you see flowers starting to open. You can also hand-pollinate by brushing the pollen from male flowers (those with straight, thin stems) onto the pistil that protrudes from the center of female flowers (those that have a swelling at the base of the flower).

Sally's
TIPS & TRICKS

Too Much Zucchini!

Zucchini sure gets a bad rap—all those jokes about keeping the lights on at night or neighbors will put their extra zucchini on your porch. But there are at least three easy cures for the problem of overproducing plants.

First, you can pick zucchini (and other squash) blossoms for eating in omelettes, stir-fries, or salads. They're delicious!

Second, never let a zucchini grow longer than 8 inches; it's those club-sized zucchini that everybody dreads. Small zucchini are more tender and tasty, and you'll still get plenty.

Third, never plant more than one or two plants. (Perhaps there should be a law...)

Withered leaves. Squash bugs suck plant juices, causing the leaves to wither or dry out and shrivel. It's hard to control squash bugs by hand-picking. Remove and destroy severely infested plants. If it's not too late in the season, try re-planting, and cover the plants with row cover from planting until blossoms open.

Plants wilt suddenly. If healthy plants wilt suddenly, the problem could be squash vine borers. Look at the base of the plant, and you'll find a hole in the stem with crumbly material by it. If you split the stem open with a knife, you may find the borers inside. Squish the borers, and bury the stem section in soil. There's about a 50-50 chance that the plant will sur-vive and bear some fruit.

White coating on leaves. Powdery mildew is a fungal disease that is especially preva-lent during wet, rainy sum-mers. If you have plants that are severely infected, remove and destroy them. You can fight powdery mildew with a safe, simple spray made from baking soda; see the instruc-tions for making it on page 227. Spray plants every ten days or after a rain.

HARVESTING

Harvest crookneck squash and zucchini when the fruits are 6 to 8 inches long. Harvest pattypan squash before they reach 4 inches across, while they're pale yellow or green. Use a knife or pruners to cut the squash off the vine so you don't uproot the whole plant.

Sally Says

"Summer squash is prime for picking when the rind is tender enough to pierce with your fingernail."

Strawberries • Fragaria × ananassa • Rosaceae

FAMILY UNIT

Strawberries are perennials and belong in the permanent section of the garden. You can plant them along with other long-term crops, like rhubarb, horseradish, or asparagus. In a new strawberry bed, try planting spinach or lettuce between the young strawberry plants.

FRIENDS

Traditional companion plant-ings pair borage with strawber-ries, and I always let some borage seed itself among my strawberries. I also plant dill, coriander, and fennel nearby and let a few Queen-Anne's-lace plants spring up. Love-in-a-mist looks wonderful planted in the center of a wide row of strawberries.

GROWING BASICS

Strawberries must have full sun and good drainage, so be sure to plant them in a raised bed with a lot of organic matter mixed into the soil. They need a pH of 5.8

Strawberries

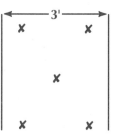

Space crowns 18" apart in a 2-1-2 pattern

to 6.5. Plant new strawberry plants when they are dormant, as early in the spring as you can. Try to plant on an overcast, windless day, and soak the plants well before you get started.

Trim the plant roots to about 5 inches from the crown. Set each crown on a small mound of soil with the roots spread evenly over the mound. Be sure that the crown is positioned just above the soil surface; otherwise, the crowns will dry out (too high) or rot (too deep).

Spacing. My standard technique for planting strawberries is to space crowns 18 inches apart in a 2-1-2 pattern. Then I harvest from the plants for three years, concentrating the fruit production by cutting off runners (long stems with new little plantlets at the ends) as they appear. After the three years, I dig out the old plants and replant new, vigorous plants.

If you don't want to replant every few years, you can use the runners to renew your bed.

Sally's
TIPS & TRICKS

Renewing Strawberries

To keep a strawberry patch producing for many years, turn the little plantlets produced at the ends of runners (long horizontal stems) into new plants. To manage a strawberry patch in this way, start by planting strawberry crowns in a zigzag pattern down a bed. Set plants 20 to 24 inches apart and offset by 12 inches.

As the runners form, guide them directly across the row, and encourage them to root there by weighting the stem with a rock. The plantlets will root and grow into new plants. Every third year, dig out the old plants, and then guide runners into those vacant spaces to start the next strawberry generation.

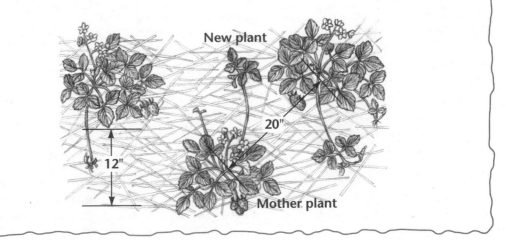

New plant

20"

12"

Mother plant

With this technique, I use a zigzag planting pattern, as shown on the opposite page.

Feeding. It's good to side-dress strawberry plants each spring with compost or foliar-feed with a fish-emulsion solution. To keep the mother plants productive, feed them again when harvest is over. Be sure to keep plants well watered while they're producing fruit.

Mulching. Mulching strawberries is crucial for maintaining soil moisture. You'll also need to apply mulch over the top of the plants in late fall to protect them from winter cold. Chopped leaves or straw are fine, but pine needles are even better.

Add winter mulch only after there have been several hard freezes, and then leave it in place until spring. Remove it gradually, and leave it nearby to be put back in place if a late frost threatens. Many new blossoms are lost to unexpected spring frosts.

PROBLEMS AND SOLUTIONS

Distorted berries. If your berries have sunken, distorted areas (called "catfacing"), the culprit is the tarnished plant bug. The berries are edible but may not ripen well. If you have problems with tarnished plant bugs, clear all old fruit and plant debris out of the patch after harvest. Weed thoroughly—tarnished plant bugs also like pigweed and lamb's quarters. The only effective control I have found is row covers, placed over the strawberries at planting time.

White coating on leaves. Powdery mildew can be a problem on strawberries, especially in overcrowded patches. Control it by removing the infected plants. Only water strawberries early in the day, never work around the plants when they're wet, and thin the plants to let in light and air.

Stunted, wilted plants. There are several serious fungal diseases of strawberries. If your plants get infected, your best bet is to dig them out and destroy them. Take a sample to your Cooperative Extension office to learn the specific disease that's to blame. Then search out varieties resistant to that disease, and replant.

Pecked fruits. To prevent bird damage, cover plants with row covers or netting. Suspend the netting over hoops or other supports so the birds can't peck through the netting. Be *very* careful to fasten down the edges so birds don't become trapped under the cover or in the netting.

HARVESTING

For a big second-year harvest, pinch off all strawberry blossoms during the first year of growth. In the second spring, you will know by tasting when strawberries are ripe. They usually ripen one month after blossoming, and harvest can last up to three weeks. Remove any rotting or old berries from the plants so that fungal diseases don't set in.

Sally Says

"I scare birds away from my strawberries with strips cut from Mylar balloons. Attach the strips to a string suspended directly over the berries."

Sweet Potatoes • *Ipomoea batatas* • Convolvulaceae

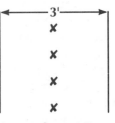

Sweet potato

FAMILY UNIT

I've grown sweet potatoes along with my regular potatoes and bush beans. You can also try a planting of sweet potatoes with an occasional scarlet runner bean or other pole bean plant left to ramble among the sweet potato vines.

FRIENDS

These "southern cousins" like the same friends as our other potatoes: dill, basil, and other aromatic herbs. There are some indications that tansy, radishes, and summer savory may repel or confuse the sweet potato weevil.

GROWING BASICS

A long warm season—from 70 to 100 days—is a must for a good sweet potato harvest. They need full sun but tolerate many kinds of soil. Soil pH of 5.5 is best. If you tend to have cold soil, plant them in a framed raised bed where soil will warm quickly.

Sweet potatoes start from "slips," which are miniature plants that sprout from sweet potato roots. If you live in a cold region and plan to order slips from a mail-order supplier, be specific about your last frost date, and ask for the shortest-season variety the company carries.

You can also try starting your own slips: Just cut some sweet potatoes in half, and place them cut side down on some moist paper towels or peat moss on a cookie sheet. Cover the potato pieces with a few more moist paper towels, and then wrap the whole arrangement with plastic wrap. When you see sprouts, remove the wrap, and place the plants in a bright location. If you start about two months before your last frost date, your slips should be ready just in time for outdoor planting.

Sweet potatoes need a good supply of phosphorus. You can supply it by working bonemeal into the soil at planting.

Spacing. Plant sweet potato slips in a single row down the center of a bed, spacing plants 14 inches apart.

Feeding. Don't give sweet potatoes too much fertilizer (especially nitrogen-rich types), or you'll have lots of sweet potato vine, but only vine!

Mulching. Sweet potato vines grow fast and form their own mulch. To keep the area around young plants moist, cover them with newspaper five or six sheets thick. Weigh the newspaper down with rocks or boards until the vines spread over them.

Don't water sweet potatoes too much because wet soil contributes to small roots. Water only when the soil feels dry to a depth of 8 inches.

Space plants 14" apart in a single row

PROBLEMS AND SOLUTIONS

Small, flavorless roots. Cold spells late in the spring or early in the fall can result in poor yields and flavorless roots. A rainy summer or a short growing season can also give the same results. For a better sweet potato crop next time, extend the season with frost protection and raised beds, and be careful to supply the right conditions for the crop's needs.

Tunnels in roots. Sweet potato weevils are common in the South. The weevils chew on the plants while the larvae tunnel through the roots. The pest can spread a serious disease as it feeds. If you have a problem with this pest, plant resistant varieties, and be sure to buy certified disease-free slips. Handpick any of the reddish orange blue-winged weevils you find on your plants, and destroy all crop debris at the end of the season.

Roots rot in storage. Careless handling results in bruised potatoes, which leads to rot. Poor curing also contributes. Sweet potatoes keep best if stored in newspaper at 55° to 60°F.

Cooked roots won't soften. If you leave sweet potatoes in the ground too long or store them in a cold place (like a refrigerator or cold root cellar), the roots may not soften even when they are cooked.

HARVESTING

Check your sweet potatoes about 70 days after planting to see if they've reached harvestable size. In the north, harvest sweet potatoes when there's even the suggestion of a frost, because the plants are very tender. If a frost blackens the vines, the decay will spread quickly to the tubers.

When you dig sweet potatoes, work gently, inserting a digging fork far from the base of the plants. Sweet potatoes need to dry in the air for a few hours before curing, but do not leave them outside overnight. Do *not* wash them. Cure in a warm, well-aired, dark place for about two weeks. Sweet potatoes bruise easily, so handle them gently.

Sally Says

"In my garden, success with sweet potatoes requires an early start and mild weather, but they're worth the try."

Sally's
TIPS & TRICKS

Sweet Potato Mountains

One Master Gardener I know, John Holnbeck, grows huge sweet potatoes near Buffalo, New York, where frosts start in September. Here's his secret: Instead of hilling soil *around* the plants (like you would with regular potatoes), he hills the soil *before* he plants.

To try his technique, make a "mountain" of soil at least 12 inches high for each slip you plan to plant. If possible, shape the hill from light topsoil. Make a slit in the top of the mound, and plant the slip 5 inches deep, with just one leaf peeking out. Firm the soil around the plants, and water gently. Be sure to protect the plants from frost at the beginning and end of the growing season, as the very first "nip" will kill the vines.

Swiss Chard • *Beta vulgaris,* Cicla group • Chenopodiaceae

Swiss chard

FAMILY UNIT

Swiss chard is also called chard or spinach beet. I grow it with other greens, such as lettuces, spinach, gourmet greens, and New Zealand spinach. Swiss chard has few pest and disease problems, so you can really add it to any bed in the garden when you have extra space. It makes a great fall crop and can work well with broccoli and cabbage planted for fall harvest.

FRIENDS

Swiss chard can be an early- or late-season star in your garden. For early-season friends, try early blooming English daisies, blanket flower, sweet alyssum, or calendula nearby. For summer and fall companions, try black-eyed Susans and tall, airy herbs like sweet Annie or fennel.

GROWING BASICS

Swiss chard is a hardy crop that tolerates light freezes and continues growing even after a hard frost. It will grow in full sun or partial shade but needs at least five hours of sun daily.

Swiss chard grows well in most soils but does best in rich soil with a pH of 6.0 to 6.8.

Plant Swiss chard from seed outdoors two to four weeks before the last expected frost, and seed more in summer four to six weeks before the first fall frost

date for fall and winter harvest.

Spacing. Seed Swiss chard in rows 4 inches apart, aiming for seed to fall every 2 to 4 inches. Thin plants to four inches apart within the row, using thinnings for salads.

Feeding. Swiss chard is a light feeder, but if you want it to keep producing for many months, spray the foliage with seaweed extract or fish emulsion once a month.

Mulching. The leaves of Swiss chard plants quickly expand to shade the roots. But to beat weeds, I sprinkle grass clippings among the seedlings when they emerge.

PROBLEMS AND SOLUTIONS

Tiny holes in leaves. Flea beetles will feed on Swiss chard, but the damage usually isn't serious. Try planting trap crops of Chinese cabbage for spring crops and eggplant for fall. Place them 10 to 20 feet away from the Swiss chard, and pull up and destroy the trap-crop plants if they become seriously infested. You can also try covering Swiss chard with row cover, but then you will miss the crop's good looks, and repeated harvests will be less convenient.

Small tunnels in leaves. The larvae of leafminer flies tunnel through Swiss chard leaves. Remove infested leaves

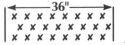

Space transplants 4" apart in all directions

as you spot them. If you harvest frequently, you'll usually stay ahead of leafminer problems. Pull all weeds like lamb's-quarters because they can harbor leafminers, too.

HARVESTING

When plants are 7 to 8 inches tall, cut the leaves off 1½ to 2 inches above ground level. Keep cutting every time the leaves regrow. You may see the recommendation to harvest outer leaves only. This will give you tougher Swiss chard, and it's a lot more trouble, too! If you like the white fleshy stalks for use in stir-fry or soups, let a few of the plants mature, strip the leaves for stewing, and cut up the stalks for cooking.

Sally's TIPS & TRICKS

Beautiful Swiss Chard

I think Swiss chard's glossy, arching leaves are gorgeous to look at as well as good to eat. For a knockout companion garden combination that has lots of good-bug–attracting power to boot, try pairing your Swiss chard with the pale blue flowers of bronze fennel and the striking foliage of borage.

Tomato • *Lycopersicon esculentum* • Solanaceae

Tomatoes

FAMILY UNIT

Tomatoes, eggplants, peppers, and potatoes all belong to the same botanical family, and they're collectively known as the nightshades (some poisonous weeds also belong to this family). I grow tomatoes with eggplant and peppers because they are prone to some serious soilborne diseases. However, these are my favorite crops, so I give them a very large neighborhood!

I keep potatoes separate from their cousins, growing them with beans. This makes rotation a bit trickier but still workable in my garden because I have six garden neighborhoods.

FRIENDS

Basil goes with tomatoes in cooking and in the garden. I also like to pair aromatic herbs such as sweet Annie, dill, or fennel with tomatoes. Tall daisy-shaped flowers like cosmos, Shasta daisies, or sunflowers work well in or beside tomato cages. I always include borage near tomatoes. Tansy is another important friend to keep in a nearby perennial bed.

GROWING BASICS

Tomatoes like fertile, well-drained soil, with a pH of 6.0 to 7.0, and 8 hours of sun daily. Most disappointments with tomatoes happen because of

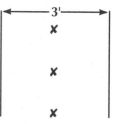

Space transplants 2'–3' apart in a single row

how they are grown—not because of pests or diseases!

Don't plant tomatoes outside unprotected until the soil is warm (over 55°F, even at night) and nighttime air temperatures don't dip below 55°F. (That's well into June in western New York, or two to four weeks after the frost-free date in most places.)

If you're starting seeds indoors, do so about six weeks before the last spring frost. Transplant on an overcast day or in the evening. Cover plants with baskets if you anticipate wind or a hot spell during their first days outside.

Planting tomatoes horizontally isn't really a secret, as old-timers have done this for generations, but lots of people still don't know about it: You can get a really good root system, a sturdier plant, and an earlier harvest if you plant your tomato transplants lying down. (No, *you* don't lie down; the plants do!)

First, dig long, narrow planting holes. Put a trowelful of compost or well-rotted manure in the bottom of each, and cover it with a few inches of soil. Then strip all the leaves off your tomato plants except for the top cluster. After planting, new roots will grow at every juncture where leaves were removed! Lay the plant in the hole, and bury the whole stem with about 2 to 3 inches of soil. (A tip: If you are caging the plant or using a plant shelter or black plastic, poke a

stick into the soil at the root ball so you won't end up putting weight on the fragile, shallow, young roots.)

If you must plant tomatoes early, surround each plant with a shelter like the one shown on page 222 to keep the plant warm and protected. And see page 152 to learn how to make sturdy cages for your tomatoes.

Spacing. Space tomato plants 2 to 3 feet apart in a single row if you plan to stake, trellis, or cage them. If you plan to let them sprawl, space them at least 4 feet apart. Plant companion flowers and herbs outside of cages or at the ends of the rows.

Cherry tomatoes often need just as much space as full-size tomatoes, although "patio tomato" types intended for containers can be planted as close as 1 to 2 feet apart.

Feeding. Tomatoes are big feeders. Foliar-feed them with fish emulsion at blossom time and every two weeks thereafter. Generous watering is probably more important for tomatoes than for any other crop, because it prevents several problems.

Mulching. I mulch around tomatoes with black plastic or sow dwarf white clover once the tomato plants are about 8 inches tall. Other mulches, such as straw or leaves, are also fine. Water transplants daily for a few days, never letting the soil get dry even 2 inches down (where the tiny roots are). Then be sure they get 1½ inches of water a week.

Sally Says

"The biggest mistake is planting tomatoes too early in the great competition for the first ripe tomato."

PROBLEMS AND SOLUTIONS

Yellow leaves, slow growth. When plants look yellow, suspect a nitrogen deficiency. To fix this fast, spray plants with a solution of fish emulsion. If this doesn't help, suspect disease problems. Take a sample of the plant to your Cooperative Extension service for a diagnosis. If only a few plants are diseased, remove and destroy them before the problem spreads!

Reddish purple leaves. Phosphorus deficiency causes purpling of leaves. This often happens in areas with acid soil (under 6.0). Test your pH for long-term correction, and foliar-feed with fish emulsion for the short term.

Slow growth, few fruit. Potassium deficiency has several symptoms beyond poor growth and fruiting. New leaves crinkle, and older leaves look pale with a lime-green margin. There are bronze spots near the larger leaf veins. Fish emulsion will correct the problem temporarily, but you must begin rebuilding soil in the fall. Greensand and crushed granite are excellent sources of potassium.

Black area on bottom of fruit. Blossom end rot happens when water levels fluctuate while fruit is developing. Once you see the black spot, you can't correct the problem. But you can cut it away and eat the remaining portion of the fruit. Fruits that develop later probably won't have the problem. In the future, mulch well and water regularly.

Scarred fruits. Scarring or "catfacing" results from environmental stress at critical times in a young plant's life. If often happens when plants are set out too early and are exposed to cold. Or they suffered from drought and high temperature.

All foliage, few fruits. Several factors can cause blossoms to drop off, including low temperatures (below 55°F) during fruit set, winds, high temperatures, heavy rains, excess nitrogen, and poor pollination.

Holes in leaves. Tomato hornworms are 3- to 5-inch-long green caterpillars that chew holes in leaves. They don't usually do serious damage and are easy to handpick. If you

Quick tomato supports. To support tomato plants quickly and easily, use stakes and twine. Hammer a stake between plants all the way down the row. Then weave twine or rope around the plants on both sides, starting 12 inches above the ground and adding more tiers of twine every 12 to 15 inches.

see white "bumps" on them, it's a sign that parastic wasps have attacked—the white bumps are wasp cocoons.

Colorado potato beetles also chew on leaves but are easy to handpick. Flea beetles can do serious damage to young plants, but you can prevent this by covering plants with row covers until they grow large enough to withstand damage.

Spots on leaves. There's a grab bag of tomato diseases that can cause dark spots, water-soaked spots, yellow specks, and other symptoms on leaves. If the problems aren't too serious, you may get fine yields even when some disease is present. If plants are severely infected, destroy them. Use a three-year rotation as a minimum to keep disease problems from becoming more serious.

With all these troubles, you may wonder whether it's worth it to grow tomatoes. It is! Most gardeners with good practices and well-prepared soil grow wonderful, trouble-free tomatoes. Every garden needs some.

HARVESTING

Once tomato season begins, check your plants daily to catch fruit at its peak. Pick tomatoes when they're red and ripe, but not yet soft. When the first fall frost threatens, harvest all remaining tomatoes, including green ones, or cover the plants with sheets or tarps to protect the fruits. Use clothespins to fasten the sheets together. (I keep a supply of old sheets in the barn. In September, my garden sometimes looks like a Halloween party with all the guests dressed as ghosts!)

There are two ways to deal with green tomatoes. You can pull up whole plants, and hang them upside down in a cool, dark, dry place (like some basements in summer). Be sure to check the plants often, as the fruits will ripen at an irregular rate. If you don't pick them soon enough, they will fall off the plants and splatter.

You can also pick green tomatoes off the vines and wrap each one in a small piece of newspaper. Store them in drawers or on shelves in a cool, dark, dry place. If you have a lot, just lay them out side by side between layers of newspaper, so you can check a bunch of them at one time. Always remove fruits that start to rot.

Sally's
TIPS & TRICKS

Tomatoes Aren't for the Birds

If you see neat, sharp dents gouged out of your ripe tomatoes, blame a smart bird with a pointed beak. Sometimes birds attack tomatoes because they need moisture, so be sure to keep your garden birdbath full of water. And to scare birds away from your tomatoes, use some recycled Mylar balloons. Just cut the Mylar into long strips, and tie them to the tops of your tomato stakes or cages. They startle the birds by fluttering in the slightest breeze and look downright festive besides!

Turnips • *Brassica rapa* • Brassicaceae

FAMILY UNIT

So many people don't grow (or eat) turnips that this crop is happy to visit just about any family! Botanically speaking, turnips are part of the Cabbage Family, but they also work well in a neighborhood with root crops and salad greens.

FRIENDS

I think the coarse leaves of turnips look nice interplanted with ferny plants, so I plant them with fennel or dill.

GROWING BASICS

Turnips like full sun and light, deeply worked soil that's been amended with compost. Sow turnip seeds outside three to four weeks before the last spring frost, or eight to nine weeks before the first fall frosts.

Spacing. Sow seeds roughly 2 inches apart in rows 6 inches apart, and thin plants in the rows to stand 6 inches apart.

Feeding. Turnips don't need extra fertilizer if they're growing in rich soil. But if you're applying fish emulsion to other crops, it won't hurt to give the turnips a spritz.

Mulching. Turnip plants have spreading leaves and are self-mulching. The only mulch I suggest is a light layer of grass clippings sprinkled among young seedlings. Turnips need regular watering (1 inch per week) for good root development.

PROBLEMS AND SOLUTIONS

Woody or corky turnips. Poor root quality is the result of hot, dry weather, too much nitrogen, or not enough potassium and phosphorus. You can't change your weather, but you can try again for a fall crop. Try applying greensand or fish emulsion to correct nutrient deficiencies, and mulch to keep the soil cool and moist.

Strong or bitter flavor. Strong flavor can also result from hot, dry weather or from letting roots get too mature before harvest. Try mulching your next crop more heavily, and pick the turnips when they're quite small.

Poor yield. Turnips won't develop well if they're overcrowded or underwatered. They also don't like heavy soil. For your next crop, space seedlings further apart in loose, well-worked soil with lots of organic matter added, and water regularly.

Roots blacken. Some diseases cause black areas in roots, and so can a boron deficiency. Try to have the problem diagnosed at your Cooperative Extension office. To correct boron deficiency in future crops, check that the soil pH is between 6.0 and 8.0, use a foliar spray of liquid seaweed extract, and improve the soil by planting a cover crop of clover.

Turnip

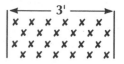

Space seeds 6" apart in all directions

For disease problems, destroy the diseased plants (roots and tops). Replant in a new area of the garden.

Wilting plants. If you see turnips wilting in moist soil, pull a few roots. If they are distorted or enlarged, with bulbous swellings, the problem is clubroot. This fungus is more likely to survive in acid soil, so test the pH, and raise it if necessary. Also, follow good garden sanitation and rotate plants. (In case of this disease, you must not grow Cabbage Family crops in the same soil for seven years!)

Tunnels in roots. The cabbage maggot tunnels through roots, leaving them open to disease. Destroy infested plants. For future crops, cover plants with row covers. You can also kill off maggots in the soil by pouring 1 cup liquid lime into the soil around each plant. (The ratio is 1 cup lime to 1 quart water, well stirred and allowed to settle for several hours before applying.)

Sally's
TIPS & TRICKS

No More Terrible Turnips

My Grandma Harper was so special that I named my daugher, Alice, after her. But I have one horrible memory of Grandma Harper—those *awful* turnips she served! My childhood memory—and maybe yours—is that turnips are tough, bitter, and blah! But try some of the varieties available today like 'Hakurei' and 'Vertus'. The flavors are mild and sweet, and the texture is smooth and tender, especially if you pull the roots while they're young. Have turnips improved, or have your tastes matured? Perhaps it's a little of both.

HARVESTING

Pull or dig turnips when they are 2 to 3 inches in diameter. The roots are most tender when they're small. Larger roots get tough and woody.

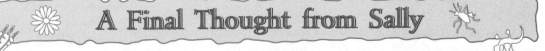

A Final Thought from Sally

THE CLOSER WE GET to the source of our food—starting in our own organic gardens—the better we eat, and the better it tastes. I want my child to eat food that isn't sprayed, coated, or soaked in anything except water, so I grow my own.

Another benefit of growing your own vegetables is the rich variety it adds to your eating. We tend to take vegetables for granted, buying the same selection of iceberg lettuce, carrots, limp cucumbers, and pale tomatoes all year long. Because I grow my own, I enjoy an ever-changing menu of incredibly fresh and flavorful vegetables as they come into season, from sweet, crunchy spring peas to zesty tomatoes and peppers in summer and hearty squash, cabbage, and turnips in fall. To increase the variety, I also buy fruit and vegetables from local farmers. Try seasonal eating—you may discover that you enjoy the surprise of fresh new seasonal tastes as much as I do.

Plants for Beneficial Insects

Use this table to find herbs, perennials, annuals, and groundcovers that will attract beneficial insects to your garden neighborhoods. Strive for a mix of plants that will keep something in flower throughout the season. Research studies confirm the beneficial-attracting power of many of the plants named below. For plants marked with a star, no studies are reported, but based on my own experience, I'm confident that they will help you maintain a steady supply of nectar, pollen, and shelter for a variety of beneficials.

Herbs				
Plant Names	**Description**	**Growing Tips**	**Garden Uses**	**Benefits**
Angelica *Angelica archangelica* Apiaceae	Early-summer-blooming biennial; celerylike stems and leaves; tiny white flowers. 5'–8' tall and 4' wide	Needs rich, moist soil; tolerates light shade; will live several years if you cut off flowers before they set seed; plant in a permanent bed	Makes a dramatic, tall centerpiece in perennial clusters	Attracts lacewings, lady beetles, parasitic wasps
Anise *Pimpinella anisum* Apiaceae	Summer-blooming annual; flat-topped clusters of creamy white flowers; feathery, sharp-toothed leaves; 2' tall	Prone to wind damage and difficult to transplant, so sow seeds directly in the garden in a protected location	Looks nice interspersed among summer-flowering vegetables	Hosts parasitic wasps, tachinid flies, lady beetles
Borage *Borago officinalis* Boraginaceae	Midsummer- to fall-blooming annual; fuzzy, gray-green oblong leaves; ¾" blue, starlike flowers; 2½' tall and 1' wide	Easy to grow in most soils; sow seeds after last frost date; transplant when young; self-seeds, but not invasive	Attractive with strawberries and any plants with red or purple foliage; allow to spring up all around the garden	Attracts bees; useful around vine crops
Caraway *Carum carvi* Apiaceae	Spring-blooming annual or biennial; flat-topped clusters of tiny white flowers; finely cut leaves; 2' tall	Prefers light, dry soil; sow seeds in early spring or fall for flowers the next summer; self-seeds easily	Good choice for fall sowing around strawberries or in herb and perennial clusters	Attracts parasitic wasps, parasitic flies
Catnip *Nepeta cataria* Lamiaceae	Mid- to late-summer-blooming perennial; coarse, gray-green leaves; tiny, tubular pale pinkish flowers; 1'–3' tall and 2' wide; Zones 4 to 9	Easy to grow in average soil; belongs to Mint Family, so beware—it spreads; plant in containers or where growth can be limited	Use it to keep cats on patrol in areas where moles are a problem; try *Nepeta faassenii*, *N. sibirica*, or *N. grandiflora* in perennial border	Attracts bees, parasitic wasps—and cats!

(continued)

Plants for Beneficial Insects—continued

Herbs—continued

Plant Names	Description	Growing Tips	Garden Uses	Benefits
German Chamomile *Matricaria recutita* Asteraceae	Late-spring- to summer-blooming annual; white daisylike flowers with yellow centers; threadlike leaves; 2'–3' tall	Tolerates a range of soil types; sow seeds in fall; self-sows once established	Pair with Cabbage Family crops or peppers	Attracts hoverflies, parasitic wasps
Roman Chamomile *Chamaemelum nobile* Asteraceae	Late-spring- to summer-blooming perennial; white daisylike flowers with yellow centers; fuzzy, threadlike leaves; apple scent. 8"–9" tall; Zones 3 to 8	Tolerates a range of soils; sow seeds in a well-worked bed in spring, or propagate by digging up offshoots from an established plant	Good low-growing groundcover in permanent perennial or herb bed; hard to control, so don't allow it to spread into vegetable beds	Attracts hoverflies, parasitic wasps
Chervil *Anthriscus cerefolium* Apiaceae	Late-spring- to summer-blooming annual; light green, deeply notched leaves resemble carrot foliage; small white flower clusters; 2' tall	Plant in part shade to prevent bolting; difficult to transplant, so sow seeds in 1"-deep trenches in the garden; leave the trenches uncovered and keep seeds constantly moist until they germinate	Use as a companion for tall or trellised crops like tomatoes	Attracts parasitic wasps
Curry plant *Helichrysum angustifolium* Asteraceae	Late-spring- to summer-blooming tender perennial; gray or whitish, woolly leaves on erect stems; small yellow flower heads; 1½' tall	Easy to grow, provided soil is well drained; drought tolerant	Plant in a perennial plot or use it as an annual in your vegetable beds	Attracts parasitic wasps, parasitic flies, other predatory insects
Dill *Anethum graveolens* Apiaceae	Summer-blooming annual; flat, 6" greenish flower clusters at the top of a hollow stalk; feathery, threadlike, bluish green leaves; 3' tall	Prone to wind damage, so plant in a protected spot; sow seeds in spring after danger of frost; self-sows readily	Looks attractive interspersed throughout the garden; try planting it between brussels sprouts	Attracts lady beetles, wasps, spiders, hoverflies, bees

Plant Names	Description	Growing Tips	Garden Uses	Benefits
Fennel *Foeniculum vulgare* Apiaceae	Mid- to late-summer-blooming semihardy perennial; branching stalks have deep green, feathery leaves; small yellow flowers; 4' tall	Prefers rich, well-drained soil; treat as an annual, sowing seeds in spring or fall	Looks pretty arching over mid-size crops; use the tall 6' bronze-colored variety for a special ornamental touch	Attracts hoverflies, lady beetles, parasitic wasps, tachinid flies
Lavender *Lavandula angustifolia* Lamiaceae	Summer-blooming perennial; bushy plant with 1"–2" gray leaves; small, lavender flowers on tall spikes; 2'–3' tall; Zones 5 to 8	Requires light soil and pH over 7.0; start new plants from cuttings; provide winter protection in Zone 5	Use in a permanent bed of perennial vegetables and herbs	Attracts bees
Lovage *Levisticum officinale* Apiaceae	Summer-blooming perennial. Celery-like plant with hollow stems; clusters of tiny yellow flowers; up to 5' tall and 2½' wide; Zones 5 to 8	Easy to grow; sow in late summer or early fall, or plant divisions; dies back to the ground each winter	Makes a striking centerpiece for a perennial and herb cluster	Attracts beneficial wasps; shelters ground beetles
Nasturtium *Tropaeolum majus* Tropaeolaceae	Summer-blooming annual; spreading vine with round leaves; bright orange and yellow funnel-shaped flowers; 6"–12" tall	Easy to grow; wait until soil warms to sow seeds	Makes an attractive groundcover, so use it to cover any bare areas; rambles well among corn or cucumbers	Provides shelter for ground beetles, spiders
Parsley* *Petroselinum crispum* Apiaceae	Early-spring-blooming biennial; curly or flat leaves at the end of slender stalks; minuscule flowers; 1½' tall	Grows well in sun or light shade; treat as an annual, sowing seeds in spring when soil is warm; often survives over winter	Harvest leaves as needed for cooking and garnishes, but allow a few plants to go to flower	Attracts parasitic wasps, but only when allowed to flower
Rue *Ruta graveolens* Rutaceae	Summer-blooming perennial; evergreen leaves made up of many small blue-green leaflets; clusters of ½" yellow flowers; 3' tall; Zones 4 to 9	Prefers well-drained soil with pH at least 7.0; start seeds indoors in late winter and transplant in late spring	Use as a filler in perennial clusters; nice companion for tall plants like lovage, rugosa roses; *caution:* causes skin irritation in some individuals	Attracts ichneumonid wasps, predatory wasps

(continued)

Plants for Beneficial Insects—continued

Herbs—continued

Plant Names	Description	Growing Tips	Garden Uses	Benefits
Spearmint *Mentha spicata* Lamiaceae	Summer-blooming perennial; square stems, sharply toothed, pointed leaves; pinkish purple flowers on tall spikes; 2' tall; Zones 5 to 9	Easy to grow; spreads by underground roots that send up plentiful shoots; to control, plant in pots or with underground barrier; tolerates partial shade	Place containers of spearmint strategically around the garden	Provides shelter for spiders; attracts predatory wasps, predatory flies
Sweet Annie* *Artemisia annua* Asteraceae Summer-	blooming annual; shrubby, gray-green leaves on branching stems; tiny flowers; anise-like fragrance; 2½'–3' tall	Grows easily in most soils; self-sows abundantly, but easy to control	Let volunteers spring up around the garden wherever they suit you	Attracts parasitic wasps, hoverflies
Sweet cicely* *Myrrhis odorata* Apiaceae	Early-summer-blooming perennial; soft, fernlike leaves; delicate white 2" flowers; to 3' tall; Zones 3 to 7	Grows in part shade; prefers moist, humusy soil	Try this underused herb in a perennial border	Attracts beneficial wasps, beneficial flies
Tansy *Tanacetum vulgare* Asteraceae	Summer-blooming perennial; long, straight stems with fernlike leaves; flat clusters of tightly packed, yellow, buttonlike flowers; 3'–4' tall and wide; Zones 4 to 8	Grows in average soil and sun to partial shade; propagate by division; spreads to form a large clump	Make permanent plantings in the corners of your garden, or plant clusters here and there around the garden	Attracts a very broad range of beneficials

Perennials

Plant Names	Description	Growing Tips	Garden Uses	Benefits
Bee balms *Monarda* spp. Lamiaceae	Summer blooming; shaggy red, rose, pink, or purple flower heads; upright stems with pointed leaves; 2'–4' tall; Zones 4 to 8	Need moist soil; prone to problems with powdery mildew, so thin stems periodically to provide good air circulation	Choose a site where you can control the spread of this Mint Family plant	Attract bees, parasitic wasps, beneficial flies; beloved by hummingbirds, too

Plant Names	Description	Growing Tips	Garden Uses	Benefits
Gayfeathers *Liatris* spp. Asteraceae	Summer blooming; tall spikes of magenta flowers open from the top down; clumps of grasslike leaves; 2'–5' tall, depending on cultivar; hardiness varies with species	Grow well in most soils; may require staking in rich soil	A must-have in perennial clusters; attractive with daisies for vertical accent	Attract parasitic wasps, hoverflies, butterflies, hummingbird moths
Golden asters* *Chrysopsis* spp. Asteraceae	Summer to fall blooming; branched stems; pointed 2" leaves; 1½" yellow, asterlike flowers; 1'–5' tall, depending on species and cultivar; Zones 4 to 9	Grow in dry, sandy soil; tolerate neglect; divide in spring; pinch during growing season to encourage bushiness; tall plants may need staking	Combine with coneflowers, goldenrods, and New England asters in a perennial cluster for long-lasting summer and fall bloom	Attract a wide range of beneficials
Goldenrods *Solidago* spp. Asteraceae	Late summer to fall blooming; golden flower plumes; lance-shaped leaves; plants form large clumps that may spread; 2'–5' tall; Zones 4 to 8	Tolerate drought; grow well in poor to average garden soil; may flop in richer soils; may spring up as weeds	Plant among perennials or let volunteers grow throughout the garden; *note:* do not cause allergies	Attract a wide range of beneficials
Hardy Marguerite *Anthemis tinctoria* 'Kelwayi' Asteraceae	Summer to fall blooming; 1"–1½"-wide yellow flowers on erect stems; finely divided gray-green foliage; 1'–2' tall; Zones 3 to 8	Needs full sun; prefers lean soil; tolerates drought; deadhead and cut back for repeat flowering	Plant with herbs in rough areas that you haven't developed into garden beds yet	Attracts lady beetles, parasitic wasps
Lavender cotton *Santolina chamaecyparissus* Asteraceae	Summer blooming; dense, branching mounds of gray leaves; buttonlike yellow flower clusters; 1'–2' tall; Zones 6 to 8	Needs good drainage and full sun; tolerates drought; cut back hard after flowering	Use as edging for perennial or herb beds	Shelters predatory beetles
Painted daisy *Chrysanthemum coccineum* Asteraceae	Summer to fall blooming; ferny foliage; 3" rose, red, or pink flowers; 2' tall; Zones 3 to 7	Grows well in average soil; won't tolerate being waterlogged; shear after flowering to encourage repeat bloom	Excellent for fall garden; try it with broccoli or red cabbage for a splash of color	Attracts tachinid flies, parasitic wasps, many other beneficials

(continued)

Plants for Beneficial Insects—continued

Perennials—continued

Plant Names	Description	Growing Tips	Garden Uses	Benefits
Pincushion flowers *Scabiosa* spp. Dipsacaceae	Summer blooming; flat, 2"–3" blue, lavender, or white flower heads atop bare stems; lance-like, gray-green basal leaves; 2' tall; Zones 3 to 7	Need well-drained soil; heat sensitive, so provide afternoon shade in hot areas; deadhead regularly	Make a permanent planting at the end of a framed raised bed; plant among strawberries	Attract hoverflies, tachinid flies
Purple cone-flowers* *Echinacea* spp. Asteraceae	Summer to fall blooming; daisylike flowers with drooping purplish pink or magenta petals and bristly centers; coarse, hairy, leafy stems; about 3' tall; Zones 3 to 8	Easy to grow; somewhat prone to powdery mildew, so thin stems occasionally to encourage air circulation; propagate by division or seed	Great for a dependable summer performance in perennial clusters or hedgerows near the garden	In my garden, attract beneficial wasps, beneficial flies, spiders, praying mantids
Rock cress *Arabis caucasica* Brassicaceae	Spring to early-summer blooming; low-growing mat of gray-green leaves; upright clusters of pink or white flowers; about 8" tall; Zones 3 to 7	Prefers cool conditions; plant 18" apart or closer for quick coverage; tolerates light shade; cut back after flowering	Use as ground-cover around early-summer crops like cabbage and broccoli or wherever ground-cover is desired	Attracts bees; shelters ground beetles, spiders
Sea hollies* *Eryngium maritimum, E. alpinum, E. bourgatii* Apiaceae	Summer blooming; stiff, leathery, blue-gray, spiny foliage; silvery blue flower heads with dome-shaped centers and silvery leaflike bracts; about 1½' tall; hardiness varies with species	Need well-drained soil; will not tolerate wet feet in winter, so mulch with gravel around the crown; difficult to transplant, so plant young seedlings in permanent location; salt tolerant	Strikingly attractive at the front of a perennial cluster	Attract tiny parasitic wasps like chalcid wasps
Yarrows *Achillea millefolium, A. ptarmica* Asteraceae	Late-spring to summer blooming; ferny, gray-green foliage; flat flower heads in gold, pink, mixed pastels, and other colors; most types are 1½'–3' tall; Zones 3 to 9	Easy to care for; need full sun; tolerate poor soils; may need staking, especially in rich soil; propagate by division	Plant in perennial clusters or hedgerows	Attract many beneficials, such as hoverflies, lady beetles, parasitic wasps

Annuals				
Plant Names	**Description**	**Growing Tips**	**Garden Uses**	**Benefits**
Annual candytuft *Iberis umbellata* Brassicaceae	Late-spring to summer blooming; mounded plants with narrow leaves; white, pink, pinkish purple, rose, or red flowers in rounded clusters; 8"–12" tall and wide	Sow seeds indoors 6 to 8 weeks before last frost, or sow seeds directly in garden in early to mid-spring	Put along edges of vine crops or Cabbage Family crops; nice edging for wide rows of salad greens	Attracts hoverflies; protects ground beetles
Bachelor's buttons* *Centaurea cyanus* Asteraceae	Late-spring to summer blooming; fluffy flowers in pink through deep purple; gray-green foliage on long stems; 1'–3' tall	Sow seeds in fall or spring; quick to bloom; cut fresh flowers often to prolong flowering	Easy starter plant for new gardeners or children; a foolproof, quick performer	Provide early nectar for many beneficials
Black-eyed Susan* *Rudbeckia hirta* Asteraceae	Summer to fall blooming; 2" daisy-like flowers with slim, dark yellow petals and deep brown centers; long, hairy leaves; about 1½' tall	Easy to grow; needs well-drained soil; plant seeds outdoors in fall or early spring; self-sows easily	Good companion for most crops; let volunteers spring up, but pull seedlings if too prolific	Attracts hoverflies, parasitic wasps
Blanket flower* *Gaillardia pulchella* Asteraceae	Midspring to summer blooming; daisylike flowers in yellow, orange, or red; narrow, hairy gray-green leaves; about 1' tall	Heat tolerant and fast growing; start indoors 6 weeks before last frost date; set transplants outside after last frost	Colorful midsize dynamo among green vegetables; select single-flowered forms rather than double	Provides nectar for many beneficials
Blue-eyed African daisy* *Arctotis stoechadifolia* Asteraceae	Summer to fall blooming; daisy-like flower, available in many colors; hairy gray leaves; 2'–3' tall	Plant seeds outside after frost, or transplant seedlings for earlier bloom; cut fresh flowers often to prolong bloom	Use as a companion plant for Cabbage Family crops and Tomato Family crops; great with all fall garden crops	Provides nectar for a wide range of beneficials
Calendula *Calendula officinalis* Asteraceae	Summer to fall blooming; bright red, orange, or gold flowers, resembling marigolds; pale green leaves; 1'–2' tall	Easy to grow; plant seeds outside in fall or spring	Plant anywhere and everywhere in the garden; good companion for Cabbage Family and other midsize crops	Attracts a variety of beneficials

(continued)

Plants for Beneficial Insects—continued

Annuals—continued

Plant Names	Description	Growing Tips	Garden Uses	Benefits
Calliopsis *Coreopsis tinctoria* Asteraceae	Midsummer to fall blooming; daisylike flowers with bands of yellow and red on petals; deeply divided leaves; 2'–3' tall	Needs well-drained soil; sow seeds thickly outdoors in early spring; sow second crop in early August for fall flowers	Good companion for tomatoes, peppers, or fall crops	Attracts hoverflies, spined soldier bugs, tachinid flies
Cosmos *Cosmos bipinnatus* Asteraceae	Summer blooming; 2"–4" white, pink, or rosy red flowers with yellow centers; fine, threadlike leaves; 4'–6' tall	Easy to grow; sow seeds outdoors after danger of frost; often self-sows; plants on windy sites may topple	Sow seed or let volunteers spring up around the garden; 'White Sensation' is very attractive to beneficials	Attracts parasitic wasps, hoverflies, tachinid flies, bees
Dwarf morning glory *Convolvulus tricolor* Convulvulaceae	Midsummer to fall blooming; vine or bushy plant with blue and white funnel-shaped flowers; rose and pink flowers also available; to 1' tall	Needs moist but well-drained soil; sow seeds outdoors 1 to 2 weeks before last frost; rub seeds with sandpaper and soak overnight before planting	Nice edging plants for raised beds; *caution:* poisonous; don't use it if children or other family members may mistake it as an edible flower	Attracts hoverflies, lady beetles
Gazania* *Gazania linearis* Asteraceae	Late-spring to summer blooming; yellow, orange, or red, daisylike flowers with dark centers; forms low mats of foliage; 6"–16" tall	Drought tolerant; needs well-drained, lean soil; flowers poorly in rich soil; start seeds indoors 6 to 8 weeks before last frost date	Good choice for companion garden for its flower shape and long bloom	Popular with lady beetles and spined soldier bugs
Marigolds *Tagetes erecta, T. patula, T. tenuifolia* Asteraceae	Summer blooming; single or double flowers in colors from yellow through orange, red, and rust; 5"–30" tall	Start seeds inside 4 to 6 weeks before last frost; pinch growing tips for bushier plants; deadhead frequently	Plant throughout the garden; choose single-flowered types; *T. tenuifolia* 'Lemon Gem' is especially attractive to beneficials	Attract hoverflies, parasitic wasps
Mexican sunflower* *Tithonia rotundifolia* Asteraceae	Summer to fall blooming; bright red-orange flowers on tall, shrubby plants; large, coarse, rounded leaves with pointed tips; 4'–5' tall	Likes a hot, dry climate; start seeds indoors 6 to 8 weeks before last frost; set out transplants after last frost; don't water or fertilize too much	Dramatic, bright flowers for the back of a perennial cluster or interplanted with tomatoes, peppers, and eggplant	Attracts beneficial wasps and flies, spined soldier bugs; shelters spiders

Plant Names	Description	Growing Tips	Garden Uses	Benefits
Common sunflower *Helianthus annuus* Asteraceae	Summer to fall blooming; 6"–12" flower heads; flowers available in many colors; heart-shaped leaves; 2'–10' tall, depending on variety	Sow seeds outdoors after last frost; thin seedlings to 1' apart	Plant among tall crops like corn or at the corners of garden beds	Attracts hoverflies, lacewings, parasitic wasps, tachinid flies, bees
Swan River daisy *Brachycome iberidifolia* Asteraceae	Midsummer to fall blooming; blue, pink, rose, or white, daisylike flowers with gold centers; deeply cut leaves; 9"–18" tall	Start seeds indoors 6 to 8 weeks before last frost; set out transplants after risk of frost is past; plant in successions for prolonged bloom	A delicate companion for fall lettuces, spinach, or late onions	Attracts tachinid flies
Sweet alyssum *Lobularia maritima* Brassicaceae	Summer to fall blooming; tiny white, pale pink, or pale purple flowers; forms low mounds; 3"–8" tall	Sow seeds indoors 4 to 6 weeks before last frost date, or sow outside 2 to 3 weeks before last frost; may self-sow	Use as a ground-cover around vegetables throughout the garden; white varieties are attractive with vegetables	Attracts and shelters ground beetles, spiders
Common zinnia *Zinnia elegans* Asteraceae	Summer to fall blooming; 1"–4" flowers bloom in a wide range of colors and shapes; coarse, pointed leaves; 4"–36" tall, depending on variety	Grows in well-drained soil; direct-seed outdoors after last frost; blooms in summer until the first frost	Plant near beans or interplant with broccoli or other summer and fall crops	Attracts lady beetles, parasitic wasps, parasitic flies, bees

Weeds/Wildflowers

Plant Names	Description	Growing Tips	Garden Uses	Benefits
Wild asters* *Aster* spp. Asteraceae	Late-summer- to fall-blooming perennials; hairy leaves; clusters of purple flowers with yellow centers at the tips of leafy branches; 2'–4' tall	Prefer moist soil; will spring up in fields and grass-lands in northern and central United States; cut back in early summer to promote bushiness	Watch for volunteer seedlings and permit them to grow all around the garden; pull up at end of season	Shelter ambush bugs; flowers may attract many kinds of beneficials
Buttercups *Ranunculus* spp. Ranunculaceae	Spring-blooming perennial; yellow, cuplike flowers atop spindly stems; ferny foliage; 1½' tall	Found in poor soils, fields, along roadsides; indicator of infertile, alkaline soil	Allow occasional volunteers to bloom in the garden; helpful clue to soil problems	Attract parasitic wasps

(continued)

Plants for Beneficial Insects—continued

Weeds/Wildflowers—continued

Plant Names	Description	Growing Tips	Garden Uses	Benefits
Corn spurrey *Spergula arvensis* Caryophyllaceae	Summer-blooming annual; loose clusters of white flowers atop slender stems; narrow, fleshy leaves; 6"–18" tall	Grows well on poor, sandy soil	Can use it as a green manure crop	Best single attractor of hoverflies
Dandelion *Taraxacum officinale* Asteraceae	Spring-blooming perennial; deeply toothed basal leaves; reddish, hollow stalk emerges topped by a mounded yellow flower cluster that turns into a puffy white seed head; 6"–10" tall	Grows in meadows and lawns and along roadsides; needs a sunny site; new plants can sprout from small pieces of root	In the garden, pull the plants and compost to capture nutrients; allow some dandelions to flower in the lawn nearby	Provides early nectar source for lady beetles; taproots bring up nutrients from deep in the soil
Lamb's-quarters *Chenopodium album* Chenopodiaceae	Early-summer- to fall-blooming annual; egg-shaped, toothed leaves on upright red-streaked stems; leaves are edible; tiny green flowers; 1'–3' tall	Thrive in poor soils; self-sow freely; pull unwanted plants before flowers form and add them to a compost pile	Permit a few to grow in the garden, but cut off flower stalks before they set seed	Attract parasitic wasps
Wild mustards *Brassica* spp. Brassicaceae	Summer-blooming annual; coarse, hairy plant; yellow flowers on erect stems; notched, bristly leaves; about 2' tall	Found in waste areas, along road-sides	Permit a few to grow in perennial clusters, herb beds, or hedgerows	Attract parasitic wasps, hoverflies, tachinid flies
Oxeye daisy *Chrysanthemum leucanthemum* Asteraceae	Early-summer-blooming perennial; 1"–2" white flowers with yellow centers; spoon-shaped leaves; 1'–1½' tall	Grows in any soil; needs staking in fertile soils	Great volunteer to let grow in place right in the garden	Attracts lady beetles, parasitic wasps, tachinid flies

Plant Names	Description	Growing Tips	Garden Uses	Benefits
Queen-Anne's-lace *Daucus carota* var. *carota* Apiaceae	Spring- to fall-blooming biennial; finely divided gray-green leaves; flat, white, lacy flower clusters; to 3' tall	Springs up in any open area; difficult to transplant	Permit volunteers to grow wherever they sprout in the garden	Attracts and shelters a wide range of beneficials
Red sorrel *Rumex acetosella* Polygonaceae	Spring- to late-summer-blooming perennial; jade green, arrow-shaped leaves on erect, branching stems; small, reddish green flowers; 2'–2½' tall	Common along roadsides and meadows throughout North America; can indicate acid or poorly drained soil	If you permit volunteers to grow, deadhead them before they set seed, because they self-sow prolifically	Attracts parasitic wasps

Cover Crops

Plant Names	Description	Growing Tips	Garden Uses	Benefits
Alfalfa *Medicago sativa* Fabaceae	Perennial; bushy plants with tiny green leaves; yellow flowers; deep taproots; about 1½' tall	Tolerates drought, but not wet soil; plant in spring for summer coverage; legume, so helps build soil nitrogen	Use as border beside or near the garden	Attracts many kinds of predatory bugs, parasitic wasps
Buckwheat *Fagopyrum esculentum* Polygonaceae	Annual; lime green, heart-shaped leaves on hollow stems; white flower clusters appear 6 to 7 weeks after planting; shallow root system	Plant 1 to 2 weeks before the last frost date; turn under when in flower; replant for continual coverage	Keep buckwheat planted in some part of the garden all season; excellent as perimeter planting	Attracts parasitic wasps, beneficial flies, bees; shelters spiders, ground beetles
Clovers *Trifolium pratense, T. repens, T. incarnatum; T. subterraneum* Fabaceae	Perennial and annual; round white, pink, or red flower heads and branched stems; round leaves in sets of three; 4"–36" tall, depending on species	Sow in spring or summer; tolerate shade and drought	Use as a cover crop on empty beds or in pathways, or as a living mulch under tall vegetables	Attract ground beetles, parasitic wasps, spiders, bees
Winter rye *Secale cereale* Poaceae	Annual; tall grain crop with grasslike leaves	Sow seeds in fall 2 to 3 weeks before first frost; turn under in spring when leaves reach 10"–12" tall	Prevents soil erosion; provides organic matter and blocks weeds	Attracts rove beetles

Plants That (May) Keep Pests Away

Here's a listing of companion plants reputed to repel garden pests. Choose some of them as plant friends for your vegetable families. Many of these recommendations are based on tradition and folklore alone, so don't rely too heavily on them for pest protection. Experiment for yourself. You may find that some of these plants do a great job in your garden.

Companion Plant	Pests Repelled	Companion-Garden Uses
Basil	Aphids, asparagus beetles, mites, mosquitoes, tomato hornworms	Plant next to paths where you'll brush it often, releasing the aromatic oil that may confuse pests; try it along the edge of asparagus beds and among tomatoes and eggplants
Borage	Tomato hornworms	Plant with tomatoes, and let it self-sow throughout the garden to attract beneficial bees and other insects
Calendula	Asparagus beetles	Definitely attracts beneficials, so plant throughout the garden as well as by your asparagus
Catnip	Aphids, asparagus beetles, Colorado potato beetles, squash bugs	Catnip's repellent qualities are backed by research; can spread uncontrollably, so plant in pots and place them near or among peppers, potatoes, tomatoes, and vine crops
Chives	Aphids, Japanese beetles, probably many insects	Excellent perennial herb to place around roses, raspberries, grapevines—or wherever Japanese beetles are a problem
Garlic	Japanese beetles, many other pests	Plant around roses or other flowers that suffer from Japanese beetles, especially in a cutting garden; or mix a spray from crushed garlic and water
Zonal geraniums	Japanese beetles	Tests show these flowers, especially white-flowered types, repel and even kill Japanese beetles; try among roses or other crops that Japanese beetles favor; may also work as a trap crop by attracting the beetle
Horseradish	Colorado potato beetles	Not a practical companion for potatoes, because it's a spreading perennial; plant among other permanent plantings, such as asparagus, raspberries, strawberries, and perhaps rhubarb
Hyssop	Cabbage moths	Some studies back this claim; try planting among broccoli, brussels sprouts, cabbage, and cauliflower
Marigolds	Mexican bean beetles, root-knot nematodes, root lesion nematodes	Strong evidence supports repellent qualities for nematodes; plant a solid block in nematode-infested areas; at flowering, chop and turn under entire crop

Companion Plant	Pests Repelled	Companion-Garden Uses
Mints	Aphids, cabbage moths, possibly other pest insects	Very invasive; surround with a solid root barrier or grow in pots
Nasturtiums	Aphids, Colorado potato beetles, Mexican bean beetles, squash bugs	Studies show conflicting evidence; plant with vine crops to protect ground beetles and spiders and to act as a pretty living mulch
Onions	Carrot rust flies	Research backs interplanting with carrots to repel rust flies; intermingle the crops or plant clusters or strips of onions and carrots side by side
Parsley	Asparagus beetles	Plant on the edges of asparagus beds; it often survives over winter; let some go to flower to attract beneficials
Radishes	Cucumber beetles	There's some evidence that radishes do confuse cucumber beetles; plant three to five seeds in every "hill" or cluster of cucumber plants; also plant among squashes and pumpkins
Rosemary	Cabbage moths, carrot rust flies, Mexican bean beetles	Plant among beans and Cabbage Family crops, or beside lettuce and carrot combinations.
Rue	Japanese beetles	Traditional reports also list rue as a growth inhibitor for some plants; not practical except among plantings of perennials; *caution:* touching the foliage may cause allergic reaction
Sage	Cabbage moths, carrot rust flies, others	Include in a perennial herb or flower border
Savory	Mexican bean beetles	Plant on the edges of tomato/bean plantings or in perennial herb areas around the garden
Southern-wood and wormwood	Flea beetles, mosquitoes	Plant in perennial clusters or herb borders near or beside the garden, and use them near areas where people congregate (we rub them on our skin as mosquito repellents)
Tansy	Colorado potato beetles, squash bugs	Some tests support tansy as a repellent, but the best reason to plant is to attract beneficial insects (see page 250)
Thyme	Cabbage moths	Studies back this claim: plant near Cabbage Family crops or in any perennial/herb combination near the vegetable garden; creeping thymes are excellent groundcovers for permanent plantings

Preventing Pest Problems

As an organic gardener, I'm sure you don't want to wage war against pests with sprays and dusts. With my companion-gardening system you won't have to. For the most part, the beneficial insects and animals your garden attracts will keep pests in check. But occasional pest problems will arise in your garden. Here you'll find my suggestions for preventing and controlling damage by 12 of the most common vegetable-garden pests. Some of the suggestions involve making barriers or traps to keep pests from reaching your crops. You'll also find summaries of the beneficial insects that target each pest and the companion plants that either repel the pest or attract the beneficial allies you need.

APHIDS (Aphididae)

ADULT
Actual
size = 1/10"

Description: Aphids are soft-bodied, pear-shaped insects that may be pale green, brown, yellow, pink, blue, or black. Aphids are usually wingless, but you'll sometimes see winged females. Adults are less than 1/10 inch long.

Damage: Aphids suck plant juices, causing leaves to curl up and turn yellow. Aphids feed on a wide range of fruits, vegetables, and flowers. You may find ants on plants infested with aphids. The ants actually protect the aphids in order to feed on the sticky "honeydew" that the aphids secrete.

Prevention and controls: Remove plant debris, till the soil in fall, rotate crops, and use row covers—especially on Cabbage Family crops. Avoid heavy nitrogen feeding, which attracts aphids. Place aluminum foil around the base of young plants, especially peppers and cucumbers. If aphid populations build up, spray plants hard with water from a hose to kill the aphids, but check plants first for lady beetles or their eggs or larvae.

Natural enemies: Many beneficials eat aphids including assassin bugs, big-eyed bugs, chalcid wasps, lacewings, lady beetles, soldier bugs, and spiders.

APHIDS ON PEA

Plant companions: To attract aphid-eating beneficials, plant companions from the Aster and Parsley Families, as well as groundcovers such as sweet alyssum or clover. Onions and garlic may repel aphids. Trap crops for aphids include early cabbage, marigolds, and nasturtiums.

CABBAGE LOOPER (Trichoplusia ni)

LARVA
Actual
size = 1½"

Description: Cabbage loopers are light green caterpillars that have two white stripes down the back. They crawl by "looping" their bodies inchworm-style. The adult is a gray moth that flies at night. Larvae grow to 1½ inches long.

Damage: Cabbage loopers chew holes in the leaves of broccoli, brussels sprouts, cabbage, cauliflower, and other Cabbage Family crops. They sometimes feed on beets, celery, lettuce, peas, and spinach.

ADULT
Actual
size = 1½"–2"

Prevention and controls: The best way to prevent cabbage loopers from feeding on plants is to cover crops with row covers at planting and leave them in place until harvest. Also be sure to remove all crop residues from the Cabbage Family after harvest. The larvae are hard to spot on plants. The first time you notice them may be when they appear in cooking water or a salad! If you suspect that cabbage loopers have infiltrated your broccoli, try soaking it in salty water for several minutes before cooking. The larvae should rise to the top of the water.

Natural enemies: Yellow jackets eat huge numbers of caterpillars, and many parasitic wasps target cabbage loopers.

Plant companions: Choose nectar-producing Aster Family plants that flower early (such as English daisies and calendulas) and late (such as asters and cosmos). Allow some seedlings of wild daisies and Queen-Anne's-lace to grow in your Cabbage Family neighborhood. Plant permanent clumps of tansy or yarrow nearby.

COLORADO POTATO BEETLE *(Leptinotarsa decemlineata)*

ADULT
Actual
size = ⅓"

Description: Colorado potato beetles are hard-shelled, round beetles with black and yellow stripes running lengthwise down their bodies. The beetles have orange heads with black dots. Eggs are orange, laid in rows on the underside of leaves. Larvae are plump orange grubs with two rows of black dots on each side of the body. Adults are ⅓ inch long.

Damage: Clusters of beetles and larvae quickly strip all the foliage off of plants. They are especially damaging to potatoes but also feed on cabbage, eggplant, peppers, tomatoes, and even petunias. You can usually spot the eggs, larvae, and adults, or you may notice black excrement on the leaves of infested plants.

LARVA

Prevention and controls: Use straw mulch to keep adults that emerge from the soil from reaching plants. Cover plants with row covers at planting. Try planting potatoes on the soil surface with a 1-foot straw mulch on top. Till the soil in fall. Look for clusters of orange eggs on the undersides of leaves and squash them. Handpick and destroy larvae and adult beetles.

Natural enemies: Colorado potato beetle predators include ground beetles, spined soldier bugs, and two-spotted stinkbugs, as well as birds and toads. One species of parasitic wasp, *Edovum puttleri,* is available commercially from mail-order firms that specialize in beneficial insects. Tachinid flies lay eggs on the beetles, and the fly larvae feed on and kill the beetles. However, the flies usually arrive too late to help prevent damage on most crops.

Plant companions: Tests show that alternating rows of potatoes with rows of bush beans radically decreases the number of Colorado potato beetles on the potatoes. To repel the beetles, try planting garlic among your potatoes and planting horseradish in a permanent bed nearby. Plant tansy, yarrow, and other Aster Family plants to encourage beneficials. Provide low water dishes and shelters to encourage toads.

CORN EARWORM *(Helicoverpa zea)*

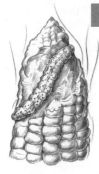

**LARVA
Actual
size = up to 1½"**

Description: Corn earworms are green or brown caterpillars with dark stripes down the side. They are also called tomato fruitworms. The adults are tan moths. Larvae can be up to 1½ inches long.

Damage: Corn earworms chew on corn tassels and bore into the ends of ears of corn. These pests also chew into tomato fruits.

Prevention and controls: Plant early to avoid damage to corn. When the silks begin to turn brown, pull back the tips of the wrapper leaves, and remove the worms. Or apply drops of mineral oil to the tips of the ears at that time.

Natural enemies: Tachinid flies and *Trichogramma* wasps parasitize this pest.

Plant companions: Plant clover or buckwheat between rows of corn. Plant Carrot Family herbs like dill and coriander with tomatoes. Allow some Queen-Anne's-lace plants to spring up in your corn and tomato patches.

CUTWORMS *(Noctuidae)*

**LARVA
Actual
size = up to 2"**

Description: Cutworms are brown or gray caterpillars with shiny heads. You may find them curled up just below the soil surface near vegetable transplants. The adults are brown or gray moths. Caterpillars grow to 2 inches long.

Damage: Cutworms chew on plant stems at night, sometimes severing plants from their roots. They feed on a wide range on vegetables and flowers.

Prevention and controls: Put collars made from cardboard tubes, heavy paper, or metal cans around the stems of newly planted transplants, and push the collars about 1 inch below soil level. Dig in the soil around damaged plants, and destroy any cutworms you unearth.

Natural enemies: Ground beetles, nematodes, and birds prey on cutworms.

Plant companions: Plant narrow borders of low-growing groundcovers such as sweet alyssum, or edge your garden with buckwheat.

FLEA BEETLES *(Chrysomelidae)*

**ADULT
Actual
size = ¹⁄₁₀"**

Description: Most types of flea beetles are shiny and black. Others have yellow or white stripes on their backs. The beetles jump when they're disturbed. The larvae are white soil-dwelling grubs. Adults are ¹⁄₁₀ inch long.

Damage: Leaves riddled with tiny holes are a sign of flea beetle feeding. Damage tends to be the worst in spring. The beetles favor eggplant, radishes, potatoes, and Cabbage Family crops, but will feed on many other crops.

Prevention and controls: Cover crops with row covers at planting. Cultivate the soil frequently to destroy flea beetle eggs. Clean up plant debris in fall. Plant radishes and Chinese cabbage as trap crops. Flea beetles don't like moisture or

DAMAGE

shade, so "hide" shade-tolerant vegetables between rows of taller crops, and water them often. Space plants closely and mulch well to keep conditions moist.

Natural enemies: Ground beetles and parasitic wasps prey upon these pests, but for best results, rely on the preventive measures above to avoid problems.

Plant companions: Interplanting crops has been shown to reduce flea beetle populations. Try alternating rows of Cabbage Family and Tomato Family plants. Plant crops closely and provide permanent mulch to attract ground beetles.

IMPORTED CABBAGEWORM *(Artogeia rapae)*

**LARVA
Actual
size = up to 1¼"**

Description: Imported cabbageworms are light green caterpillars with a single yellow stripe down their backs. The adult is a small white butterfly that flits around gardens in the daytime. Larvae grow to 1¼ inches long.

Damage: Imported cabbageworms chew large holes in leaves and leave dark green droppings on plants. They feed on all Cabbage Family crops.

Prevention and controls: Cover plants with row cover at planting and leave it in place until harvest. Destroy all Cabbage Family crop residues after harvest. If you suspect that your broccoli has cabbageworms, soak the broccoli in salty water before cooking. The worms will rise to the water's surface.

Natural enemies: Yellow jackets and parasitic wasps target these pests.

**ADULT
Actual
size = 1½"**

Plant companions: Plant Aster Family plants that flower early (such as English daisies and calendulas) and late (such as asters and cosmos). Let some wild daisies and Queen-Anne's-lace sprout among your Cabbage Family crops. Permanent clumps of tansy or yarrow nearby will also attract parasitic wasps.

JAPANESE BEETLE *(Popillia japonica)*

**ADULT
Actual size = ½"**

Description: Japanese beetles are very shiny, blue-green beetles with bronze wing covers and spiny-looking legs. The larvae are fat white grubs with brown heads that live in the soil. Adults are ½ inch long.

Damage: Japanese beetles chew on leaves, leaving a skeletonized effect. They also feed on flowers. The beetles attack a broad range of vegetables, fruits, and ornamentals. The larvae feed on roots of garden plants and lawn grasses.

Prevention and controls: Use trap crops to lure beetles away from your garden plants. Shake beetles off plants into a bucket of soapy water.

Natural enemies: The most effective natural enemies of this pest are milky spore disease and parasitic nematodes. You can buy products containing these organisms from garden-supply firms. Follow label directions for use.

LARVA

Plant companions: Four-o'clocks are one of the best trap crops for Japanese beetles. Check the trap plants daily, and shake the beetles off into soapy water, or uproot the trap-crop plants and dunk them in a large bucket of soapy water.

MEXICAN BEAN BEETLE *(Epilachna varivestis)*

ADULT
Actual size = ¼"

Description: Mexican bean beetles are oval, tan beetles with 16 black spots arranged in three rows on the back. They resemble lady beetles. The larvae are spiny, plump yellow grubs. Eggs are bright yellow ovals laid on leaf undersides. Adults are ¼ inch long.

Damage: Mexican bean beetles and their larvae chew on bean leaves, leaving leaf "skeletons" behind. They are especially prevalent in early summer, sometimes damaging leaves so severely that yield is reduced.

Prevention and controls: Mexican bean beetles cause the most damage in weed-free, beans-only sections of gardens, so companion gardening is the perfect cure. Just mix beneficial insect-attracting plants generously in your bean plantings. Try planting varieties that are resistant to Mexican bean beetles. Dig bean plant residues into the soil immediately after harvest. Plant soybeans as a trap crop. You can search out and squash egg clusters and handpick any larvae you find on the leaves.

Natural enemies: Spined soldier bugs and assassin bugs attack Mexican bean beetles, and many parasitic wasps also use this pest as a host.

Plant companions: Interplant beans with potatoes, chamomile, sage, savory, or dill. Let some flowering weeds like Queen-Anne's-lace, goldenrod, and wild daisies grow among your beans. Soybeans work well as a trap crop for Mexican bean beetles.

LARVA

SLUGS *(Mollusca)*

ADULT
Size varies with species

Description: Slugs are not insects. These soft-bodied gray or tan creatures are actually mollusks (related to shellfish). They leave a trail of mucus behind as they crawl. Adults are generally from ⅛ inch to 1½ inches long. Some species are as large as 8 inches.

Damage: Slugs chew large ragged holes in leaves and leave behind their slimy trails. They will feed on most garden plants, especially in damp or shaded conditions. Slugs particularly favor lettuce and low-growing greens.

Prevention and controls: To keep slugs away from your plants buy copper strips and use them as a boundary around plants or whole beds. Or sprinkle wood ashes or ground-up eggshells around plants. Set out boards, large cabbage leaves, and overturned grapefruit rinds in your garden as slug traps. Knock slugs out of the traps into soapy water to kill them. Sink dishes of beer or yeast into the soil to attract and drown slugs. Hand-picking slugs early in the season can eliminate a large number of these pests.

Natural enemies: Ground beetles, rove beetles, birds, snakes, toads, and lizards eat slugs. Centipedes and firefly larvae (glowworms) eat slug eggs.

Plant companions: Plant clover, sweet alyssum, buckwheat, and other low-growing plants to shelter predatory beetles. Put out rock "houses" to encourage toads and lizards to stay nearby and hunt slugs.

SQUASH BUG *(Anasa tristis)*

**ADULT
Actual size = ⅝"**

Description: Squash bugs are oval, dull black or gray bugs. The immature stages (nymphs) resemble the adults but may be pale green or red. The eggs are yellow or red, laid in clusters on leaf undersides. Adults are about ⅝ inch long.

Damage: Squash bugs suck plant juices from leaves and stems of vine crops, including cucumbers, gourds, melons, pumpkins, and squash. The leaves shrivel, and growing tips blacken and die; the plants may look diseased.

Prevention and controls: Plant resistant varieties. Avoid heavy mulches, which can shelter the bugs. Cover plants with row covers at planting and leave the covers on until the plants are in flower. Handpick the bugs and squish egg masses. At fall cleanup, leave a few plants in the garden to attract the remaining squash bugs. Then collect these plants, seal them inside plastic trash bags, and dispose of them with your household trash.

Natural enemies: Tachinid flies parasitize squash bugs.

Plant companions: Plant clover, dill, fennel, and yarrow with your Squash Family crops, and allow some Queen-Anne's-lace plants to spring up among the vines.

TARNISHED PLANT BUG *(Lygus lineolaris)*

**ADULT
Actual
size = ¼"**

Description: Tarnished plant bugs are oval, fast-moving insects, with a mottled brown, yellow, and black pattern on their bodies. The wings show a triangle design. The nymphs are yellow-green, wingless insects that look similar to the adults. Adults are ¼ inch long.

Damage: Both adults and nymphs suck plant juices and emit toxic saliva that causes distorted leaves and buds. Buds will drop off plants, and branch tips die back. Plants may be stunted. In strawberries, feeding on the fruit causes "catfacing." Tarnished plant bugs may attack almost any plant in your garden—they feed on a wider range of plants than any other insect pest.

Prevention and controls: Cover plants with row covers at planting. Clean up all plant debris near plants that have suffered damage in the past.

Natural enemies: Minute pirate bugs, big-eyed bugs, and damsel bugs prey on tarnished plant bugs.

Plant companions: Plant clover, alfalfa, hairy vetch, and other groundcovers in your garden to attract the predators. Daisies and yarrow will attract minute pirate bugs.

Sources

I LIVE NEAR SOME wonderful nurseries and garden centers, so I buy almost all of my plants locally. I like to shop at these local businesses because I want them to stay in business, and I encourage you to do the same.

However, I don't recommend buying plants or supplies from all-purpose chain stores. I don't think the quality of the plants or the service can measure up to good local businesses or good mail-order companies.

If you're not as fortunate as I am when it comes to local sources for garden supplies and plants, you can trust the companies listed below for quality seeds, supplies, and plants.

Contact these businesses to find out how to get copies of their catalogs. Some catalogs are free, while others may be available for a small fee; this fee is often credited toward your first order.

SEEDS

The Cook's Garden
P.O. Box 535
Londonderry, VT 05148
Phone: (802) 824-3400
Fax: (802) 824-3027

Johnny's Selected Seeds
Foss Hill Rd.
Albion, ME 04910
Phone: (207) 437-4301
Fax: (800) 437-4290 (in USA)
(207) 437-2165 (outside USA)
E-mail: homegarden@johnnyseeds.com
Web site: http://www.johnnyseeds.com

Nichols Garden Nursery
1190 N. Pacific Hwy.
Albany, OR 97321-4580
Phone: (541) 928-9280

Pinetree Garden Seeds
Box 300
New Gloucester, ME 04260
Phone: (207) 926-3400
Fax: (207) 926-3886

Ronniger's Seed Potatoes
P.O. Box 1838
Orting, WA 98360

Shepherd's Garden Seeds
30 Irene St.
Torrington, CT 06790
Phone: (860) 482-3638
Fax: (860) 482-0532
E-mail: garden@shepherdseeds.com
Web site:
    http://www.shepherdseeds.com

Territorial Seed Co.
P.O. Box 157
20 Palmer Ave.
Cottage Grove, OR 97424
Phone: (541) 942-9547
Fax: (541) 942-9881

GARDEN SUPPLIES

Bountiful Gardens
18001 Shafer Ranch Rd.
Willits, CA 95490-9626
Phone: (707) 459-6410

Gardener's Supply Company
128 Intervale Rd.
Burlington, VT 05401
Phone: (800) 863-1700
Fax: (800) 551-6712
E-mail: info@gardeners.com
Web site: http://www.gardeners.com

Gardens Alive!
5100 Schenley Pl.
Lawrenceburg, IN 47025
Phone: (812) 537-8650
Fax: (812) 537-5108
E-mail: 76375.2160@compuserve.com

The Green Spot
Department of Bio-Ingenuity
93 Priest Rd.
Nottingham, NH 03290-6204
Phone: (603) 942-8925
Fax: (603) 942-8932

A. M. Leonard, Inc.
241 Fox Dr.
P.O. Box 816
Piqua, Ohio 45356
Phone: (800) 543-8955
Fax: (800) 433-0633

Peaceful Valley Farm Supply
P.O. Box 2209
Grass Valley, CA 95945
Phone: (916) 272-4769
Fax: (916) 272-4794

PERENNIALS

Bluestone Perennials, Inc.
7211 Middle Ridge Rd.
Madison, OH 44057
Phone: (800) 852-5243
Fax: (216) 428-7198

Heronswood Nursery
7530 NE 288th St.
Kingston, WA 98346
Phone: (360) 297-4172
Fax: (360) 297-8321

Milaeger's Gardens
4838 Douglas Ave.
Racine, WI 53402-2498
Phone: (800) 669-9956

Roslyn Nursery
211 Burrs Ln.
Dix Hills, NY 11746
Phone: (516) 643-9347

Shady Oaks Nursery
112 10th Ave. SE
Waseca, MN 56093
Phone: (800) 504-8006

Andre Viette Farm and Nursery
Rt. 1, Box 16
Fishersville, VA 22939
Phone: (540) 943-2315
Fax: (540) 943-0782

Wayside Gardens
1 Garden Ln.
Hodges, SC 29695-0001
Phone: (800) 845-1124
Fax: (800) 457-9712

White Flower Farm
P.O. Box 50
Litchfield, CT 06759-0050
Phone: (800) 503-9624
Fax: (860) 496-1418
Web site:
    http://www.whiteflowerfarm.com

Recommended Reading

GARDENING AND READING go hand in hand. Reading leads us to try new plants and techniques in our gardens, and then new questions lead us back to read some more. You can't be a good gardener just by reading, but I can't imagine being a gardener *without* reading.

To me, the following list of books is like a gathering of dear friends. I offer these books with love and appreciation for the authors and editors who brought so much to my life. I give them credit for a great deal of what I know and believe about gardening.

ORGANIC GARDENING

Benjamin, Joan, ed. *Great Garden Shortcuts.* Emmaus, PA: Rodale Press, 1996.

Bradley, Fern Marshall, ed. *Rodale's Garden Answers: Vegetables, Fruits and Herbs.* Emmaus, PA: Rodale Press, 1995.

Bradley, Fern Marshall, and Barbara W. Ellis, eds. *Rodale's All-New Encyclopedia of Organic Gardening.* Emmaus, PA: Rodale Press, 1992.

Bubel, Nancy. *The New Seed-Starter's Handbook.* Emmaus, PA: Rodale Press, 1988.

Campbell, Stu. *Let It Rot.* Charlotte, VT: Garden Way Publishing, 1975.

Coleman, Eliot. *The New Organic Grower.* Chelsea, VT: Chelsea Green Publishing Co., 1995.

Creasy, Rosalind. *The Complete Book of Edible Landscaping.* San Francisco: Sierra Club Books, 1982.

Ellis, Barbara W., ed. *Rodale's Illustrated Encyclopedia of Gardening and Landscaping Techniques.* Emmaus, PA: Rodale Press, 1990.

Garrett, J. Howard. *J. Howard Garrett's Organic Manual.* Dallas, TX: Lantana Publishing Co., 1989.

Jeavons, John. *How to Grow More Vegetables Than You Ever Thought Possible on Less Land Than You Can Imagine.* 5th ed. Berkeley, CA: Ten Speed Press, 1995.

Michalak, Patricia S., and Cass Peterson. *Rodale's Successful Organic Gardening: Vegetables.* Emmaus, PA: Rodale Press, 1993.

Raymond, Dick. *Down-to-Earth Gardening Know-How for the '90s: Vegetables and Herbs.* Pownal, VT: Storey Communications, 1991.

Smith, Miranda, and members of the Northeast Organic Farming Association and Cooperative Extension, eds. *The Real Dirt: Farmers Tell about Organic and Low-Input Practices in the Northeast.* Burlington, VT: Northeast Organic Farming Association, 1994.

Wallace, Daniel, ed. *Getting the Most from Your Garden.* Emmaus, PA: Rodale Press, 1986.

INSECTS (BENEFICIALS AND PESTS)

Carr, Anna. *Rodale's Color Handbook of Garden Insects.* Emmaus, PA: Rodale Press, 1983.

Ellis, Barbara W., and Fern Marshall Bradley, eds. *The Organic Gardener's Handbook of Natural Insect and Disease Control.* Emmaus, PA: Rodale Press, 1992.

Flint, Mary Louise. *Pests of the Garden and Small Farm.* Oakland, CA: ANR Publications of the University of California, 1990. (Available from Publications, Division of Agriculture and Natural Resources, University of California, 6701 San Pablo Ave., Oakland, CA 94608.)

Gilkeson, Linda A., Pam Peirce, and Miranda Smith. *Rodale's Pest & Disease Problem Solver.* Emmaus, PA: Rodale Press, 1996.

Hoffmann, Michael P., and Anne C. Frodsham. *Natural Enemies of Vegetable Insect Pests.* Ithaca, NY: Cornell Cooperative Extension, 1993.

Michalak, Patricia S., and Linda A. Gilkeson. *Rodale's Successful Organic Gardening: Controlling Pests and Diseases.* Emmaus, PA: Rodale Press, 1994.

Milne, Lorus, and Margery Milne. *The Audubon Society Field Guide to North American Insects and Spiders.* New York: Alfred A. Knopf, 1980.

Nancarrow, Loren, and Janet Hogan Taylor. *Dead Snails Leave No Trails.* Berkeley, CA: Ten Speed Press, 1996.

National Audubon Society. *The Audubon Society Field Guide to North American Butterflies.* New York: Alfred A. Knopf, 1981.

Olkowski, William, Sheila Daar, and Helga Olkowski. *Common Sense Pest Control.* Newtown, CT: The Taunton Press, 1991.

Starcher, Allison Mia. *Good Bugs for Your Garden.* Chapel Hill, NC: Algonquin Books of Chapel Hill, 1995.

COMPANION PLANTING

Carr, Anna. *Good Neighbors: Companion Planting for Gardeners.* Emmaus, PA: Rodale Press, 1985.

Jones, Louisa. *The Art of French Vegetable Gardening.* New York: Artisan, 1995.

Kourik, Robert. *Designing and Maintaining Your Edible Landscape Naturally.* Santa Rosa, CA: Metamorphic Press, 1986.

McClure, Susan, and Sally Roth. *Rodale's Successful Organic Gardening: Companion Planting.* Emmaus, PA: Rodale Press, 1994.

Philbrick, Helen, and Richard B. Gregg. *Companion Plants and How to Use Them.* Old Greenwich, CT: The Devin-Adair Company, 1966.

Riotte, Louise. *Carrots Love Tomatoes.* Pownal, VT: Storey Communications, 1975.

———. *Roses Love Garlic.* Pownal, VT: Storey Communications, 1983.

NATURAL LANDSCAPING

Kress, Stephen W. *The Audubon Society Guide to Attracting Birds.* New York: Charles Scribner's Sons, 1985.

Lovejoy, Sharon. *Hollyhock Days.* Loveland, CO: Interweave Press, 1994.

Mahnken, Jan. *The Backyard Bird-Lover's Guide.* Pownal, VT: Storey Communications, 1996.

Roth, Sally. *Natural Landscaping.* Emmaus, PA: Rodale Press, 1997.

Tufts, Craig, and Peter Loewer. *The National Wildlife Federation's Guide to Gardening for Wildlife.* Emmaus, PA: Rodale Press, 1995.

PERENNIALS AND OTHER ORNAMENTALS

Appleton, Bonnie Lee, and Alfred F. Scheider. *Rodale's Successful Organic Gardening: Trees, Shrubs, and Vines.* Emmaus, PA: Rodale Press, 1993.

Art, Henry W. *A Garden of Wildflowers.* Pownal, VT: Storey Communications, 1986.

Bradley, Fern Marshall, ed. *Gardening with Perennials.* Emmaus, PA: Rodale Press, 1996.

Burrell, C. Colston. *A Gardener's Encyclopedia of Wildflowers.* Emmaus, PA: Rodale Press, 1997.

Holden Arboretum Staff. *American Garden Guides: Shrubs and Vines.* New York; Pantheon Books, 1994.

Kowalchik, Claire, and William H. Hylton, eds. *Rodale's Illustrated Encyclopedia of Herbs.* Emmaus, PA: Rodale Press, 1987.

McKeon, Judith C. *The Encyclopedia of Roses.* Emmaus, PA: Rodale Press, 1995.

Phillips, Ellen, and C. Colston Burrell. *Rodale's Illustrated Encyclopedia of Perennials.* Emmaus, PA: Rodale Press, 1993.

Proctor, Rob, and Nancy J. Ondra. *Rodale's Successful Organic Gardening: Annuals and Bulbs.* Emmaus, PA: Rodale Press, 1995.

Roth, Susan A. *The Four-Season Landscape.* Emmaus, PA: Rodale Press, 1994.

Taylor, Norman. *Taylor's Guide to Annuals.* Rev. ed. Boston: Houghton Mifflin Co., 1986.

PERIODICALS

Common Sense Pest Control Quarterly
Bio-Integral Resource Center (BIRC)
P.O. Box 7414
Berkeley, CA 94707-0414
Phone: (510) 524-2567

National Gardening
National Gardening Association
180 Flynn Ave.
Burlington, VT 05401

Organic Gardening
Rodale Press, Inc.
33 E. Minor St.
Emmaus, PA 18098

Photo Credits

Fern Bradley/Rodale Press: page 171 (center).

Rob Cardillo/Rodale Press: pages 58 (top), 66 (top).

David Cavagnaro: pages 55, 56, 57, 58 (bottom), 59, 60 (bottom right), 69, 70.

Deanne D. Cunningham/*Wings and Things*: pages 60 (left), 61, 62 (left), 63 (top right), 64, 65, 66 (bottom), 67 (bottom), 68 (bottom left), 167, 168 (bottom), 169, 171 (bottom), 172, 173 (top), 174–75 (bottom), 176, 177 (top), 178, 179, 180, 181, 182.

Sally Cunningham: pages 168 (top), 170, 171 (top).

T. L. Gettings/Rodale Images: pages 67 (top), 68 (bottom right), 173 (bottom), 174 (top left), 175 (top).

Dency Kane: pages 62–63 (bottom: taken at The Cook's Garden, Londonderry, VT), 68 (top).

Ed Landrock/Rodale Images: page 177 (center left).

Rodale Images: page 177 (center right, bottom).

On the cover: photos by Deanne D. Cunningham; T. L. Gettings/ Rodale Images; John P. Hamel/ Rodale Images (portrait); Ed Landrock/Rodale Images; Alison Miksch/Rodale Images; Maslowski Photography; Rodale Images; Margaret Skrovanek/Rodale Images; Delilah Smittle/Rodale Press; Kurt Wilson/Rodale Images.

Illustration Credits

Nancy Smola Biltcliff: pages vii (left), 46, 47, 79, 80, 145 (top), 185 (top), 186, 188, 190, 192 (top), 194, 195, 197, 199, 202, 204 (top), 206, 207, 208, 210, 212, 213, 215 (bottom), 217, 218, 221, 223, 226, 228, 230, 231, 233, 235, 238, 240, 241, 245, and electronic art on pages 185–245.

Kathy Bray: pages vii (bottom right), 1, 10, 11, 13, 29, 32, 33, 35, 37, 39, 41, 43, 81, 87, 111, 125, 127, 137, 138, 139, 140, 141, 143, 145 (bottom), 149, 152, 153, 154, 155, 162, 183, 203, 204 (bottom), 215 (top), 222.

Louise Smith: pages vi, ix (top right), x (top right), 2, 3, 5, 14, 19, 20, 22, 25, 26, 27, 30, 45, 48, 50, 52, 54, 71, 72, 73, 75, 76, 77, 78, 85, 86, 113, 116, 117, 118, 119, 121, 123, 124, 129, 130, 131, 132, 134, 146, 156, 159, 160, 164, 185 (bottom), 187, 192 (bottom), 196, 200, 201, 209, 216, 219, 225, 232, 236, 243.

Amy Wright: pages ix (bottom left), x (middle and bottom right), 8, 17, 82, 84, 88, 89, 90, 91, 92, 93, 94, 95, 96, 97, 98, 99, 100, 101, 102, 103, 104, 105, 106, 107, 108, 109, 110.

INDEX

NOTE: Page references in italic indicate photographs. Boldface references indicate illustrations.

USDA Plant Hardiness Zone Map

This map was revised in 1990 to reflect changes in climate since the original USDA map, done in 1965. It is now recognized as the best estimator of minimum temperatures available. Look at the map to find your area, then match its pattern to the key on the right. When you've found your pattern, the key will tell you what hardiness zone you live in. Remember that the map is a general guide; your particular conditions may vary.

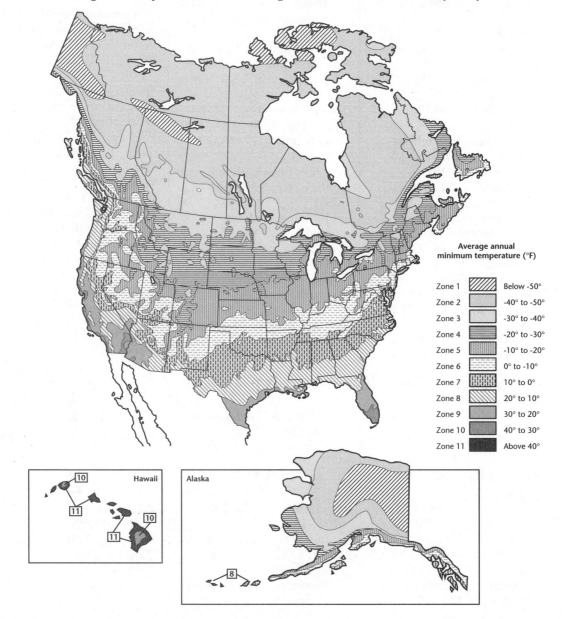

Average annual minimum temperature (°F)

Zone 1	Below -50°
Zone 2	-40° to -50°
Zone 3	-30° to -40°
Zone 4	-20° to -30°
Zone 5	-10° to -20°
Zone 6	0° to -10°
Zone 7	10° to 0°
Zone 8	20° to 10°
Zone 9	30° to 20°
Zone 10	40° to 30°
Zone 11	Above 40°

Hawaii

Alaska